FORTHCOMING BOOKS

Legend of the Overfiend
Death Note
Naruto
Bleach
Vampire Knight
Mushishi
One Piece
Nausicaä of the Valley of the Wind
The Twilight Saga
Harry Potter

APPLESEED

MASAMUNE SHIROW

THE *MANGA* AND THE *ANIMÉ*

APPLESEED

MASAMUNE SHIROW
THE MANGA AND THE ANIMÉ

JEREMY MARK ROBINSON

Crescent Moon

First published 2024.
© Jeremy Mark Robinson 2024

Set in Book Antiqua, 9 on 12 point.
Designed by Radiance Graphics.

British Library Cataloguing in Publication data available for this title.

ISBN-13 9781861719249

Crescent Moon Publishing
P.O. Box 1312, Maidstone, Kent
ME14 5XU, U.K.
www.crmoon.com
cresmopub@yahoo.co.uk

CONTENTS

Acknowledgements ◆ 9

PART ONE ◆ MASAMUNE SHIROW

01 Masamune Shirow: Biography and Works ◆ 17
02 Masamune Shirow and the Japanese *Manga* Industry ◆ 54
03 The *Intron Depot* Series and Other Works ◆ 91

PART TWO ◆ THE *APPLESEED MANGA*

01 *Appleseed*: The *Manga* ◆ 125
02 Other *Appleseed* Stories ◆ 146
03 The Story of the *Appleseed Manga* ◆ 158

PART THREE ◆ THE *APPLESEED ANIMÉ*

01 *Appleseed* In *Animation* ◆ 208
02 *Appleseed* ◆ 219
03 *Appleseed: Ex Machina* ◆ 234
04 *Appleseed XIII* ◆ 245
05 *Appleseed: Alpha* ◆ 260

Resources ◆ 273
Filmographies ◆ 276
Masamune Shirow: Key Works ◆ 281
Bibliography ◆ 283

ACKNOWLEDGEMENTS

To Masamune Shirow (Masanori Ota).
To the authors and publishers quoted.

PICTURE CREDITS

NOTE

This book uses material that also appears in the two volumes *The Art of Masamune Shirow: Volume 1: Manga* and *The Art of Masamune Shirow: Volume 2: Animé* (published by Crescent Moon Publishing in hardcover black-and-white and also hardcover colour editions).

PART ONE

MASAMUNE SHIROW

士郎 正宗

青心社

01

MASAMUNE SHIROW:
BIOGRAPHY AND WORKS

BIOGRAPHY.

Famously regarded as something of a recluse,[1] Masamune Shirow (not his real name, which is Masanori Ota), was born on November 23, 1961 in Higashinada, Kobe, Hyogo, and grew up in Kobe[2] (where he still lives. Kobe, pop. 1.5m, is 15 miles West of Osaka, in Kansai). He studied art (traditional techniques, like oil painting) at Osaka University, and his well-known *Appleseed manga*, which started out as a *dojinshi* (fan-based) work, was published in 1985 (by Seishinsha; later animated in a number of versions, beginning in 1988). During this time Shirow worked as an art teacher for five years.[3] Biographical information about Shirow is difficult to find outside of the published, official biogs, which are all short and all repeat the same data. (There's nothing on his background, his parents,[4] his marital status, etc).

Not only are there very few photographs publicly available of Masamune Shirow,[5] he has also declined to do TV interviews and audio interviews. When interviewed, journos tend to have to travel to meet him (in Kobe), rather than him travelling to Tokyo. You can spot the occasional satirical self-portrait in his *manga*, however:[6] sometimes as an octopus, sometimes as a *mangaka*. There are thus no filmed interviews with Shirow, and no audio interviews, on radio or in other audio formats.

Why are many *manga* artists and writers (and *animé* staff, too) so private? – to the point that photos of them are hard to find (let alone video footage)? Several reasons have been put forward. (1) *Mangakas* are

---

1 Shirow's media image is of a reclusive loner, rather like the Puppet Master and the Laughing Man in *Ghost In the Shell* (J. Clements, 2009, 309).
2 Kobe features prominently in the incredible *animé* series *Earth Maiden Arjuna* (dir. Shoji Kawamori, 2001).
3 How cool would it be to have the author of *Appleseed* and *Ghost In the Shell* as your art teacher!
4 In the 1990s he was looking after his ageing father.
5 Just one is widely available online. But is that really Masanori Ota?
6 Tho' not as many as Toshio Maeda (*Urotsukidoji*), who's fond of sending himself up.

private, often shy people;[7] they like to keep their personal lives separate from work. (2) They are not comfortable with being in the public spotlight. (3) They are workaholics, and being well-known could impinge on their work schedules (they wouldn't want to be approached by *otaku* – or anything or anybody that would take them away from their work).

Private, retiring, shy *mangaka* include the author of *Death Note* and *Bakuman* (Tsugumi Ohba), Yana Toboso (*Black Butler*), Kentaro Miura (*Berserk*) and Himoru Arakawa (*Fullmetal Alchemist, Silver Spoon*). And when a photo is required for publicity purposes, a *mangaka* will often draw a silly self-portrait instead (Arakawa pictures herself as a black-and-white, spotted cow, for example – she harks from rural Hokkaido). There *are manga* artists, tho', who're happy to be seen and interviewed: Katsuhiro Otomo, Hayao Miyazaki, Masashi Kishimoto, Tito Kubo, Hiro Mashima, etc.

It is striking, though, that someone so well-known, who's such a great artist, can avoid appearing – for his entire career – in newspapers, magazines, books, web pages, TV documentaries, filmed or radio interviews, photographs, articles, essays, etc.

So Masanori Ota – a.k.a. Masamune Shirow – remains a mystery: is he married? With kids? Is he straight? Gay? Is he a woman? Or a cyborg? (Shirow mentions he has a brother-in-law,[8] so presumably he has (or had) a sister).

Shirow-sensei started out writing fan stories (which he got into thru friends at Osaka University of Arts). Most comic artists are self-taught. Fans create *dojinshi manga*, which can range from simple home-made publications to high quality productions. Some *dojinshi* artists go on to become professional *manga* artists and writers. *Dojinshi* creators are often part of a group called *saakuru*.[9] While companies in the West often pursue copyright infringement (especially in the litigious U.S.A.), fan publications are more tolerated in Japanese culture. Most *dojinshi* portray existing *manga* characters; and often *dojinshi* are erotic (thus, many *dojinshi* depict well-known *manga* characters having sex).

Shirow-sensei was not one of those *mangaka* who drew comics as a child, starting out by copying by their favourites (*Dragon Ball* or *Tetsujin 28*, say). Shirow painted and drew as a child, but only really got into *manga* when he went to Osaka to study.

Like many successful *mangaka*, Masamune Shirow has produced a host of miscellaneous material, to be used for promotional work, for ads, for posters, for calendars, for collector's cards, and for the title and contents pages of *manga*. Plus commercial work, covers/ illustrations for novels, numerous magazine covers, designs and ideas for many *animé* shows, advice and designs for video games, designs for phone cards, etc. Shirow's work has also appeared in digital form in formats such as I-Phone, Android, I-Pad, E-books, websites and streaming.

7 If they do interviews, they still prefer to remain anonymous, without showing their faces (in either print, online or video interviews – some interviews are audio only).
8 In the notes to *Ghost In the Shell*.
9 It was estimated that there were 50,000 *manga* circles in Japan in the 1990s (F. Schodt, 2002, 37).

In *Intro Depot: Ballistics*, Masamune Shirow portrays the familiar anxiety of the workaholic artist, which many *mangaka* can relate to:

> Maybe in my heart of hearts I just want to escape, since I spend so much time locked up in my studio. Yet when I do take a trip somewhere, I feel antsy without any work to do.

Among the elements and interests in the art of Masamune Shirow are: insects; tanks; guns and weaponry; utopias; political systems; nature; *mecha*; new technologies (with cyborgs, artificial intelligence and nanorobots a speciality); the future; alternative societies; and sexy warrior women.

In a 1995 interview, Shirow noted:

> Emphasizing a combination of females and mecha, as I do, is something that's been around for a long time, and neither the idea of computer brains nor Special Forces units are themselves new, either. But as with cooking, even if the ingredients are the same, the way they are mixed together and the goal of the person doing the mixing creates a different flavor. In that sense, if the result of cooking can be called original, so, too, can my work. I always try to draw manga that are true to myself.

Masamune Shirow started out as a *manga* fan, and has mainly worked on his own ('I personally like working alone'): he has not been an apprentice or assistant to established *manga* artists, tho' he has employed assistants – such as Hagane Kotetsu (actually a pseudonym for Shirow, or 'the other Shirow', the evil twin, as he calls him),[10] and Pure.[11]

WORKS.

The impact of the work of Masamune Shirow[12] has been immense in *animé* and *manga*: *Ghost In the Shell* alone led to not one but two classic movies, two outstanding TV series (plus a third, the *Arise* series), and spin-off movies. Add to that the live-action *Ghost* of 2017, and more *Ghosties* on the way. Then there's the *Appleseed* computer-aided animations and *Appleseed* cel animation, plus *Black Magic, Real Drive, Ghost Hound* (*Unseen World*) and *Dominion: Tank Police*. It all adds up to a remarkable presence in TV and cinema.

The 'golden age' of Masamune Shirow's output would be the mid-1980s to the early 1990s, the era of his most celebrated works (*Ghost In the Shell, Appleseed, Dominion: Tank Police, Orion, Black Magic,* etc). This was also the period of the first *animé* adaptations of Shirow's *manga* (culminating in the *Ghost In the Shell* movie of 1995).

In the West, the *Appleseed manga*, Shirow's first big hit in comics, was published initially by Eclipse Comics and Studio Proteus (1988-1992),

10 Since 'Kotetsu's' departure, Shirow has been working on his own.
11 Pure produced the *manga Pixy Junket* (Seishinsha, 1992).
12 In the West, we're reading Shirow in translation. It gets irritating at times when Shirow's dialogue is translated into quippy, North American English – 'jeez', 'man', 'uh', 'crap' (and in *Appleseed* Briareos always calls Deunan 'girl').

and then in four volumes by Dark Horse[13] (in 1995), with the titles: 1. *The Promethean Challenge*, 2. *Prometheus Unbound*, 3. *The Scales of Prometheus* and 4. *The Promethean Balance*.

Among Masamune Shirow's early works are: *Areopagus Arther* (1980), *Atlas* magazine; *Yellow Hawk* (1981), *Atlas* magazine; *Colosseum Pick* (1982), *Funya* fanzine and (1990), *Comic Fusion Atpas* fanzine; *Pursuit* (1982), *Kintalion* fanzine; *Optional Orientation* (1984), *Atlas* magazine; *Battle On Mechanism* (1984), *Atlas* magazine; *Metamorphosis In Amazoness* (1984), *Atlas* magazine; *Alice In Jargon* (1984), *Atlas* magazine; and *Bike Nut* (1985), *Dorothy* fanzine.

Other *manga* works include: *Gun Dancing* (1986), *Young Magazine Kaizokuban*; *Pile Up* (1987), *Young Magazine Kaizokuban*; and *Neurohard: The Planet of a Bee* (1992-1994), in *Comic Dragon*. Both *Gun Dancing* (1986) and *Pile Up* (1987) were detective stories published in *Young Magazine*. The *manga* were later released in a CD-ROM format (as 'e-manga'). Shirow has created many covers for magazines such as *Comickers*, *Young*, *B-Club*, *Newtype*, *Groove*, *Manga Max*, *Comic Box* and *Comic Gum* (many of which are republished in his calendars or other collections).

Masamune Shirow's other works include his first comic, *Black Magic M-66* (made into an animation in 1987),[14] and *Dominion: Tank Police* (1988, published in *Comi Comi*, and also animated, in 1988, *Dominion: Tank Police*, directed by Koichi Mashimo), with a sequel in 1992, in *Comic Gaia*. *Dominion Tank Police* revealed Shirow in a lighthearted mood, a departure from his usual more serious pieces – altho' there is a lot more humour in the *Ghost In the Shell manga* than in its animated adaptations.

A story set on Mars in the future seems to have been planned then abandoned by Uncle Shirow; it would probably have centred around a police team[15] or the private detectives in the *W Tails Cat*, *Galgrease* and *Galhound* books (with Poseidon Industrial featuring prominently as a setting). In the end, what we have are the fragmentary plots collected in the *W Tails Cat* and *Galhound* volumes, where the emphasis is on erotic scenarios and depicting the girls as glamorous pin-ups. (Based around a female cop team, the Mars story would've featured tons of *mecha* – robots, robot tanks, motorcycles, cybernetics, and of course guns a-plenty).

There are collections of images related to *Ghost In the Shell*, including: *Cybergirls Portfolio*, *Cyber-world*, *Cyberdelics* and *Pieces Gem 01 – Ghost In the Shell Data + Alpha*. Shirow, however, has produced more extra material featuring Deunan Knute of *Appleseed* than Major Motoko Kusanagi. And he has focussed more recently on a bunch of other female characters, rather than Motoko, such as Cyril Brooklyn and her chums at

13 Dark Horse, one of the publishers in the Occident of Shirow-sensei, was founded in 1986 (or 1988) by Mike Richardson (b. 1950). Early publications included *Outlanders* by Joji Manabe and *Godzilla #1*. Dark Horse became the third largest publisher of *manga* in the New World. Dark Horse has specialized in horror, sci-fi and action *manga*, and published *Akira*. Its other titles include *Oh My Goddess!* and *What's Michael?* Dark Horse also licensed properties such as *Star Wars*, *Buffy the Vampire Slayer*, *Aliens*, *Predator*, *The Incredibles* and *Indiana Jones*. Dark Horse's Western products included *Sin City*, *The Amazing Adventures of the Escapist*, *Barb Wire*, *Grendel*, *X*, *Hell-boy*, *Concrete* and *300* (many of these were published under the *Dark Horse Presents* label).
14 This featured Shirow as animation director, but the experience was not good.
15 The space police team, a.k.a. S.S.A.A.T. (they appear in many of Shirow's erotic works).

the detective agency on Mars (in the *W Tails Cat* and *Calgrease* series), and Toguihime, the warrior-princess in historical Nihon (in the *Hellhound* books).

Masamune Shirow has also contributed designs to *Blue Uru* (1992, unmade), *Landlock* (Yasuhiro Matsumura, 1996) and *Gundress* (Katsuyoshi Yatabe, 1999).16 Shirow provided the story for *Ghost Hound* (a.k.a. *Unseen World*, Ryutaro Nakamura, 2007) and *Real Drive* (2008), more animated shows.

Masamune Shirow's interviews have been published in a huge number of magazines, including: *Melti Lemon, Young, Metal Kids, Comics Informational, B-Club, Comic Box, Cyber Comics, Out, Anime V, Super Game, Hobby Japan, Comickers, Groove, Screentone, Monthly Newtype, Afternoon, Magazine S, Canopri Comic, Comic Ryu, Videoboy, Kissui Bijin, D.M.M., Newtype A,* etc. (So he's happy to chat about his work, but not in video or audio form).

An exhibition commemorating the 25th anniversary of *Ghost In the Shell* was shown in Japan in 2014. It featured artwork by Shirow, *genga* and sketches from each of the animated versions of *Ghost In the Shell*, etc (an artbook was published, too).

Masamune Shirow is a geek's *mangaka*, an *otaku*'s artist. In Japan, *otaku* signifies a nerd, geek or obsessive fan, while in the West it simply means a fan.17 The 1990s term *moe* is also employed (it means 'to sprout'); for Toshio Okada, a *moe* fan is obsessed, but an *otaku* learns the background and details. Magazines sympathetic to *otaku*-dom include *Monthly Shonen Ace, Dragon Age, Comic Gum, Ultra Jump* and *Dengeki Daioh. Otaku* culture has been famously celebrated in *animé* in *Otaku no Otaku* (1991), and later works such as *Comic Party* (1995), *Maniac Road* (2002), *Genshiken* (2002) and *Pretty Maniacs* (2004). *Otaku* elements crop up in *animé* such as *Eden of the East, Ghost In the Shell: Stand Alone Complex* (Aoi is an *otaku*), *Paranoia Agent* and *Neon Genesis Evangelion.*

Editors play a vital role in the development of *manga* and a *mangaka*'s work and career: for Masamune Shirow, his editor at Seishinsha in Osaka was Harumichi Aoki (Aoki was an important early supporter of Shirow: he invited Shirow to publish *Appleseed* after seeing his *dojinshi* work – and *Black Magic* in particular). Shigehiko Ogasawara was one of Shirow's long-time editors. (Although Shirow had assistants, he said that often the only visitors he got in Kobe were Aoki and Ogasawara).

Koichi Yuri (b. 1947) was one of the editors of Masamune Shirow's early output – Yuri worked for *Young Magazine*, where *Ghost In the Shell* was published (it was Yuri who asked Shirow for a flashier title than *Ghost In the Shell*; so Shirow came up with *Shell Squad*, a.k.a., *Mobile Armored Riot Police.* Thus, altho' *Ghost In the Shell* is known as *Ghost In the Shell* outside Japan, in Japan it is *Mobile Armored Riot Police* as well as *Ghost In the Shell*).

---

16 On *Gundress* and *Landlock*, Masamune Shirow was credited as a 'planning assistant': the shows were released partly to cash in on the success of *Ghost In the Shell.*
17 Retreating from society was a growing trend in the 1990s, dubbed *hikkomori* (the issue has also been explored in *animé*).

In his "Afterword" to *Appleseed* (volume one), Masamune Shirow acknowledged that he wasn't as prolific as the commercial *manga* artists working in Tokyo. He wasn't producing 20 or more pages for the weekly and 30+ pages for the monthly *manga* magazines. Instead, he was publishing once a year: 'I've been very lucky'. To produce *Ghost In the Shell*, Shirow said (in 1995) that it took him about forty days to draw forty pages (i.e., one chapter):

> For *Ghost in the Shell* I drew an average of forty pages per episode and it took me around forty days to do one episode. But the number of hours I can work, and the efficiency of my work fluctuates, so it's not always possible to do a page a day.

The fifth volume of *Appleseed* has been rumoured for a long time (Shirow-sensei tended to deflect questions about the 5th book apologetically – he had already moved on to other things).

The many publishers of the work of Masamune Shirow have happily exploited it in many formats. The *manga* have been published, for ex, in digest (*bunkobon*) and *Wideban* (wide edition) sizes, as limited editions (and collector's editions = *Kanzeban*), and as part of special sets. Shirow's work has been released with booklets, posters, CDs, puzzles, etc. In ring binders. As booklet posters. As CD-sized booklets or posters. In plastic folders.

It's worth remembering that much of Masamune Shirow's work has been published in series, not all at once: his *manga* works, for instance, such as the big three – *Ghost In the Shell, Dominion: Tank Police* and *Appleseed* – were published in chapters over a long period of time (as with almost all longer *manga*). Only *later* were they collected into volumes. Thus, not only did each comic alter over the months and then years of publication (like any *manga*), they were also adjusted when they were collected together and published as *tankobon* (for instance, pages would be left out, or added, or changed). There are further changes when comics are published for overseas editions; Shirow sometimes revises his *manga* considerably for the collected editions.

By the time of the success of the *Appleseed* and *Ghost In the Shell manga*, in the late 1980s/ early 1990s, Masamune Shirow's publishers and editors would've informed the *mangaka* that if he kept producing *manga* like that, he would be rich (and so would they!). Indeed, many fans of Shirow-sensei would be very happy if he had simply gone on drawing *Appleseed* and *Ghost In the Shell* – and *Dominion* and *Orion* and *Black Magic*. The thought of *Ghost In the Shell* and/ or *Appleseed* extending into a long-running *manga* series, like *Berserk, Urusei Yatsura* or *Oh! My Goddess*, is mind-boggling (tho' hoping for a 700-chapter *manga* like *Naruto* from Shirow is probably too much!). But just think where Shirow might've taken the stories of *Appleseed* and *Ghost In the Shell*, if someone had locked him in a room from 1991 to 2011, and told him to write, to draw, to make *manga*!

No doubt publishers and editors have over the years pleaded and begged Shirow Masamune to produce either: (1) more of *Ghost In the Shell* (and/ or *Appleseed*), or (2) something in a similar manner.

MASAMUNE SHIROW'S WORK SINCE THE 1980s.

Masamune Shirow has received plenty of negative criticism over the years. Some fans don't like his digital artwork, with its images manipulated in Photoshop, Lightwave or similar digital software (the plasticky, floaty look of digital imagery, like computer-aided scenes in movies, aren't to everybody's tastes. It *looks* photo-realistic, but it's still a *cartoon*). Some fans hanker after the watercolour and gouache artwork. Some fans find his stories too obscure (in the later *Ghost In the Shell* outings, for instance), or muddled, or way too arcane. Some fans don't want the out-there porn, where man-beasts, monsters and aliens do naughty things with oiled, pneumatic, young women, and some find the emphasis on eroticism too much and too bizarre.

What does his family think? My guess is that they are aware of it, but seldom or never look at it.

But there's no doubt that Shirow Masamune is the King of 'Fan Service' (despite *strong* competition from other *mangaka*!) – whether it's *mecha*, cybernetica, esoterica or erotica. And by now Shirow is a Super-Class-A artist in the hyperspace of digital art, an artistic version of the Super-Class-A hackers in his *Ghost In the Shell*.

'Fan service' in Japanese pop culture means delivering to audiences something fetishized and glamourised: *mecha* (robots and machines), for example, lovingly depicted, or something sexy – glimpses of underwear or parts of the body.

Masamune Shirow has been creating erotic art throughout his career, but in his later career, it has greatly increased in proportion to his other published work. Also, it hasn't changed too much for twenty or more years: posterbooks published in 2019 (such as *Greaseberries 4*), employ the same approach as pin-ups and erotica appearing in 2000. But erotica is what Shirow wants to do: 'I always try to draw *manga* that are true to myself.'

Masamune Shirow has published his erotic imagery and stories in anthology magazines of erotica such as *Canopri Comic* and *Comic Anrthurium*. In those magazines, Shirow's digital art sits alongside the usual porn comic strips of schoolgirls and teachers, brothers and sisters, mom and her son's best friend, gang rape in the school store room, etc. The *Pieces*, *W Tails Cat*, *Greaseberries*, *Galgrease et al* series are marketed as 'collections of Shirow Masamune's full colour indecent works', in individual, colour book form.

Notice, though, that none of the regular publishers of Japanese *manga* in the West – Viz, Dark Horse, Del Rey, Yen Press, etc – have produced English-translated editions of Shirow's erotica. There is a market for it – there are many collectors of Shirowania in the Western world – but maybe not enough of a market to justify publishing a full-colour[18] English edition. The troublesome nature of some of Shirow's erotica wouldn't put off many publishers of similar material. (Erotica is a long-established sub-genre of the comics market in Europe and the U.S.A., producing artists such as Manara, Altuna, Serpieri, von Gotha, Coq, Ferocius, Lemay, Noe, Molinari, etc).

The *Hellhound* series and the *Toguihime/ Japanesque* series in particular cry out for a Western/ English edition. This is some of Shirow's finest art, a unique, inventive and luscious Dream of Japan (you could leave out the more explicit erotica from *Hellhound*).

Negative reactions to Masamune Shirow's art include the wish that Shirow had spent more of his talents and time on projects 'worthy' of his skills, instead of so many erotic pin-ups, posters and mini-stories. A girl getting assaulted on a train by a black guy, a girl being gang-raped in a swimming pool, and lubed-up ladies being set upon by spiders and aliens just aren't up to Shirow's artistic standards for the critical complainers (tho' the girls changing into high fashion outfits and steam-punk accessories every ten seconds is very Shirowian, and the quality of the artwork is outstanding).

When you know just what Masamune Shirow is capable of, in terms of storytelling and conjuring up fantasy worlds, it can seem way below his talents to produce yet another Photoshop file of a girl pulling her panties up into her crotch. (But all of the paraphernalia surrounding that girl, the clothing, the accessories, the props, the furniture, etc, is amazing).

But wait – this is what Masamune Shirow *wants* to do, part of the time. He likes to produce erotica. And artists have depicted sexual acts for millennia. And a great artist has earned the right, perhaps, to do what they like (or at least they've achieved the economic independence to be able to do that). Picasso, Renoir, Titian, Moreau, Fuseli, Schiele, Klimt, Ingres, Rodin, Correggio, Goya, Boucher, Cranach, Michelangelo, and thousands of other artists have created erotic material. Some other *manga* artists have produced erotica as a sideline, such as: Kohta Hirano (*Hellsing*) and Sakurako Gokurakuin (*Sekirei*).

It's true that Masamune Shirow has probably spent more time on his erotic artwork than on the *Ghost In the Shell* and the *Appleseed mangas* put together! Instead of cyber-punk fantasies and urban thrillers, Shirow has, for many years now, been more interested in portraying pretty, young things in fetish gear being ogled and molested by monsters.

Masamune Shirow acts as the Great God of Digital Art, creating the template of a young woman and dressing her up in astonishing costumes and accessories. Shirow is very much like a puppeteer with his dolls – his art comes across sometimes like that old toy of childhood which had cardboard figures and paper clothes that you could cut out and pin to a figure (where you could endlessly switch round the combinations of items). Or like a doll with miniature clothes. Shirow's art is the digital version of playing with Barbie (with sex added).

18 Shirow would likely insist on full colour – he is picky about the colour reproduction of his works (which would also mean good quality paper, etc).

To satisfy every fan or consumer is probably impossible – but many fans would be happy for Masamune Shirow to create as many erotic images as he likes – but only <u>if</u> he was <u>also</u> writing further installments of *Appleseed* or *Ghost In the Shell,* or if he was conjuring up new sci-fi/ fantasy stories.

We can all wish…

I wish – to pick just a few in the fantasy realm – that J.R.R. Tolkien hadn't spent so long fiddling around with his Middle-earth legends and had put them into final published form (they were published after his death, unfinished and incomplete, as *The History of Middle-earth*).

And I wish that Robert E. Howard hadn't killed himself at the age of 30 (in 1936),[19] so we could have 100s of *Conan* and other fantasy tales.

In cinema, we lament the early deaths of F.W. Murnau and Andrei Tarkovsky; the persecution of Sergei Parajanov; and the long gaps between movies (and the struggle to find backing) of Orson Welles and Carol Theodor Dreyer.

The poster(book)s, pin-ups, calendars and other erotica produced by Masamune Shirow from the late 1990s onwards *do* tell stories – stories that can be evoked in a single image. A woman as a pirate on a galleon, a woman as a vampire surrounded by blood-drained victims, a woman as a secretary, etc. But these are not long-form *manga* stories, with many characters, with dramatic interactions and action scenes. They are one-off vignettes which emphasize one element above all: eroticism. (Or, you could argue, they stress design and art above all: these are images which call attention to themselves as artworks).

Who knew that Masamune Shirow would revert to the pin-up, nudie and *Heavy Metal*-style art and comics that he grew up on in the 1970s? Who imagined that Shirow-sensei would devote weeks and months of his precious time to creating images of sexy babes in clichéd scenarios out of the genres of horror, science fiction and fantasy (the big three)?

Well, yes – but Masamune Shirow had *already* been doing that with the *Appleseed* and *Ghost In the Shell* comics! There is erotic material *already* in the first *Ghost In the Shell* collected book and the four *Appleseed* volumes!

Here's another way of looking at this issue: maybe Masamune Shirow wanted to be an artist who creates erotic art all along, and the years of producing *Ghost In the Shell, Appleseed* and other *manga* were simply a side-show, something he got distracted by for a while (but also just happened to make him a millionaire).

For Jason Thompson in *Manga: The Complete Guide,* Masamune Shirow squanders his terrific ideas and scenarios in endless footnotes, obscure storytelling, and a depressing move towards erotica/ porn.

One of the popular views of Masamune Shirow in the Western world

19 Robert E. Howard was born in Peaster, Texas, in 1906. Howard spent most of his life in Cross Plains, Texas. He committed suicide in 1936 following his mother's death. Although literary critics often cite J.R.R. Tolkien as the creator of the sword and sorcery genre, Howard defined much of it with his *Conan* stories. These included "The Phoenix and the Sword", "The Scarlet Citadel", "The Tower of the Elephant", "Black Colossus", "The Slithering Shadow", "The Devil In Iron" and "Jewels of Gwahlur".

is that his *manga* work was outstanding in the 1980s and 1990s (tho' quirky, over-written and sometimes obscure), but that in the second half of his career he has sunk to the lows of producing weirdo porn.

Yes, it's true, much of Shirow-sensei's work in the late 1990s until the present day has involved a *lot* of erotic material (erotic for some, porn for others). But this is not all that Shirow has been doing! Of course not: for ex, he has worked in *animé*, magazine covers, computer games, and novels.

(1) Shirow has advised on the two *Ghost In the Shell: Stand Alone Complex* TV series, the *Ghost In the Shell: Stand Alone Complex* spin-off movie *Ghost In the Shell: Solid State Society*, the *Ghost In the Shell: Arise* series (and movie), the *Appleseed* computer-aided remakes, the *Appleseed* TV series, and the *TANK S.W.A.T. 01* show.

(2) Shirow has creator credit on several *animé* series including: *Ghost Hound, Real Drive, W Tails Cat* and *Pandora In the Crimson Shell: Ghost Urn*.

(3) Shirow has continued with commercial commissions and design work.

(4) Shirow has created covers for books, and insert illustrations;

(5) Shirow has produced cover artwork for magazines (such as *Comic Gum* and *Canopri*);

(6) Shirow has made artwork, illustrations and covers for spin-off books from his *manga* (including *Black Magic, Appleseed, Real Drive, Dominion: Tank Police* and *Ghost In the Shell: Stand Alone Complex*);

(7) Shirow has developed further installments of the *Intron Depot* series (*Blades, Ballistics, Battalion*, etc);

(8) And Shirow has contributed to the designs and ideas of computer games based on his *manga*.

Further recent Shirow artwork includes: *Seven Traps, Cover Girl Fragments, Dead Drive*, and the *Shirow Masamune Studio Diary*.

❊

Meanwhile, other artists and writers have produced tie-in comics based on each of the animated adaptations of Shirow's works, including *Ghost In the Shell* by Akinori Endo (1995, 1998) • novels of *Ghost In the Shell: Stand Alone Complex* by Junichi Fujisaku (2004-05) • two comics for the *Stand Alone Complex* (in 2009) and *Arise* (in 2013) versions of *Ghost In the Shell* • *Black Magic* by Hideki Kakinuma (2005-08) • *Real Drive* by Yoshinobu Akita (2008) • *Appleseed XIII* by Yoshiki Sakurai (2012) • *Appleseed: Alpha* by Iou Kuroda (in 2014) • light novels and collections of short stories have appeared • a theatrical play (in 2015) • a tribute anthology to *Ghost In the Shell* by contemporary *mangaka* (in 2017) • a history of *Ghost In the Shell* in animated form, *Perfect Book* (in 2017) • art books for the live-action movie (in 2017) • and an original *manga* spin-off (in 2019). Shirow has produced artwork, including book covers, for some of those tie-in/ spin-off works.

RESEARCH AND INFLUENCES.

Masamune Shirow has probably been influenced by, well, everybody (like everybody else). It's easy to see just how much Shirow has consumed of books, TV shows, movies, photos, art and music (Shirow has remarked that he's of the TV generation, the baby boomer generation, and TV and movies have influenced him more than comics; he got into comics later, at university). Numerous influences are easy to detect: the usual North American sci-fi movies (*Alien, Blade Runner, RoboCop, War Games, 2001: A Space Odyssey, The Terminator*, etc).[20] The usual roster of sci-fi authors: Arthur C. Clarke, Phil Dick, Isaac Asimov, Robert Heinlein, etc. Reference and scientific books and magazines. *Akira* and Katsuhiro Otomo (an influence on *Appleseed*).[21] *Thunderbirds* and other Gerry Anderson adventure (and team) shows. And Osamu Tezuka (of course!).

Hayao Miyazaki was a big influence on Masamune Shirow – especially when he was making the *animé* of *Black Magic* (the influence of *Laputa: Castle In the Sky* and of course *Nausicaä of the Valley of the Wind* is enormous on all subsequent fantasy and sci-fi *animé* and *manga*. Miyazaki's *Nausicaä manga* likely influenced the style of Shirow's subsequent comics – such as the use of very dense panels, crammed with information, and the rounded, organic forms).

For research, Masamune Shirow consumes (imported) books on military hardware, on art and sculpture, on cars, on micro-machinery, on military robots, on insects ('I have quite a lot of books on bees'), on bio-technology, on Greek mythology, plus 17 or 18 magazines a month, and as many *manga* as imported books.[22]

As his notes on his images relate, Masamune Shirow has a vast library of imagery and material which he draws on to create his art. Some come from photographs, some from photos he's taken himself, some from photocopies, and some from books. The backgrounds are constructed, piece by piece, rather than being a complete photo (tho' Shirow will occasionally use a whole photograph – of something like a deep-sea submersible). Shirow is known for using a photocopier to generate interesting textures (such as photocopying rocks, metallic images or the cloth of *kimonos*). The humble photocopier is an often overlooked tool in the creation of *manga*; it's used for all sorts of tasks. In 1995, Shirow commented:

> I use a color copy machine and copy rock or metallic images onto a 'transparent film with an adhesive on one side' (reversing or flipping positive and negative images, altering colors, and changing sizes), and then cut and paste them into the drawing. I usually use acrylic paint and apply several thin layers.

For many Japanese *animé* filmmakers, Masamune Shirow included,

---

20 *Animé* filmmakers have been hugely influenced from seeing a number of Western movies: *2001: A Space Odyssey, Blade Runner, Alien, Star Wars, The Terminator, Thunderbirds* and *King Kong* (and to a lesser degree *RoboCop* and Ray Harryhausen's monster movies).
21 Shirow has cited *Macross* as an influence.
22 Masamune Shirow, in T. Ledoux, 1997, 42.

Blade Runner has been a major inspiration, a storehouse of possibilities. No matter what you think of *Blade Runner*, its importance for Japanese *animé* is enormous. *Blade Runner* has influenced *Akira* (Katsuhiro Otomo, 1988), *Patlabor*, *Legend of the Overfiend*, and of course *Appleseed* and *Ghost In the Shell*. And Mamoru Oshii has spoken repeatedly of the influence of *Blade Runner* on his cinema.

Probably the most influential aspect of *Blade Runner* was its *mise-en-scène*, copied and developed in many subsequent films, such as *Judge Dredd* (1995), *Brazil* (Terry Gilliam, 1985), the *Star Wars* prequels (1999-2005), the *Batman* series (1989-), *Twelve Monkeys* (Terry Gilliam, 1995), *Cyborg* (Albert Pyun, 1989), *Total Recall* (Paul Verhoeven, 1990), *Strange Days* (Kathryn Bigelow, 1995), *Johnny Mnemonic* (Robert Longo, 1995), *The Salute of the Jugger* (David Peoples, 1990), the *Matrix* series (1999-2003), and *The Fifth Element* (Luc Besson, 1997).[23] The influence continued in the 2000s and 2010s.

INFLUENCED BY MASAMUNE SHIROW.

There are numerous instances of the influence on Masamune Shirow's art on Asian and Western art and artists. Some of the obvious examples include: *Gunnm* (a.k.a. *Battle Angel Alita*) by Yukito Kishiro, a futuristic comic about a female cyborg/ robot which's really a footnote to *Ghost In the Shell*. The *Burst Angel* (2004) *animé* series is a mere replay of *Appleseed* and *Ghost In the Shell*, as is the *Vexille*[24] movie of 2007 and the *Psycho-Pass* series (2012).

Hyper Police (1994-, by Mee) was influenced by Masamune Shirow. *Pixy Junket* (1992), by one of Shirow's assistants, Pure, bears his imprint. *Silent Möbius* (1988-99, Kadokawa Shoten) by Kia Asamiya 'borrows liberally'[25] from Shirow. *Alice In Lostworld* (2000-01) was influenced by Shirow. There's an amusing *hommage* to Shirow in *xxxHolic* (by the Clamp collective), when the magical girls play with a Tachikoma tank toy.

In Western/ Hollywood cinema, Masamune Shirow's influence is easy to spot in the *Star Wars* prequels, in the *Matrix* movies, in *Avatar*, in *Minority Report*, in the *Avengers* series, and in many a superhero flick.

---

23 Other flicks linked to Phil Dick's work include *A Nightmare On Elm Street*, *Mulholland Drive*, *Fight Club*, *Vanilla Sky*, *Donnie Darko*, *Videodrome*, *Existenz*, *Being John Malkovich*, *Adaptation*, *Eternal Sunshine of the Spotless Mind*, *Dark City*, *The Truman Show*, *Gattaca* and *Memento*.
24 *Vexille* shamelessly combines *Appleseed* and *Ghost In the Shell* (and uses some of the same personnel, such as the voice of Batou, Akio Otsuka). We're back in a futuristic world of robots, androids, mobile suits, an *élite* S.W.A.T. team (called Sword), terrorism and info-war. Aside from some fun *James Bond*-scale stunts (like a plane slicing thru the whole wing of a mansion so the super-villain Saito can make his escape hanging onto it), and over-stuffed design work (robots're everywhere), the most compelling aspect of *Vexille* is the concept of a Japan that seals itself off from the rest of the world for ten years. This is a cyber/ digital version of Japan's self-imposed political isolation during the Edo period, vividly portrayed with 3-D graphics to evoke hi-tech barriers which prevent information – and people – from entering or leaving Nihon.
25 J. Thompson, 2007, 340.

GHOST IN THE SHELL.

Masamune Shirow's *manga Kôkaku Kidôtai* (*Ghost In the Shell*)[26] – his signature work – was first published in 1989, in the Kodansha magazine *Young* (where *Akira, Initial D, 3 x 3 Eyes* and *Basilisk* also first appeared). Shirow maintained his distance from the world centre of *animé* and *manga*, Tokyo, remaining in Kobe. It's no surprise that Shirow (like most Japanese), hasn't travelled outside of Japan (he says he'd like to visit the U.S.A., but, ironically for such a *mecha* junkie, he's afraid of planes). 'I've never been overseas, but I do think it's necessary' (he said that years ago, but it's likely he still hasn't been outside Nippon).

In Japan, *Ghost In the Shell* is called *Kôkaku Kidôtai*, which means *Mobile Armored Riot Police* – a more suitable title, really, than the more poetic, abstract title of *Ghost In the Shell* (Shirow's preference – which became the subtitle). In Spanish, it's *Ghost in the Shell: Espectro Virtual*, in Italian, it's *Lo Spirito nel Guscio*, in Portuguese it's *O Fantasma do Futuro*, and in Polish it's *Duch w Pancerzu*.

The *manga* refers to artificial intelligence, medicine, science, British politics, a lot of Japanese politics, the *Bible,* Hayao Miyazaki, and writers such as A.E. van Vogt and Isaac Asimov. (More people consume science fiction in Japan than anywhere else. There are many science fiction clubs in Japan, often in schools and colleges[27]).

You'll hear (or read) certain words recurring in the *Ghost In the Shell* world: *ningen* (humans), *gosuto* (ghost), *robotto* (robot), *tamashi* (soul), *saibogu* (cyborg), and *mashin* or *kikai* (machine).

There are six animated movies of *Ghost In the Shell* and four TV series. All are from Production I.G., Bandai, Kodansha, Dentsu, Nippon TV and associated companies: two movies directed by Mamoru Oshii, three spin-off movies from the TV series directed by Kenji Kamiyama, and the *Arise* Original Video Animations, TV series and movie. Add the *manga* by Masamune Shirow to that, and the spin-off *manga* (which re-tell the *Ghost In the Shell: Stand Alone Complex* TV series), and the merchandizing and the video games, and the live-action flick of 2017 (from Paramount/ DreamWorks/ Reliance/ Shanghai Film/ Huahua/ Arad), and you have a pretty big franchise. (There are more *Ghost In the Shell* adaptations in the pipeline: a new (fourth) TV series was announced by Production I.G. in April, 2017, to be called *Ghost In the Shell S.A.C. 2045*; it bowed in 2020. Every few years, it seems, the President of Production I.G., Mitsuhisa Ishikawa,[28] announces, *OK!*, it's time for another *Ghost* series).

That idea that Masamune Shirow had for *Ghost In the Shell* in his early twenties has made him a millionaire. It's 'The Franchise That Won't Quit'. Other producers and artists of *animé* and *manga* must look at the *Ghost In the Shell* franchise and think, *hell, how does he do it?* After all, it's a multi-million earner from only three *tankobons*!

No – it's *one book*! – the entire *Ghost In the Shell* franchise has been

---

26 *Gosuto In Za Sheru* and *Kokaku Kidotai* mean *Ghost in the Shell* and *Mobile Armoured Riot Police.*
27 G. Poitras, 2001, 35.
28 Ishikawa says his favourite animated movie is *Ghost In the Shell.*

based in the main on just one volume of *manga*. Yes, just 350 pages for a franchise that's generated million$ and influenced so many people. The other two *Ghost* books came later (in 2001 and 2003), and, besides, most of the adaptations have drawn on that all-important first *Ghost In the Shell* comic.

Of course, Shirow-sama has had plenty of help: the *Ghost In the Shell* franchise has been exploited by Production I.G., Bandai Entertainment in the U.S.A., and Manga Entertainment in Europe for every cent it can muster: thus, the TV series and the movies have been sold singly and in box sets for home entertainment formats such as video, DVD and Blu-ray; the movies have been re-mastered and updated (*Ghost In the Shell 2.0*); the TV shows have been broadcast in Russia, Germany, Italy, Canada, Spain, Oz, etc; the *Ghost In the Shell manga* has been re-issued (including recently in large format books). Add games, novels, artbooks. And on and on it goes. Same with any big franchise. Look at the *Harry Potter* or *Star Wars* franchises for textbook examples of commercial exploitation; and of course, the Walt Disney corporation still leaves everybody else behind when it comes to finding new ways of drumming up $$$$$.

Masamune Shirow has exploited aspects of the world of *Ghost In the Shell* in print media: the *Cybergirls Portfolio*, *Cyberworld* and *Cyberdelics* collections are images which focus on Motoko Kusanagi.

Each *Ghost In the Shell tankobon*, meanwhile, has been published in short (cut) editions and longer editions (some include appendices).

On a selfish, fan-based note, I would like to see Production I.G. sell the rights to *Ghost In the Shell*, and let's see a completely new bunch of companies have a go at Masamune Shirow's famous work. It would be great, for ex, to see a version of *Ghost* which *really* captures the goofy humour and joshing among the team at Public Security Section 9, instead of the usual too-serious approach. (There's more to *Ghost In the Shell* than a kick-ass cyborg girl who beats up bad guys and spends the rest of her time moping about and philosophizing). I'd like to see the *One Piece* or Toei Animation version of *Ghost In the Shell*.[29]

The *Ghost In the Shell* movies and TV shows explore numerous aspects of science fiction, and science fiction cinema. Cyborgs, robots and artificial intelligence or life is an obvious one. But also the significance of time and memory;[30] the sublime; the role of the individual in society; how societies should be policed; and metaphysics, the soul and the divine.

The *Ghost In the Shell* world boils down to four principal characters, really:

• Major Motoko Kusanagi (Atsuko Tanaka),
• Batou (Akio Otsuka)
• Togusa (Kôichi Yamadera),
• and their boss, Daisuke Aramaki (Tamio Ôki).

Most of the time the *Ghost In the Shell* TV series (and the movies) stay with either Kusanagi and Batou, or the Chief and Kusanagi, or Batou and Togusa, or Togusa and Kusanagi. In the *animé* TV shows, Motoko often

29 The closest animation to that is *Dominion: Tank Police*.
30 There are disquisitions on how memory has been externalized in the digital era.

spends more time with Aramaki than Batou or Togusa, but Aramaki tends to appear only to set the narrative rolling – the exposition scene following the opening set-up scene (it's the same in the *Ghost In the Shell manga*). Or he'll appear halfway thru to head-up the operation which'll climax the show's Part B.

Some of the later *animé* adaptations of the *Ghost In the Shell manga* have *sidelined* Motoko Kusanagi: *Ghost In the Shell 2: Innocence*, for instance, focusses on Batou and Togusa, and *Ghost In the Shell: Stand Alone Complex: Solid State Society* followed that example. Yet for Masamune Shirow, Motoko is absolutely central to *Ghost In the Shell* – Shirow is mad about putting women in the central roles in his stories. In fact, Shirow has gone in the *opposite* direction from the *animés*, and made Motoko *even more* central to *Ghost In the Shell* (in the *Ghost In the Shell* sequel *manga*, for instance, Batou, Aramaki, Boma, Togusa *et al* are either relegated to cameos, or don't appear at all. The sequel is *The Motoko Kusanagi Show*).

Let's remind ourselves that the two best-known and most successful of Shirow's creations – *Appleseed* and *Ghost In the Shell* – feature *women* as the main character. And women of action, too. In the world of television and movies, that is very rare. (It continues in other works, such as *Dominion: Tank Police, Orion, Pandora In the Crimson Shell* and *Real Drive*.)

Shirow-sensei might've stopped publishing books of *Ghost In the Shell* stories in 2003 (with *Ghost in the Shell 1.5: Human-Error Processor*), but he didn't stop drawing Major Kusanagi and the gang. Motoko, for ex, was a regular guest star in Shirow's calendars.

◆

MASAMUNE SHIROW'S WORKS IN *ANIMÉ*.

Among the works by Masamune Shirow that've been made into TV, Original Video Animations and movies are:

Black Magic (1987), Original Video Animation
Appleseed (1988), Original Video Animation
Dominion: Tank Police (1988), Original Video Animation
New Dominion: Tank Police (1994), Original Video Animation
Ghost In the Shell (1995), movie
Ghost In the Shell: Stand Alone Complex (2002-03), TV series
Ghost In the Shell: Stand Alone Complex: 2nd Gig (2004-05), TV series
Ghost In the Shell 2: Innocence (2004), movie
Appleseed (2004), movie
Ghost In the Shell: Stand Alone Complex: The Laughing Man (2005), movie
Ghost In the Shell: Stand Alone Complex: Solid State Society (2006), movie
Tank S.W.A.T. 01 (2006), Original Video Animation
Appleseed: Ex Machina (2007), movie
Ghost In the Shell: Stand Alone Complex: Individual 11 (2007), movie

Ghost Hound (2007), TV series
Real Drive (2008), TV series
Appleseed XIII (2011), TV series
W Tails Cat (2013), Original Video Animation
Appleseed: Alpha (2014), movie
Ghost In the Shell: Arise (2013-15), TV series/ Original Video Animation
Ghost In the Shell: The New Movie (2015), movie
Pandora in the Crimson Shell: Ghost Urn (2015-16), TV series
Ghost In the Shell (2017), live-action movie
Ghost In the Shell: S.A.C. 2045 (2020), TV/ net series

Masamune Shirow is one lucky *manga* artist: he has had *Ghost In the Shell* made into two classic movies by one of Japan's premier animation *auteurs*, Mamoru Oshii; he has had not one but two outstanding *animé* series made for TV from *Ghost In the Shell*; he's had three spin-off movies from the TV show; he's had not one but five *animé* adaptations of *Appleseed* (tho' the first, in 1988, is the best at capturing the *Appleseed* world); and other adaptations, such as *Black Magic* (made when Shirow was 26), and two versions of *Dominion: Tank Police*.

Lucky – because we all know how many less than stellar *manga* adaptations there are in *animé*. (However, several Shirowian adaptations are patchy – *Real Drive* and *Ghost Hound* – or downright dreadful: *Appleseed XIII* and *Tank S.W.A.T. 01*. In fact, adaptations of Shirow's work and concepts went off the rails between the mid-2000s and mid-2010s, with many shows being well below par: *Appleseed XIII*, *Ghost Hound*, *Real Drive*, *Tank S.W.A.T. 01*, *W Tails Cat* and *Pandora in the Crimson Shell: Ghost Urn*. The *Ghost In the Shell: Arise* series of 2013-15 delivered a much-needed improvement in quality).

Masamune Shirow also has credits on other animations apart from his well-known pieces like *Appleseed* and *Ghost In the Shell*: *Gundress* (character design), *Hyakki Sho*, unmade (original creator), *Landlock* (original character design), *Real Drive* (original creator), *Ghost Hound* (original creator), *W Tails Cat* (original creator and designer), *Bounty Dog* (character design), and *TANK S.W.A.T. 01* (original creator).

The flow of creativity hasn't all been one way, from *manga* to *animé*: Masamune Shirow would very likely have been influenced by seeing the 1995 *Ghost In the Shell* movie – not least because the movie was a masterpiece. Imagine writing and drawing a *manga* as a 28 year-old starting out as a *mangaka* (Shirow was 28 in 1989), and watching a bunch of filmmakers in Tokyo turn it into this extraordinary, hi-tech action thriller! That's got to influence your later work, right?

ADAPTING MASAMUNE SHIROW'S WORKS

Masamune Shirow's involvement in *animé* adaptations of his work following the troubled *Black Magic* Original Video Animation has usually been in an advisory capacity, at a distance. But that includes story ideas, designs for characters and *mecha,* and other ideas.

Shirow has acknowledged that comics and television are two different ways of telling stories, and ideally he preferred animation that adapted *manga* as a stand alone work, drawing on the strengths of animation. In 1995, he said:

> I think there are ways to demonstrate and produce animation that are unique to animation. Also, in order to establish animation as a truly unique medium of expression, I think it's better to work from an original concept than to base the work on a manga, or, if producing animation based on a manga work, I think it's better to at least rewrite the story for the animation.

Shirow came to realize early on that adaptations of his comics into other media were fraught with issues (he had first-hand experience of this during the difficult production of *Black Magic*). So he developed a way of submitting a bunch of ideas and designs instead of finished stories, as he explained in 1993:

> If I create a regular 'story comic', it can't really be adapted to animation or games without radical changes. So, rather than offering a completed story to the various companies that have expressed interest in my work, I'm just putting together 'do-it-yourself' packages of various bits and pieces, such as mechanical and character designs, and basic storylines. So, from that, they can develop whatever they want, without feeling restricted by the existing work. (1994)

Many of the *animé* adaptations of the work of Masamune Shirow add psychodramatic and melodramatic elements that simply don't exist in the originals. To *Appleseed,* the writers added suicide and a troubled cop Karen Mawserus; to *Dominion: Tank Police,* the filmmakers focussed far too much on the villain Buaku's anxieties about his origins and being artificial; in the two *Ghost In the Shell* movies of '95 and '04, the Public Security Section 9 team mope like teenagers; and in the two *Ghost In the Shell: Stand Alone Complex* series narratives of suicide and self-loathing occur several times (which continues in the *S.A.C. 2045* series).

All of which reflects the concerns of the adapters and scriptwriters, and twist Masamune Shirow's stories to address issues like teenage alienation (the 'shut in' and *otaku* syndrome), social misfits, and, most disturbingly, self-harm and suicide. Yes, some of those issues *are* addressed by Shirow-sensei, but not in the same melodramatic manner, and certainly not in the same quantity. (There are far more evocations of self-hatred and suicide in the three *Ghost In the Shell: Stand Alone Complex* TV series, for instance, than in all of Shirow's *manga*).

The production teams behind the *Ghost In the Shell* franchise in TV and film are all mad, crazy *cinéastes*: executive producers Mitsuhisa Ishikawa and Shigero Watanabe, directors Kenji Kamiyama and Mamoru Oshii, and writers Dai Saito, Junichi Fujisaku, Yoshiki Sakurai,

Shotaro Suga *et al*, have consumed movies by the ton and absorbed them: Jean-Luc Godard (*Breathless, Vivre Sa Vie, Alphaville, Pierrot le Fou*), Stanley Kubrick (*2001: A Space Odyssey, A Clockwork Orange, Full Metal Jacket*), Tsui Hark, Jackie Chan, John Woo (they love over-the-top Hong Kong action movie gunplay), Takeshi Kitano, Federico Fellini, François Truffaut, Akira Kurosawa (*The Seven Samurai, Yojimbo*), Martin Scorsese (*Taxi Driver, Raging Bull*), *The Terminator, Alien, Star Wars, RoboCop, Star Trek*, Hayao Miyazaki (*Laputa: Castle In the Sky, Princess Mononoke, Porco Rosso*), and of course *Blade Runner.*

As you study the adaptations of the *Ghost In the Shell manga* of Masamune Shirow, you are amazed at just how much of the comic made it into each movie and TV series. The filmmakers must've gone thru the *manga* literally 100s of times, to squeeze out every idea, detail and image. 'I looked at that book so much that it's all dog-eared now', remarked *mecha* designer of the *Ghost* TV series, Kenji Teraoka.

None of the adaptations of either *Appleseed* or *Ghost In the Shell*, two of the key franchises in the world of Masamune Shirow, have been able to translate his very distinctive character designs and figures into animation. They come close, but are never quite Shirowian through and through (Shirow's young women are a critical element in his *manga*, but the animated versions can't render them, and always make them too plump. The character designers have included Hiroyuki Okiura, Makoto Shimomura, Tetsuya Nishio, Takayuki Goto, Tetsuro Ueyama, Yumiko Horasawa, Hiroki Takagi, Noboru Furuse, Hiroyuki Kitakubo, Masaki Yamada, Kazuchika Kise, Takuya Tani and Ilya Kuvshinov).

It's a pity, but none of the video/ film versions of the *Ghost In the Shell manga* by Masamune Shirow have attempted to reproduce his crowded street scenes, where cyborgs and humans and robots jostle shoulders and spinal cords. Shirow, in full, post-punk *Star Wars*, *Blade Runner* and *Road Warrior* mode (the streets in *Blade Runner*, the cantina scene in *Star Wars*), loves to imagine ridiculous cyborgized augmentations for humans: weirdos with pipes running from a box on their shoulder into their nostrils; guys in biohazard suits; snooty folk holding opera glasses; a bozo with a *kawaii*, baby-shaped earring; and robots that're nothing more'n a tin box with flailing arms.

Only the home life of Togusa is depicted with any depth or detail in the *Ghost In the Shell: Stand Alone Complex* TV series and the *Ghost In the Shell* movies. The TV shows depict a family man with a wife and daughter (*Ghost In the Shell 2: Innocence* portrays Batou and his pooch, of course). Masamune Shirow's *Ghost In the Shell manga* goes *much* further in delineating the everyday lives of the principal characters. The audience gets no idea of what Aramaki, say, or Ishikawa, or even Major Kusanagi are like at home in the animated versions (the 1995 *Ghost In the Shell* movie has an eerie and hypnotic scene showing Kusanagi waking up in her apartment[31] – of course it has a *fab* view of the city outside the giant

31 The shot holds and holds as Kusanagi walks offscreen then back into shot – a self-conscious, European New Wave motif which filmmakers such as Woody Allen have employed to an enormous degree.

window – she lives alone, naturally (and it's beyond minimal, it's empty). And the 2004 *Ghost In the Shell* sequel has a lengthy sequence showing what life is like *chez* Batou – supping beer from cans and preparing food for dawgs is what it is).

If you know the *manga* of *Ghost In the Shell,* you will notice right away that the TV series *Ghost In the Shell: Stand Alone Complex* has consciously gone for something far, far more political and social than Masamune Shirow's cyber-thriller *manga*. The philosophical, metaphysical and scientific issues, so central to Shirow's *manga,* are still explored by the Japanese filmmakers (the adaptations have scenes with ministers and politicos), but they have grounded the three TV series of *Ghost In the Shell: Stand Alone Complex* very much in contemporary political and social issues.

One of the simple but crucial reasons that the two *Ghost In the Shell: Stand Alone Complex* TV series are so good is that the filmmakers have something to say (it helps that they know how to say it, too). Whereas in much of TV and cinema, the producers don't have much to say (but insist on saying it anyway).

However, the second *Ghost In the Shell* movie, *Ghost In the Shell 2: Innocence*, and the *Arise* version of *Ghost In the Shell* (2013-15), and the live-action movie of '17, don't have much to say that hasn't already been said before in the previous *Ghost In the Shell* outings.

The same companies have handled all of the animated versions of *Ghost In the Shell* – Bandai, Dentsu, N.T.N., Tokuma, Victor, Production I.G., etc. The *Arise* series was partly intended to be a new take on the *Ghost In the Shell* material, but ended up being essentially a prequel/ origins story to the two *Stand Alone Complex* series. I'd like to see Toei Animation (*One Piece*) or A-1/ Satelight (*Fairy Tail*) or Studio Pierrot (*Bleach, Naruto*) or Madhouse (*Memories, Death Note*) or Studio Bones (*Cowboy Bebop, Fullmetal Alchemist*) tackle Masamune Shirow's cyberpunk comic.

I'd love to see Shoji Kawamori (*Macross, Escaflowne, Aquarion*), Noriyuki Abe (*Bleach, Arslan*), Yasuhiro Irie (*Fullmetal Alchemist*), Koji Morimoto (*Memories*), Tetsuro Araki (*Death Note*), Hayato Date (*Naruto),* or Konosuke Uda (*One Piece*) adapt *Ghost In the Shell.*

Live-action versions of *anime* and *manga* are occasionally produced, though seldom in the West. Inevitably, rumours of a live-action version of *Ghost In the Shell* have circulated from time to time (James Cameron and Steven Spielberg were linked to live-action remakes of *Ghost In the Shell,* and also *Akira*).[32] My question is always the same with remakes of classic movies: why bother? These are incredible movies.[33] Don't do it. Go think up your own story instead! (There is also a very mistaken assumption here that an <u>animated</u> version of a story isn't as 'important' or 'serious' as a <u>live-action</u> version. Live-action is culturally promoted above animation).

---

32 Rumours often turn out to be rumours, and often the rights have not been bought up.
33 As director Christophe Gans put it: '*Ghost In the Shell* is already perfect. What would you do, reproduce it frame for frame?'

Also, you can bet that the ideas of making a live-action TV series of both *Ghost In the Shell* and *Appleseed* have been discussed many times in Tokyo. Shirow's most famous *manga* are ideal starting-points for a long-running TV series, or a shorter mini-series. (Rights and costs would be issues – many charas and elements require computer-aided animation).

VIDEO GAMES.

Games are popular *anime* spin-offs – role playing games, card games, chess, jigsaw puzzles and board games are widespread in Japan (and you often see charas playing games in *anime*).

Video games are also tied in very closely with *manga* publishing: *manga* for elementary children, such as *Comic Bombom* and *Corocoro Comi*, have many game and *anime* tie-ins.

Masamune Shirow's art and storytelling is perfect for computer games (his three signature works, *Ghost In the Shell, Appleseed* and *Dominion: Tank Police*, are cop shows, ideal for shoot-em-up video games. It's not only Public Security Section 9 who blam-blam away, it's also the Tank Police of *Dominion* and the mobile suits of *Appleseed*). And we all know that the computer game industry generates billions, as *anime* producers in Japan know well.

Shirow-sensei has been involved with video games created from his works, including for PlayStation (*Ghost in the Shell, Yarudora Series Vol. 3: Sampaguita, Project Horned Owl* and *Gundress*), for PlayStation 2 (*Ghost in the Shell: Stand Alone Complex* and *Appleseed EX*),[34] for PlayStation Portable (*Ghost in the Shell: Stand Alone Complex* and *Yarudora Series Vol. 3: Sampaguita*), for Super Famicom (*Appleseed*), and games for Arcade, P.C. (*Aoki Uru, Black Magic, Emil Chronicle*), social media and cel phones, flight simulator games, and Nintendo D.S. There are also artbooks/ guidebooks published for the computer games, and most of the games include Shirow's artwork and cover art. (Some of Shirow's work for video games was collected in *Intron Depot 5: Battalion*, 2001-09). So although film critics often deride action *anime* (including the shows based on Shirow's work) as being too much like shoot-em-up computer games, gaming has been part of Shirow's output for decades (and Shirow is a big fan of gaming himself).

COP SHOWS.

The cop show format is employed by Masamune Shirow many times: it is the basis of *Ghost In the Shell*, of course (the Japanese title of *Ghost In the Shell* is *Mobile Armored Riot Police*), but also *Dominion: Tank Police* and *Appleseed*. That means that Shirow's works are usually using the team format (*sentai*), which's common in sports *manga*, adventure *manga*, and giant robot *manga*.

Ghost In the Shell, in any of its manifestations, as *manga*, movies or TV series, is basically a cop show (if you call it *Mobile Armored Riot Police*, it explains what it's about much more than 'ghost in the shell'). Yes,

---

34 There have been video games of *Appleseed* for PlayStation 2 (*Appleseed EX*), Super Famicom, online games, and cel phones/ social media.

it's a cyber-punk, hyper-space classic, with its philosophical musings on the digital realm, on life and death, on artificial life vs. organic life. But it's still a cop show. You've got the super-cop, Major Kusanagi,[35] her burly, gruff buddy, seen-it-all-b4 veteran, Batou, the sensitive, put-upon, long-suffering family man Togusa, the wry, seasoned, computer specialist, Ishikawa,[36] and of course the stern, patriarchal boss Daisuke Aramaki (who keeps the squad in line, and also juggles with being answerable to the politicos in command above him). As with all cop shows, there are mysteries to solve, murders to avenge, people to protect, bad guys to chase, civilian casualties to avoid, and politicians to out-manœuvre. (And, being a cop show, that means that *Ghost In the Shell* inevitably promulgates right-wing, pro-military, pro-government, and pro-State politics. The Major might pretend to be rebellious and independent, as in the *Arise* series, but she's working for the State, for The Man[37]).

Apart from Motoko Kusanagi, the *Ghost In the Shell* franchise employs two principal cops, the hulking Batou, a world-weary cop with cropped, white hair, blank, implanted eyes and a vast battery of weapons, and Togusa, a younger cop, with a family (and fewer technological additions to his body).

Batou is a type in Japanese animation of the guy who can't express his feelings – towards Major Kusanagi: these guys, as Gilles Poitras pointed out in *Anime Essentials*,

> have trouble clearly stating their feelings and struggle to express themselves to the one they love. It is not just men; female characters can also hold back or be confused by their emotions, as in the case of Madoka in *Kimagure Orange Road* or Kyoko in *Maison Ikkoku*. (2001, 56)

The cops in the *Ghost In the Shell* world're battling against crime, as cops've always done in the *policier* or thriller genre. Except the criminals in *Ghost In the Shell* are operating partly in cyberspace – hacking into networks, or creating viruses or dodgy software, or copying people's spirits, or selling e-brains on the black market. The cops're protecting society, as usual, and the Japanese nation, too; but a lot of their time is spent preventing attacks or countering attacks on minds, spirits and bodies.

Masamune Shirow makes computers and hacking sexy and thrilling: he takes working with computers far away from the clichéd image of lonely, spotty, fat slobs living in cheap motels, so it becomes beautiful super-babes in shiny, rubberized cat-suits who turn hacking into floating about in dreamy, golden realms like a slinky cat burglar.

---

35 As a character type, Motoko Kusanagi has numerous forebears in both Western and Japanese cinema.
36 The name Ishikawa in *Ghost In the Shell* might come from Goeman Ishikawa XIII, a samurai warrior sidekick of Lupin III. Goeman refers to a legendary thief character in Japanese culture, subject of *Kabuki* plays, such as *Ishikawa Goemon* of 1680 (G. Poitras, 2001, 42).
37 Shirow's own politics seem liberal and socially-conscious, but right of centre.

PUBLIC SECURITY SECTION 9.

The *manga* of *Ghost In the Shell* portrays the creation of the Public Security Section 9 unit itself, with Chief Aramaki telling M. Kusanagi that they have been granted the budget for the kind of team they've been talking about. (Notice that critics and fans talk about Section 9, leaving out the all-important 'Public Security' part of the team's name. You could also say, 'Japanese Government Section 9'. The 'Public Security' bit reminds us that these are agents of the Japanese government. They're not rebels, or outsiders: they are cops – they *are* the State).

Public Security Section 9 is defined in the *Ghost In the Shell: Man-Machine Interface manga* thus:

> Section 9 of the Public Security Bureau is original to the *manga*.
> According to the information that I have on hand, the real Public
> Security currently consists of General Affairs (including special
> support troops), Section 1 (in charge of investigating student move-
> ments and radical activities), Section 2 (labor disputes and organized
> crime), Section 3 (right-wing activities), Section 4 (information
> gathering, statistics, etc), External Affairs Section 1 (in charge of
> investigating non-Asian foreigners), and External Affairs Section 2
> (Asian foreigners). (54)

Authority is seldom questioned among the Public Security Section 9 team in *Ghost In the Shell:* only three of the main characters ever question Chief Aramaki: Motoko, Batou and Togusa (which is quite the norm in Japanese pop culture. They *never* yell at Aramaki or even mildly grouse). It's intriguing that in the second *Ghost In the Shell* TV series, the Major doesn't voice her concern over the influence of Kazundo Goda as loudly or as often as Batou does (and Togusa too). Rather, Motoko seems to be going along with Aramaki, maybe opting to wait until Goda and his regime definitely does something immoral or wrong.

Similarly, within the hierarchy of the Public Security Section 9, no matter what they're up against, or how they're feeling, they all jump to attention when Aramaki or Kusanagi say *jump*. And Aramaki, too, doesn't argue with his superiors often, and also tends to go along with Prime Minister Yoko Kayabuki, in the *2nd Gig* series (Kusanagi reckons he might have a crush on her).

Masamune Shirow's heroes are heroes – they are not anti-heroes, nor are they villains. They fight on the side of 'right' (even if some of their methods are obscure, as with Motoko Aramaki in *Ghost In the Shell: Man-Machine Interface*). The Major, Batou, Deunan Knute, Briareos Hecaton-chires, Leona Ozaki *et al* are not really flawed, either (tho' some of them have 'issues'). Detractors might carp that they're not fully-rounded characters, either. True – Shirow's charas tend to grow on you deeply only if you read and re-read his comics (that's when you take in all of the little details that Shirow packs into the corners of his *manga*). And they don't go thru many psychological changes – like most charas in *manga* and animation, they remain pretty much the same from start to finish.

GUNS.

Despite the scary amount of weaponry and gun-related violence on display in the *Ghost In the Shell* animations, and in a large amount of other *animé,* Japan has a low crime rate, and very low gun crime, according to Gilles Poitras (48 murders with hand-guns in 1979 compared to 9,848 in the U.S.A.).[38] As Poitras pointed out in *The Anime Companion*:

> Japan's Firearms and Sword Possession Control Law is the strictest weapons control law in the world. Police officers are not even allowed to carry firearms unless they are on duty, and many police never even draw their weapon during their entire career, much less ever fire their gun. (136)

But *Ghost In the Shell* is wholly a genre outing, and a cop show without guns ain't going to fly – like a Western without horses, or a soap opera without scenes of people in bars, stores and hospitals wittering on and on and on about absolutely nothing.

Animé movies and shows fetishize guns to an extraordinary degree. Yes, of course that partly derives from the forms and genres that Japanese filmmakers have taken from North American cinema and Hong Kong cinema (everybody took from those American detective and *film noir* motifs, including the *sensei* himself, Akira Kurosawa). You can see the North American fetishization of weaponry in loads of national cinemas around the world. French cinema is the obvious example: for instance, there's always a gun lying around in a Jean-Luc Godard movie (in some of Godard's films, people sit around brandishing guns while reading books, which's classic Godardism – guns and books! The intellectual assassin! A cowboy who reads Guy de Maupassant novels!).

In *Intro Depot: Ballistics*, Masamune Shirow voices concerns over the morality of including images of women in military uniform[39] in these troubled times. This apology or doubt seems hypocritical from an artist who has been drawing aggressively pro-military and pro-government images since the beginning of his career! Few comparable artists have depicted so many characters wielding guns, for example.

TANKS.

We know that Masamune Shirow is fond, like Hayao Miyazaki and Katsuhiro Otomo,[40] of tanks (as well as every form of *mecha,* from guns to helicopters to all manner of cyberization). In Shirow's *manga* work, tanks're everywhere: they are a *very* big deal in the *Ghost In the Shell* franchise, especially on screen (to the point where some of the TV episodes are devoted solely to the Tachikoma tanks). In the *Appleseed manga,* the first big action sequence involves a tank attacking Deunan Knute and

---

38 Guns were used in only 0.8% of robberies, and only 5.3% of murders involved guns.
39 Women in uniform and action women are recurring characters in Japanese animation – shows like *Ghost In the Shell, Patlabor, Gunbuster, Dominion: Tank Police, Bubblegum Crisis* and *Cat's Eye* embody that.
40 Tanks pop up all over Otomo-sensei's work.

Briareos.[41] And Masamune Shirow created a whole series centred around cops plus tanks: *Dominion: Tank Police* (and the main character, Leona, lavishes more love on her cute, little tank Buonaparte than anything or anyone else in her life). The enshrinement of tanks is a gift to animators in Tokyo, most of whom seem to be as crazy about tanks as Shirow is. Thus, every adaptation of a Shirow work includes at least one tank scene.

BUGS.

Masamune Shirow is fond of bugs – insect and spider forms appear throughout his work (and have been taken up by the designers of the *animé* versions of his *manga*). For instance, the Tachikoma robots in *Ghost In the Shell: Stand Alone Complex*, the armed platforms in *Appleseed*, the nasty tanks in *New Dominion Tank Police*, the tanks in *Black Magic*, and many other tanks and robots are based on spiders (the Tachikoma even spin elasticated ropes, and leap about like spiders). In his erotic work, Shirow has depicted naked women being ensnared and tupped by giant spiders. Thus, altho' Shirow's *manga* employs circles as a primary motif (like so many artists, including Katsuhiro Otomo in *Akira*), many of his designs are organic, drawing on the insect world (Kentaro Miura, of *Berserk* fame, is another *mangaka* fond of bug designs, as was the 'god of manga', Osamu Tezuka).[42]

STYLE.

The art of Masamune Shirow is not in love with white space! No! Shirow will fill every *manga* page with marks.[43] And if the frame isn't crowded enough, there'll be lengthy speech bubbles, plus sound effects,[44] and also the idiosyncratic footnotes, in which the Master shares his thoughts on, well, everything. The love of detail continues in Shirow's erotic art. (*Mangaka* who employ lots of white space include Himoru Arakawa (*Fullmetal Alchemist*), Katsuhiro Otomo (*Akira*) and Tite Kubo (*Bleach*)).

Masamune Shirow is a perfectionist – as is obvious by looking at any of his work. He has been known to throw away completely finished artwork – pages of the later *Appleseed* volumes, for example, were ditched, after being inked. (This is one reason why Shirow takes a long time to complete his artwork – like Kentaro Miura (*Berserk*), he won't let something sub-standard leave his studio).

In 1994, Masamune Shirow said that he used a *kabura* pen (which's shaped like a turnip), with a pen holder he made himself. He had a Canon photocopier (one of the *mangaka's* chief tools). He used a regular X-Acto eraser. He worked on regular smooth Kent paper. He employed Maxon

---

41 Just Deunan in the 2004 version of *Appleseed*.
42 Tezuka named his company Mushi, after the *kanji* for insect (which he used for his pen-name).
43 Masamune Shirow uses a good deal of screen tone (also known as 'zip'), as a means of quickly supplying shading and tones to images.
44 'Shirow's scratchy-pen artwork has great energy and fantastic detail: the near-future is nifty and unusually practical' (Julie Davis in *Manga: The Complete Guide*, 85).

screentones,[45] mainly 60 line, 10%, 20%, 30%, etc. Shirow often talks about looking for the right 'tension' or 'life' in a picture.

For computer work, in the 1990s, up to the early 2000s, Shirow used Apple computers, including a 9600/ 350 machine, a G4 machine, and OS 9.2.1, and software such as Photoshop for 2-D work, Lightwave for 3-D modelling, and Cinema 4-D for rendering and layouts.

Most of Masamune Shirow's art has employed the portrait format, rather than the landscape format. All of Shirow's erotic art, for instance, uses the portrait format. Shirow has produced his art chiefly for publication in printed form, and mainly in book form[46] (which are in portrait format, like this book and most books). He uses fewer double-page images than some artists (such as Kentaro Miura (*Berserk*) or Eiichiro Oda (*One Piece*)). As his notes show, he is very conscious of issues such as colour and contrast, and how his art will finally look when it's printed.

Water and the ocean is a significant ingredient in the work of Masamune Shirow: it's striking how many works are set next to water – for all the usual reasons of looks, movement, symbolism, etc. (Maybe for Shirow growing up and living in Kobe has been an influence here: Kobe is by the sea,[47] with the city built onto hills rising above the port. And Kobe being the epicentre of a major earthquake (in 1995), which killed 6,000+ people and destroyed over 100,000 buildings (including Shirow's house),[48] has likely influenced Shirow.)

'A PHILOSOPHY TEXT WRITTEN BY ALIENS'.

In *Ghost In the Shell: Man-Machine Interface*, Motoko discovers a file by a professor which she reckons looks like 'a philosophy text written by aliens'. And that is exactly how many fans and critics regard the footnotes and side-notes to Masamune Shirow's *manga*!

For some, Masamune Shirow's style is too dense, too difficult and confusing to follow, too easily distracted, with a tendency to wander off the point, and too pretentious. True – this is not easily-to-digest comic art, like *Oh! My Goddess, Love Hina, Naruto* or *Urusei Yatsura*. Shirow's *manga* asks for much more of your attention and your committment. But certainly, Shirow-sensei is a world-maker, and a lot of people find the worlds he creates fascinating.

Shirow-sensei provides references to many books in the *Ghost In the Shell manga* that he recommends: *Sensors and the Eyes of Living Things* (1985) • *Jintai no Shori* (= *Victory For the Human Body*) • *The Recursive Universe: Cosmic Complexity and the Limits of Scientific Knowledge* by William Poundstone • *The Relationship of Fungi To Human Affairs* by W.D. Gray • *Adam Link – Robot* by Eando Binder • *Biomaterials: An Approach To Artificial Organs* by Dr Yoshito Ikada, etc.

---

45 Screen tone or zip in *manga* is a big part of the artist's armoury: there is screen tone of all kinds, including readymade cityscapes and skies.
46 With a sideline in magazine, video game and book covers.
47 Shirow used to live very near the sea, then he moved about five miles from the coast.
48 The epicentre of the quake flattened a huge area of Kobe.

FASHION AND CLOTHES.

One aspect of Masamune Shirow's art is obvious to anybody: it features a feeling for costumes, accessories and fashion which I would contend is the equal (and in many respects the superior) of any of the celebrated fashion designers of recent times: Tom Ford, Alexander McQueen, Thierry Mugler and even England's Queen of Fashion, Vivienne Westwood (not to mention the classic brands, such as Coco Chanel, Christian Dior, Yves St-Laurent, D. & G., etc). The use by Shirow of corsets and steam-punk paraphernalia has obvious counterparts in the fashion designs of Westwood, John Galliano and Jean-Paul Gaultier.

Meanwhile, Japan has produced many celebrated fashion designers, including Issei Miyake, Takoda Kenzo, Mori Hanae, Janya Watanabe, and Kansai Yamamoto[49] (b. 1944), known for his flamboyant stage costumes manufactured for David Bowie, which drew on *Kabuki* theatre.

In *Intron Depot: Ballistics*, Masamune Shirow admits that his cutaway costumes revealing lots of skin are not always practical: of one of his slim-hipped, big-breasted, young police officers with only a thong below her waist, Shirow noted: 'a high-exposure costume like hers has no particular rationale to justify it except that it's fun to draw (for me, anyway)'. The *animé* adaptations have followed the maestro's example: some of the costumes worn by Deunan Knute and Motoko Kusanagi sure aren't practical.

HUMOUR.

Like many *mangaka*, Masamune Shirow has produced 4-*koma* (four-panel) strips of his *manga* works such as the *Appleseed* and *Ghost In the Shell* stories (which feature the usual light-hearted, single gags of *yonkoma*). There are also many *chibi* (super-deformed) versions of the cast of *Appleseed*, for instance: Deu and Bri in a flying *Yellow Submarine* machine, or Deunan and Bri as pirates in a pirate galleon, or dressed as Native Americans, or Deu and Bri astride a scooter, or a mechanical fish, etc. The *chibi* forms in the *Appleseed manga* emphasize, again, the humour in *Appleseed*, which the *animé* adaptations insist on ignoring.

It's the same story in other adaptations of Shirow-sensei's work: the action, the serious themes, and the detailed futuristic worlds[50] are played up, while the humour is sidelined. Mistake! Humour is a *vital* ingredient in the Shirowian cosmos. All of Shirow's key works feature humour – *Ghost In the Shell*, *Appleseed*, *Dominion: Tank Police* – and some, such as *Orion*, are much more comedic than serious.

The first *Tank Police animé* adaptation, released in 1988 as *Dominion: Tank Police*, caught the essential element of humour in the *manga* by Masamune Shirow. It focussed very much on Leona Ozaki, but also

---

49 The famous Japanese-themed costumes for the Ziggy Stardust persona were designed by Kansai Yamamoto, who met David Bowie in 1973. The clothes included satin cloaks that were made to be pulled off Bowie with a flourish (you can see this in *Ziggy Stardust* movie. The device comes from Japanese *Kabuki* theatre). The layered approach revealed another costume underneath or sometimes just glam underwear.
50 Unfortunately, the O.A.V.s/ TV series/ movies of *Ghost In the Shell* opted for a much safer, more recognizable futuristic vision of Japan.

offered a very entertaining portrayal of yet another team in *animé*.[51] Thus, *Dominion: Tank Police* might be the most successful film or animated version of the Shirowian heroine, in capturing her humour, compared to *all* of the adaptations of *Appleseed* and *Ghost In the Shell*, etc.

'MADE IN JAPAN.'

Masamune Shirow's *Ghost In the Shell manga* is 'made in Japan' – as if it could be made anywhere else! To remind readers, Shirow sometimes includes the words 'MADE IN JAPAN' tattooed onto the chest or rear of some of the slinky, young characters (on page 123 of the first *Ghost In the Shell manga,* one of the maids working for the Colonel is seen in close-up, her svelte *derrière* bare under frilly panties, and stamped with 'MADE IN JAPAN'). Yes, the finest cyborgs in the future will by made in Japan (which, as we know, is actually going to be true! Japan leads the world in robotics and cyborgization).[52] In his "Afterword" to *Appleseed*, volume one, Masamune Shirow noted that 'this comic was originally written for Japan'.

CYBORGS.

Cyborgization makes for great science fiction stories, but it is problematic on many levels. Politically, it's a time bomb. Only the privileged few would be able to afford it (look at who can afford plastic surgery and body augmentations at the moment). Ideologically, it has deeply suspect elements, many bordering on fascism, the 'survival of the fittest', and other post-Nietzschean philosophies.

Manga author Yukito Kishiro (*Gunnm* a.k.a. *Battle Angel Alita*) said that 'from an ideological point of view, I'm against the idea of cyborgs'. But Kishiro agreed with Donna Haraway that, in a way, we are all already cyborgs:

> urbanites of the modern age are a lot like cyborgs, you know. They become immediately incapacitated when you cut off their juice. Isn't that what being a cyborg is all about...?[53]

The more sophisticated *animé* and *manga* explore some of these issues[54] (such as *Ghost In the Shell* and the work of Katsuhiro Otomo), but many other Japanese sci-fi stories are content to go, 'cool, a robot!'

Other names for robots or androids in *animé* and *manga* include the *jinzo ningen* in *Dragonball*, 'perso-coms' in *Chobits*, 'boomers' in *Bubblegum Crisis*[55] and 'bio-androids' (or 'bioroids') in *Appleseed.*

---

51 The animation of *Dominion: Tank Police* is very late 1980s – that is, colours include deep blues and reds, the action is very broad, with plenty of squash and stretch, and giant close-ups.
52 Japan still uses more robot technology than any other nation, and was also the first country to employ robotization in industry.
53 Quoted in T. Ledoux, 1997, 58.
54 How Motoko and the cyborgs are powered is left aside by Shirow; they must use a *lot* of fuel.
55 *Pace Bubblegum Crisis*, Philip Brophy noted that 'the hyper-sexed construct of a woman with an incredible figure who is also a crack marksperson is a complex assemblage of male, female, gay, straight, heroic and S. & M. fantasies' (2005, 58).

The love in Japanese pop culture of robots (who grow souls), dolls, puppets, toys, ghosts in the machine and ghosts in the shell is well-known (the dolls are called *ningyo,* and the automata are *karakuri ningyo* (automata from the Edo period).)

Certainly Masamune Shirow's fiction and art is among the finest in the giant robot sub-genre of science fiction. His mobile suits and automated machines look like they could really work or exist, whereas most giant robot TV shows don't bother with piffling, distracting details like real science or physics; they just crack on with the loud action scenes.

Jeopardy is of a different order for a cyborg heroine – smashed to bits, she can commission a new body from one of the mega-corporations in Nihon. Thus, the threats in *Ghost In the Shell* are to the ghost inside that shell – the brain, the mind, consciousness, the self, identity, memories, etc, via hacking, viruses, 'cyber-crime' and infiltration (from Puppeteers and Super-Class-A hackers).

Why are there so many *female* robots and cyborgs in the world of Masamune Shirow? In the appendix of *Black Magic,* Uncle Shirow comes up with some reasons – all pretty dodgy. Because, Shirow insists, a female shape has a lower centre of gravity. Because, Shirow says, a female cyborg would put off enemy troops for a moment, making them hesitate in firing (at a 'woman'). Because, Shirow asserts, pervs might put their life at risk. But then he comes clean, and admits that it's 'to make this manga more attractive'.

RELIGION IN THE SHIROWWORLD.

The work of Masamune Shirow refers to religion at times, and a whole *manga* story is devoted to it: *Orion*. In the posterbooks and pin-ups, there are Buddhist shrines and religious artefacts. But the *animé* adaptations of Shirow's material included far more references to religion, and Western religion very obviously, than occurs in his comics. Angels, crosses, crucifixions and the like were added to the *Ghost In the Shell: Stand Alone Complex* series and the *Ghost In the Shell* movies.

Steeped in Shintoism and Buddhism, the use of Christian and pagan/ occult imagery and motifs in *animé* reflects a flirtation with foreign religious influences which typically occur in teenage (the Christian wedding ceremony, for instance, or *Harry Potter*-esque occultism and Greek mythology). And if Western religion is cited, it's often as something exotic, strange, other, and even sinister (as in *Hellsing, Black Butler, Samurai Champloo, The Qwaser of Stigmata* and *Urotsukidoji*).

Animé will take motifs and symbols from all sorts of places, often just for the look or the feel, disregarding the theological, religious or cultural attributes (and often drawn from foreign movies). As long as it look exotic and other-worldly, that's cool. Thus, the Star of David[56] is employed without the filmmakers seeming to be aware of its enormous cultural and religious significance. It's the same with cruciform and church imagery.

---

56 Often in magical scenes or rites, where the pentagram would be more suitable.

The *Ghost In the Shell* movies/ TV series, like many *animé* products of this type, revolve around very familiar dualisms and oppositions:

Body	Soul or spirit
Body	Mind
Organism	Machine
Brain	Computer
Individual	Network

The terminology changes, so sometimes it's the 'ghost', or the 'soul', or the 'spirit', or the 'mind'. But the dualities are very familiar. Indeed, they are contained in the title 'the *ghost* in the *shell*'. The 'ghost in the machine' might be an alternative (and perhaps more accurate) title for *Ghost In the Shell*.[57]

Of course, there *are* slight differences between someone's 'soul' and their 'spirit', or between the 'soul' and the 'mind', or the 'mind' and the 'ghost'. But it's the bigger differences, between being organic and being a machine, between the body and the mind or spirit, between organic life and artificial life, btn being natural and man-made, that're really important.

As Masamune Shirow notes in the notes to the *Ghostly manga*:

what we refer to as the "spirit" or "soul" is a very vague concept, including things programmed into, or closely related to, the physical body, such as memory, the results of chemical reactions, and emotions, etc. (357)

Is the body just a 'shell'? Does it matter what body you have attached to the mind or the spirit? Can a spirit exist inside another body, different from its own? Or inside a machine?

In fact, Masamune Shirow prefers to use the term 'spirit' rather than the more Western 'soul'. His work is very Oriental in its use of religion in this respect: it's not about individual souls, but about spirits which link to a universal spirit, a mystical oneness which chimes with the ontological unities central to the religions of Shintoism, Taoism and Buddhism.

The point about cyborgization and replacing parts of the human body with artificial organs for Shirow is that there is more to humans than just a physical self, plus a brain (and possibly a mind). Spiritual or religious aspects need to be considered (even if they are not 'scientific' or 'real'). In short, we are not only flesh and blood.

Whispering ghosts (one of Motoko Kusanagi's mantras is 'my ghost whispered to me') is Masamune Shirow's hi-tech version of intuition or sixth sense or people (like shamen or psychics) who can channel the unseen. (Thus, even Chief Aramaki recognizes the significance of espers and spiritual mediums).

Ghost In the Shell, as Shirow-sensei explains in the notes, employs the notion of bodies linking to a higher level spirit. This is a true ghost, 'the

57 But it has been used many times – from the Arthur Koestler book.

higher level spirit attached to human bodies'. In other words, the 'ghost in the shell' (*Ghost*, 362). For Shirow, spirits and physical bodies are (ideally) in harmony; cyborgs, such as Motoko Kusanagi, confront this issue head-on, experiencing the difficulties of fusing their spirit with a new, artificial body. (Shirow also employs the terms 'phase' and 'mode' (*Ghost*, 363), which is the entire body-brain-spirit entity).

The *Ghost In the Shell* franchise uses cybernetic technology to deliver what are essentially stories of ghosts, or spirits (*ayakashi*), or the dead, or *yokai* (demons). In Japanese pop culture, ghosts, the deceased, demons and the like are everywhere. Only a few (special/ magical/ disturbed) people can see them. Many times in several of the *Ghost In the Shell* outings vision is hacked, and scenes play out only in the perceiver's cyberbrain. Batou can make someone think he's been decapitated; Aoi can hack Batou so he's invisible; and the Major is a genius at manipulating perception and cyberbrains.

The companion *mangas* to *Ghost In the Shell* are usually regarded as *Appleseed* and *Dominion: Tank Police*; but for the religious/ metaphysical/ philosophical issues, it's *Orion*. Here Shirow-sensei delved deeper into how bodies relate to minds and spirits. (In the *Ghost* sequel comic, Shirow ventured further into the spiritual issues of cyborgization and artificial intelligence).

Orion is a 13-chapter *manga* of 266 pages in total, yet Shirow still provided 15 pages of notes and a dictionary of his invented terms. The dictionary offers explanations of terms such as 'anti-dharma master spell', 'cubular warheads', 'harmonic core disintegration' and 'hexapole solar reactor'.

Ghost In the Shell works superbly within a Japanese religious context – Shintoism is the main religion of Japan – because that's where it comes from (with some Buddhism and Taoism, too. There are numerous references to Buddhist religion in Shirow's work). In the notes for *Ghost*, Shirow cites some concepts from Shintoism:

> Shinto also considers things in terms of three stages – the *ikumusubi* or conscious self, the *tarumusubi* or unconscious self, and the *tamazu-memusubi* or the self that transcends the self. (363)

But *Ghost In the Shell* also works within a Western (and a Christian) context, and you can leave aside the Shintoist/ Buddhist philosophy. Of course: because this kind of *manga* and movie/ *anime* is a hybrid. As well as being very Japanese, *Ghost In the Shell* is also very Western (and very North American).

Take the form: the 1995 movie is a hi-tech thriller, which's primarily a Western form (and, in cinema at least, also a North American form). It employs the cop or detective form, which's North American. It uses *film noir* elements, too, which're again North American.

There's no doubt that *Ghost In the Shell* and Masamune Shirow's other works have been popular in the West partly because of their North

American elements. It's the same with Katsuhiro Otomo and *Akira*, and Toshio Maeda and *Urotsukidoji*. Yet some franchises which're popular in the West – such as *Naruto*, *Bleach* and *Pokémon* – are very Japanese. And of course *Akira*, *Ghost In the Shell* and *Overfiend* are also distinctly Japanese.

SHIROW, DE SADE AND SURREALISM.

The art of Masamune Shirow has several links to the Surrealist movement in Europe of the 1920s-40s. The Surrealist artists did not seriously alter notions of sexuality, but they did question them. Indeed, Surrealism focused on sex obsessively, as obsessive as Symbolist art, from which it derives much. The Surrealists were well-known for their concepts of *l'amour fou*, of sex and death, of æsthetics and poetry. As André Masson wrote, 'eroticism and death are always coexistent.'[58] Typical among Surrealist images and philosophies is Salvador Dali's *Phenomenon of Ecstasy*, showing several photos of women (supposedly) in orgasm, a collage that targets the main areas of Surrealist discourse which are always connected: eroticism, death and 'the feminine'.[59]

Nearly all the major Surrealist artists made erotic art, or included erotic elements in their art: René Magritte produced the *Rape*, showing a woman's body as a face, with breasts for eyes and the vagina for the mouth,[60] Salvador Dali drew many erotic pictures, including bizarre, moustachioed men being serviced by prepubescent girls entitled *Choice Treats For Children* (child abuse images which are distinctly un-PC), and Man Ray produced films that evoked pornography. Hans Bellmer created a series of erotic images based on dolls (which were used in the second *Ghost In the Shell* movie).

One of the gods of the Surrealism movement was the Marquis de Sade. The high priest of metaphysical eroticism was championed by the European, artistic élite, such as Charles Baudelaire, Jean Cocteau, the Surrealists, Algernon Swinburne, Lautréamont, Fyodor Dostoievsky and John Cowper Powys. Among visual artists, the inheritors of the Sadeian pornographic ethic include Pablo Picasso, Hans Bellmer, Jean Cocteau, Max Ernst, Allen Jones and David Salle. Many artists have had a go at illustrating de Sade's work. Shirow's work draws on the Western/ European tradition of Sadeian erotica, of art created under the influence of the Divine Marquis. (The Sadeian approach to erotic material has certainly influenced Shirow's own erotic art).

58 André Masson: *Entriens avec Georges Charbonnier*, Paris, 1958, 138.
59 S. Dali: *Phenomenon of Ecstasy*, in *Minotaure*, nos. 3-4, 1933, 77.
60 R. Magritte: *The Rape*, 1934, pencil drawing, 14 x 9.5in, Menil Foundation Collection, Houston, Texas.

Masamune Shirow a.k.a. Masanori Ota
(this is a rare photograph of Shirow).

Below: Shirow's home town Kobe (photo: I-Stock).

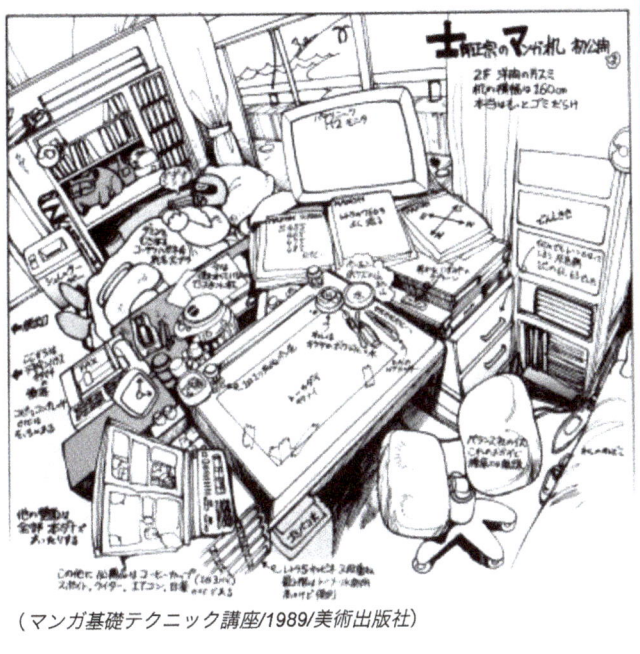

（マンガ基礎テクニック講座/1989/美術出版社）

Masamune Shirow's sketch of his studio in 1989.

Masamune Shirow's self-portrait, included
in the manga of Ghost In the Shell

●士郎さんに直撃 Q&A!

【攻殻の単行本2巻はいつ頃に?】

●1998年の中～後半の労力ほとんどを使って仕上げる予定です。単行本1巻のように並べやすい内容ではないので、調整が難航しています。大幅な加筆、「外科手術」が必要になっていますね。可能な限り早く仕上げるべく努力してますので、もうしばらくお待ちください。

【これから発売予定の作品は?】

●「INTRON DEPOT 2」が1998年前半に青心社から出ます。1992年から1997年にかけて描いたイラストの内、ファンタジー系を中心にまとめた画集です。サブタイトルをつける予定です。いずれは「攻殻」1と2のカラー部分だけを集めた「ID・3」を講談社から出します。「攻殻」以外の1992年から1997年のメカ系イラストは「ID・4」になる予定ですが、これもそう遠くない将来に形にできると思います。

それと、青心社から出版される(仮)「イスラエル」という小説に格闘&エロ系カラーイラストを描きました。著者は「メガブレイド」の出海まこと氏です。

●士郎正宗完全BIBLIOGRAPHY

『アップルシード1』	青心社	1985
『アップルシード2』	青心社	1985
『ブラックマジック』	青心社	1985
『ドミニオン』(絶版)	白泉社	1986
『ブラックマジック M66 絵コンテ集』	青心社	1986
『アップルシード3』	青心社	1987
『1988アップルシード・カレンダーブック』(絶版)	青心社	1987
『アップルシード4』	青心社	1989
『アップルシード・データブック』	青心社	1990
『攻殻機動隊』	講談社	1991
『仙術超攻殻オリオン』	青心社	1991
『INTRON DEPOT 1』	青心社	1992
『ドミニオン』(白泉社版の再刊+番外編を収録)	青心社	1993
『ドミニオンC1・コンフリクト編 第1話』	青心社	1995
『コミックガイア版 アップルシード総集編 士郎正宗ハイパーノーツ』	青心社	1995
『1997ドミニオン・カレンダー』(絶版)	青心社	1996
『攻殻機動隊 Cyberdelics』(ポスターBOX)	講談社	1997
『1998士郎正宗カレンダー GEMCAT』	青心社	1997

※青心社・問い合わせ先 ☎06-543-2718

●攻殻Tシャツ&ポスター発売!

●講談社が漫画のキャラクターグッズ制作に本格的に取り組むことになり、「攻殻」ではTシャツと超大判ポスターを計画中。予約限定生産方式で、来年2月頃からヤンマガ誌上で告知&予約開始。「サイバデリックス」ほど高いものにはならんでしょう。

1997年、士郎さんは久々に漫画家であった。サイバやゲームやいろんな動きもあったけど、なんといっても「連載」がYMにとっては記憶されるべき大事件だったよ。そして今回の赤BUTA……。士郎さん、来年も漫画家でいてくれよ～!

●未確認!? 情報、乱れ打ち!

●秋に発売予定だったゲーム「攻殻」のアニメメイキングビデオは、4月発売予定。●Windows版ゲーム「ブラックマジック」、価格9800円(税別)でウィズから発売中。●『ヴァレリア・ファイル』シリーズ(谷甲州・作)のさし絵を士郎さんが執筆予定。中央公論社から。●富士見書房から発売中のトレーディング・カードゲーム「モンスター・コレクション」に士郎さんも少し参加。●講談社から「攻殻」のメカ系解析本とノベライゼイション第2弾が。

SHIROW NEWS!

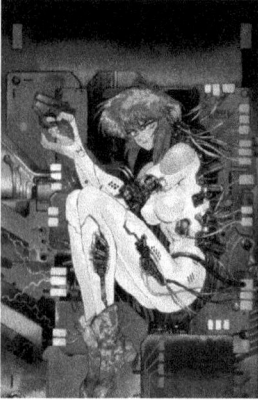

Manga and artwork by Masamune Shirow.

TV and movies based on the work of Masamune Shirow

02

MASAMUNE SHIROW AND THE JAPANESE *MANGA* INDUSTRY

THE *MANGA* INDUSTRY.

Manga (comics1) are huge in Japan, and more so than in any other country (though they are on the increase in some places). North America doesn't have a comics tradition anything like *manga* culture in Japan: in Japan, a *manga* like *Shonen Jump* might sell 6 million copies a week, enormous numbers.2 (Some claim that the North American comic industry has never recovered since its run-in with media watchdogs in the 1950s).

Japan has the most sophisticated, the most varied, the funniest, the most entertaining, and by far the most imaginative comics culture in the world. Yes, we know that France, Germany, Spain, Italy, China, Korea, Britain and U.S.A. (among others) have thriving comic industries, but none of 'em come anywhere near Japan.

In Japan, the audience for *manga* is pretty much everybody: the stigma in the West attached to comics simply doesn't exist: everyone reads *manga*. The Japanese *manga* market is bigger than the *animé* market. *Manga* also requires far fewer personnel to create, and is cheaper to disseminate.

The market is led by three big publishing houses: Kodansha, Shogakkan, and Shueisha.3 Other notable *manga* publishers include Hakusensha, Futabasha, Shonen Gahosha, Kobunsha, Akita Shoten, Media-Works, Square Enix, Kadokawa Shoten, Ohzora, Shuppan, and Nihon Bungeisha. Shirow has worked for the big companies and some of the smaller ones.

In 2000 in Japan there were 15 monthly magazines, 10 twice-weekly magazines, and 12 weeklies. Some have print runs of over a million copies. *Manga* accounted for about a quarter of all publishing sales (about

1 The term comics covers everything – 'comicbook' seems too fussy and 'graphic novel' is a commercial term (both 'comicbook' and 'graphic novel' are attempts to reposition comics as prestige or literary items).
2 In a 1994 speech, Hayao Miyazaki compared that 6 million with the video sales of *Beauty and the Beast* in the U.S.A.: 20 million, for a nation with twice the population of Japan. Selling 20 million in America would be like selling 10 million in Japan, Miyazaki suggested, and *Shonen Jump* sells 6 million *manga* a week!
3 The Japanese companies have links to Western companies: Shueisha and Shogakukan, for instance, own Viz, Kodansha has worked with Del Rey, and Square Enix with Yen Press.

550 billion Yen (there are about 100 Yen to the U.S. dollar).[4]) *Manga* absorbed around 40% of Japan's printed matter. The average spend on *manga* was ¥4,500 for everybody living in Japan. According to VIZ Media, the *manga* market in Japan in 2006 was worth US $4.28 billion (and $250m in the U.S.A.).

There were around 3,000 *manga* artists working in Japan in 2000 (not including assistants or contributors to anthologies). Using assistants is commonplace, altho' they are only occasionally credited (sometimes, assistants are given part of a *manga* to show off their work).

Manga are read very fast. Readers in Japan flip thru *manga* at speed. They don't linger over the artwork: not when a weekly *manga* magazine contains 400 pages! *Manga* is thus quick and disposable. *Manga* are read once then chucked away, like a newspaper.

All *manga* are published for either males or females. Only magazines aimed at very young children cater to both, and a few others. The gender separation, then, is fundamental to *manga* publishing: it's either boys *or* girls, men *or* women. *Not* both.

And then the market's divided into *manga* for two or three age groups (typically, teen and adults, or youngster, teens and adults). Of course, readers within each category can be anyone.

Whatever you think about that, in marketing terms it works wonders – because the sales of *manga* magazines are stupendous in Japan. The gender split is separated into five categories of *manga*: *shonen* = boys; *shojo* = girls; *seinen* = young men (also called *dansei*); *residu* = women; and *seijin* = adult (including erotica for men). The work of Masamune Shirow is pretty much exclusively targetted at the young men and adult male categories. (Shirow has very rarely entered *shojo* territory: an attempt was made in 2012 with *Pandora In the Crimson Shell*, tho' the artwork wasn't by Shirow).

In 1995, there were 23 *manga* magazines (*shonen*) aimed at boys, and 45 magazines aimed at girls (*shojo*). Boys' magazines accounted for 662 million copies in sales (about 38% of the market in the 2000s); girls' magazines for 145 million copies. Magazines like *Shonen Jump* and *Weekly Shonen* sold over 2 million copies each week in the 2000s. *Shonen* and *shojo manga* have had the highest profile in the West. *Seinen* (young men's magazines sold 551 million copies (the biggest category for sales) with 37 titles (about 31% of the market in the 2000s). Women's magazines (*redisu*) accounted for 103 million copies, with 52 titles.[5] *Manga* for adults as a whole (including golf, *pachinko*, *mah jongg*, *tanbi mono*, 4-panel and others), accounted for total sales of 786 million copies, from 197 titles.

In Japan, *manga* made up 40% of all books and magazines in 1995. As Fred Schodt put it:

> Japan is the first nation in the world to accord "comic books" –
> originally a "humorous" form of entertainment mainly for young
> people – nearly the same social status as novels and films. (2002, 19)

4 113 to 1 dollar in 2017.
5 Source: Research Institute For Publications, *Suppan Geppo*, Mch, 1996.

Japan has the most sophisticated and *by far* the biggest comic tradition in the world. Sales in 1995 amounted to 2.3 billion *manga* books and magazines printed (or 15 for every citizen annually). In 1995 there were 265m magazines published on a regular basis. The big magazines can sell millions a week, while others might be a few thousand copies.

There are two types of magazines physically: stapled and folded ones, and glued, square-backed ones (which might be as big as telephone directories). Most *manga* are published in the B5 format (10 x 7 inches) or A5 (8.2 x 5.8 inches). This book is 9.25 x 6.14 inches.

As well as *manga*, the word *komikkusus* is also used (usually by folk trying to be intellectual), as well as *comics* and *gekiga* (= 'drama pictures'), for more serious or realistic works.6 (The term *gekiga* was introduced partly to distinguish comics aimed at older readers from those aimed at kids).

In Japan, *manga* are very cheap, compared to comics in the U.S.A. and Europe, where comics are typically 30 or 40 pages long, in colour, are published monthly, and cost a few bucks. In Japan, *manga* are nearly always black-and-white,7 run to 100s of pages, come out weekly, and cost far less per page. A *manga* in Japan might also run to 1,000 pages, and include 20 or more stories.

The huge quantities sold per issue are a key factor in the *manga* industry: *manga* can be so cheap and so large because they sell in such enormous amounts (advertizing, as in all magazine publishing, contributes significantly to supporting the business). They also allow artists to spread their stories out over many issues, as well as expanding story beats within an installment.

MANGA IN THE WEST.

Manga has become more popular in North America and Europe in the 21st century, with new *manga* magazines being launched by the big Japanese publishers (such as *Daisuki, Banzai* and *Manga Power* in Germany, *Shonen* in France, and *Shonen Jump* in the U.S.A.).

In the mid-2000s, the *manga* market in the U.S.A. was $40-50 million, and the *animé* market $400-500 million. Tokyopop were one of the pioneers of Japanese-style *manga* (in 2002), which they called '100% Authentic Manga'. The artwork wasn't flopped, the art retained the Japanese sound effects and layout, and the books were printed in the same compact format of Japanese *manga*. Tokyopop sold nearly 200,000 books in 2002. Other publishers (such as Viz) followed suit. *Shonen Jump* was published by Viz (it sold 300,000 copies in 2002). Tokyopop had started out as Mixx Entertainment, the company (founded by Victor Chin, Stuart Levy and Ron Scovil) behind *Sailor Moon*, a great success in the West in the Nineties.

Publishing *manga* in the English language has only really taken hold since the 1980s, when *Barefoot Gen* was an early success (a group of

6 Fred Schodt notes that *manga* can mean comicbook, cartoon, comic strip, caricature and animation (2002, 34).
7 The cover and a few pages inside might be in colour.

volunteers, called Project Gen, translated the classic wartime story by Kenji Nakazawa, beginning in 1976, inspired by its strong political message).

Manga have moved into many Asian territories, such as Taiwan, Hong Kong, Thailand and South Korea (Thailand is a major market for Japanese *manga*, and all of the main Japanese boys' and some girls' magazines are published there).

France has a tradition of comics known as *bandes desinées*: many Japanese *manga* are published in translation in *bandes desinées* (including the long tradition of erotic comics publishing in France).

Manga magazines and books read right to left; some translations in the West (such as from Dark Horse and Viz in North America), have tried to maintain the right-to-left format, without flipping the artwork (there are good arguments for both methods). Some publishers in the West have brought out translated versions of magazines such as *Shonen Jump* (such as Viz).

As well as flipping the artwork, Western publishers also translate the speech bubbles, and alter or remove the sound effects (in Japanese *manga*, the sound effects, written in Japanese *katakana* characters (and sometimes using *hiragana*), are regarded as part of the artwork, not as separate elements. Indeed, *manga* feature a range of sound effects *far* more sophisticated than Western comics: *mangaka* have developed sound effects for everything, from the sound of rain (*para para, za, botsun*) to noodles being eaten (*suru suru*)).

The audience for comics in the West is still largely young males and the comics reflect that, with their superhero stories, their emphasis on action, sci-fi, fantasy and horror. In Japan, the audience for *manga* is everybody – and thus *manga* stories include any kind of story that has been of interest to anybody. (Fred Schodt compares *manga* in Japan to populist media like television, which broadcasts to everybody: but in the West, the market is much smaller and narrower).

THE *MANGAKA*.

From the *manga* artist a whole industry is created: the stories and the characters are able to generate *animé* adaptations (which might be updated or rebooted as well as spun off into other series), Original VIdeo Animations and TV specials, toys, plays, radio dramas, musicals, 'operas', CDs, video games, and movies. (The industry formed around the work of Masamune Shirow isn't as large as some of the famous *mangaka* such as Masashi Kishimoto (*Naruto*), Rumiko Takahashi (*Urusei Yatsura, Ranma 1/2, Inuyasha*) and Eiichiro Oda (*One Piece*), but it's still considerable).

Artists will often have a number of stories running concurrently, in different magazines. They work hard, Fred Schodt pointed out, because they love what they're doing, and hard work is part of Japanese society (you only have to read any *manga* of any kind to realize that!).

Altho' *manga* artists have assistants and a manager, it will be their story, concept, layout, pencilling and inking. The artist is very much the engine in the *manga* factory. 'Individual artists, with the aid of their publishers, are what power and feed the entire system', remarked Fred Schodt (1997, 138). So if the artist becomes ill, everything stops. (Thus, vacations, long breaks, travelling overseas, etc, are not top priority; indeed, Shirow-sensei has not travelled much, and has admitted to feeling antsy if he hasn't worked for a while).

Most *mangaka* are not professionally trained, did not go to art school, and did not graduate from high school. What counts is stamina, imagination, and the ability to keep coming up with new stories.

Because they don't employ huge teams to produce them (unlike cinema and television), and they don't have committees and groups writing them, *manga* often contain quite a bit of the artist, including their autobiography: in *Dreamland Japan,* Fred Schodt opined:

> manga represent an extremely unfiltered view of the inner workings
> of their creators' minds... In Japan, a single artist might employ many
> assistants and act as a sort of "director," but he or she is usually at
> the core of the production process and retains control over the rights
> to the material created. (31)

Shirow's form of comic art could not be constructed by a committee: Shirow is not a team player (as he found out when he worked with the animation team on the adaptation of *Black Magic*). No, he prefers to work on his own (with an assistant or two over the years). But he does work with editors and publishers.

In Japan, the really successful *mangaka* become celebrities and millionaires.[8] They retain the rights to their work (and will also earn revenue from licensing deals (including merchandizing), rights for *animé*, and royalties on sales of *tankobon*). They are the subject of newspaper and TV attention (including documentaries), do public signings and appearances, have comics written about them, and record albums. Masamune Shirow has of course famously *avoided* all of that attention – to the point where not many folk even know what he looks like.

In the *manga* industry, editors have a lot of power. They have a close relationship with their *manga* artists, for a start, to the point where they travel in person to collect the pages (they like them even in this computer age to be on paper). Editors liaise with their authors, and sometimes cajole them to produce the weekly pages (even locking them in a room until they come up with the goods!). Editors discuss the storylines, and occasionally they'll also help to write them. (*Mangaka* regularly satirize their relationship with their editors in their *manga*). Shirow has noted the significance of his editors (such as Harumichi Aoki and Shigehiko Ogasawara), who trek out to Kobe to visit.

---

8 *Dr Slump's* creator, Akira Toriyama, made $2.4 million in 1981.

MANGA AND ANIMÉ.

Manga and *animé* are closely aligned commercially as well as culturally.[9] Many *animé* shows are based on *manga* (and some of the big shows have their own *manga* spin-offs – reworkings from the *animé*, for instance, or 'film comics' using still frames from the animation). *Manga* can be a cheaper means of testing out if a story will work with an audience. There are many more *manga* stories than *animé* stories. Thus, *animé* has a huge source of stories to draw on, alongside novels, plays, TV shows, video games[10] and all the other products that can be adapted.

Certainly *manga* and *animé* have been important in depicting Japanese culture overseas – and it will be for many their first encounter with Japanese culture.[11] Masamune Shirow's *manga* and artwork is utterly Japanese, and celebrates all things Japanese. *Manga* and *animé* are popular in many Western markets, including France, Britain, Italy, Spain, Germany, and into Hong Kong, South America, and South-East Asia.[12] The U.S.A. is the primary market outside Japan. In Europe, *animé* is most popular in France (and France has a substantial animation industry). Sci-fi, cyber-punk and steam-punk are also much admired in France, as are comics.

Most consumers of *animé* and *manga* in the U.S.A. are young males (90% of the market is consumed by men between the ages of 18 and 36, according to a Viz survey). The art of Masamune Shirow is perfect for that market.

MANGA STYLE.

Characters speak in bubbles, but also have commentaries or asides included in panels (Shirow-sensei famously turns the side panels into long-running disquisitions on numerous topics). Characters speaking in different attitudes/ tones are indicated by different typefaces. It's common for characters to be depicted in *chibi*/ super-deformed versions as well as their usual forms on the same page (the *chibi* versions of the *Ghost In the Shell* characters, which Shirow includes in the comics, have sadly been ignored by all adaptations). *Manga* make much of double-page spreads, exploiting the increased page count that allows for more designs spread over two pages than their Western counterparts. Bleeding over the page is common. Sometimes a single word or idea in text is placed in an empty panel, to emphasize it. Abstract 'auras' are sometimes arranged around characters in *shojo manga*, indicating mental states

For Buichi Terasawa (*Space Adventure Cobra, Red Brand Takeru*), it's the storytelling that is the most important part of *manga,* not the art:

> …*manga* is a visual medium, so people might think the art is the most

---

9 The crossover between *manga* and *animé* is well-known (many animations are *manga* first, and *manga* are in turn produced from movies.) There is also a crossover into computer games, board games, card games, pop music and online gaming.
10 Among the well-known *manga* and *animé* that were based on computer games were *Final Fantasy, Pokémon,* and *Sakura Wars.*
11 See G. Poitras, 2001, 8.
12 H. McCarthy, 1996, 7.

important aspect. But actually, the story is far more important. A series of pretty pictures does not a *manga* make. (T. Ledoux, 1997, 131)

If an artist is working for a weekly *manga* magazine, that means a whole chapter of 20 (or even 40) pages has to be produced each week. Sometimes artists have to create up to 80 pages a week. That is *a lot* of drawing! After the pages have been picked up the editor (in person),[13] there is still plenty of work to do, such as adding texts to the speech bubbles, and getting the pages ready for the printer (the dialogue, called *nemu* (name) is printed on paper, cut into strips, and pasted into the speech balloons.)

The pressure can be intense. No wonder, then, that magazine editors have been known to try all sorts of tactics to squeeze out the required number of pages from their artists, including cajoling and threatening, and locking them up (called *kanzume* or 'canning'), and forcing them to draw the pages. Some *manga* artists will use their own families, as well as assistants and friends, to create the weekly pages. Editors will act as ghost writers, and massage big egos. The editor-artist relationship is often parodied or the subject of its own skits and jokes.

The typical *manga* story extends over 20-30 pages per week (= one chapter), far more than its North American counterpart. So that when they're published together as *tankobon*, stories might run to over 2,000 pages.[14] Shirow-sensei has seldom produced comic strips on a weekly basis; he admits that he is far too slow for that.

Collected paperback editions of *manga* appear as *bunkobon*, compact and cheap paperback editions (of about 300-400 pages in a 4 x 6 inch size), or the more expensive *tankobon* (about 200 pages, in a 4.375 x 6.875 inch format). Single issue comics are 24-48 pages. *Kanzeban* (= complete edition, a.k.a. *aizoban* = collector's edition) are usually 300-400 pages, sometimes with colour, and additional material. *Wideban* (= wide edition) are printed larger than the original work, usually on cheap paper (with pages up to 1,000). Shirow's work has been published in all of the chief formats for *manga* (and he has been known to re-draw and polish art for the collected editions).

The *manga* cycle begins with stories being produced in magazines which're typically published bi-weekly, weekly, bi-monthly, monthly, or quarterly. Later, *manga* are often re-published as collected volumes or *tankobons* (in both paperback and hardcover formats). An *animé* will often be produced from a successful *manga*, with spin-offs such as a theatrical movie, spin-off O.V.A.s, updated or re-booted *animé* series, plus tie-in video games, toys, CDs, and stationery, plus live-action versions, radio versions, musicals, 'operas', *manga* based on the movies, and novels.

The collections of *manga* that are published in magazines (sometimes in hardback) are called *tankobon*. This is where the most revenue is

---

13 *Manga* editors and publishers tend to collect the finished pages from their artists in person, instead of the pages being sent in the mail, or by messenger. Leaving the artist without the pages would mean 'a great loss of face', said Fred Schodt (1997, 144). Most *manga* editors are male (and usually older men).
14 F. Schodt, 1997, 18.

generated in the *manga* market.[15] Famous *manga* works such as *Ghost In the Shell*, *Akira*, *Nausicaä of the Valley of the Wind* and *Fullmetal Alchemist* are republished as *tankobon*. *Tankobon* have a longer shelf life than throwaway magazines, and usually stay in print much longer than magazines.

There are four writing systems employed in Japan: *kanji*[16] (ideograms), imported from China; *hiragana,* a cursive script (the script most often used in *manga*); *katakana*, a more angular script; and Roman letters. *Furigana* (a.k.a. *yomigana* or *rubi*) are training wheels for young readers. *Mangaka* employ all four writing systems. Nouns are both singular and plural. Pronouns are usually left out. Definite articles are not used. And there are thousands of *kanji*.

Manga, as Fred Schodt noted, tend to be melodramatic, exaggerating everything, including the visual style and the story. That exaggeration may stem from *Kabuki* theatre, an 'indigenous love of stylization', but also because *manga* are entertainment, after all (1997, 79). Shirow is conscious that he is producing entertainment for readers. All good *mangaka* know that they're putting on a show.

The great thing about drawings is that one can do anything in them – including things that real actors might refuse to do! Filmmaker and *mangaka* Takashi Ishii, for instance, told Fred Schodt: 'I could put the 'actresses' in my manga in any position I wanted. In the films now they often refuse!'[17] And one can imagine some actors (even porn stars) balking at performing some of the scenes in Shirow's erotic work.

There is an enormous emphasis on the eyes in all *manga* (and *animé*). Highlights are usually included (deriving in part from the use of the eye light in cinematography – even in night scenes, where it's apparently dark, you'll see little eye lights shone into actors' eyes). As well as highlights, stars are featured, adding extra gleams and emotion (what Fred Schodt called 'liquid pools of rapture'). Plus tears, of course (there is a *lot* of weeping in *manga*, but often it's in frustration/ exasperation/ embarrassment/ anger rather than sadness).

Osamu Tezuka is sometimes credited with introducing big eyes to Japanese animation and *manga*; Tezuka was in turn influenced by the Disney Studios. In fact, as Gilles Poitras correctly notes (1999, 102), big eyes have been a staple of animation all over the world (partly because so much acting and expression is in the eyes). However, in *animé* and *manga* big eyes have become part of the whole look and culture, and they often do appear *very* large (and often coupled with a cute – *kawaii* – ingredient). Shirow continues that tradition – his character designs are firmly embedded within the context of Japanese popular culture.

Fantasy is absolutely central to the *manga* tradition (and the *animé* tradition) in Japan. As Fred Schodt noted in *Dreamland Japan:*

Most stories – even if they depict normal people doing normal things,

15 G. Poitras, 2001, 66.
16 The meanings of *kanji* are modulated by the phonetic *katakana* and *hiragana* on either side.
17 Quoted in F. Schodt, 2002, 286.

or impart hard information on history or the tax code – at their core are pure, often outrageous fantasy. (30)

Despite the astonishingly fantastical and violent nature of *manga* and *animé*, Japan has one of the lowest crime rates in the world. There is a huge sex industry, as Fred Schodt notes, and occasional outbursts of violence (such as the suicide cults, and downtown shootings), but Japan is far more well-behaved than most Western nations.[18] Shirow has addressed the issue of crime and the portrayal of the authorities and the security services (he likes his characters to be armed to the teeth, when he also knows that in Japan guns are very rare).

Racial stereotyping is all over *manga* (and *animé*): foreigners are often portrayed as foreign in a clichéd manner: Chinese and Korean characters, for instance, will have slanted eyes and buck teeth. Westerners are depicted as hairy hulks, altho' Japanese characters will be given Caucasian features. (Remember that only one per cent of the Japanese nation are from other territories: Japan remains very much an isolated island in that respect).

However, Japanese characters are often presented as idealized versions of Westerners or Caucasians: women, for instance, will take on the look of fashion models from the Occident, to the point of having blonde hair and blue eyes, while remaining thoroughly Japanese. The issue of 'whiteness' in relation to Japanese characters sometimes confuses Western readers: whatever their skin colour, even if it's appears white, these are *Japanese* characters.

It isn't unknown for *manga* artists to photograph real scenes on the streets of Tokyo, xerox them and incorporate them directly into their *manga* stories. That can be quicker and easier than re-drawing a complicated image (such as a city street or a machine. For some *mangaka*, this enhanced the feeling of making a movie, because it added photographic techniques to their drawings, so that the *manga* came over like storyboards for a live-action production).

Masamune Shirow didn't do that in his early *manga* (or in the first *Ghost In the Shell*) – photocopies of the 'real world' just aren't dense or eccentric enough for Shirow. But when he took the digital art route, we saw photographic elements appearing throughout his art. So that recently, Shirow's art contains 100s of bits of photographs – but they've been cut up, used for textures, and reworked.

MANGA HISTORY.

In Japan, there is a long tradition of line drawings and woodblock art that goes back beyond the 19th century. The tradition includes fantasy and eroticism as well as humour and domestic topics (the emphasis on blood and guts and exaggerated eroticism mirrors the 'penny dreadfuls'

18 Akira Fukushima has researched the effect of *manga* on its readership (in 1992), and discovered that altho' *manga* contain plenty of sexual imagery, exposure to *manga* might lessen the amount of sex crime. Fukushima claimed that young Japanese were late developers sexually, and were more repressed, compared to other nations.

and schlocky magazines of 19th century Europe). Early examples of Japanese art include mediæval scrolls (such as those legendarily produced by the Buddhist priest Toba, hence the name *toba-e* = 'Toba pictures' or *Chojugiga*,[19] describing 18th and 19th century picture books), the yellow jacket books (*kibyoshi*), which combined b/w prints and stories, the woodblock prints and *ukiyo-e* of the Edo period, and erotic prints (*shunga*). (According to Fred Schodt, 'townspeople in the Edo period were crazy about humorous woodblock illustrations and trashy illustrated storybooks' [2002, 138]).

There is also a long tradition going back beyond woodblock prints of the 19th century of *humour* – and of including comedy right in the middle of serious scenes.

Masamune Shirow has dug deep into Japan's history for some of his artwork – the mythology in *Orion*, for instance, or the many historical elements in the pin-up and posterbook works, featuring samurai warriors, monsters, wooden houses, etc (in the *Hellhound* and *Japanesque* series).

The visual styles of Japanese *manga* are far wider than those in the West, which are still shackled to Renaissance and post-Renaissance space and perspective, to figurative art, and to photo-realism. By contrast, Japanese *manga* employ a huge variety of visual approaches, including super-deformation or *chibi* forms, and all sorts of abstraction. (As Donald Richie put it, 'Japan has no tradition of the common style known as realism'). Surely one of the reasons for Shirow's popularity in the West is that his *manga* art has been relatively 'realistic', or at least, contains elements which conform to Western styles.

---

19 Shortened from *Choju jinbutsu giga* = 'Scrolls of Frolicking Animals and Humans'.

From the Black Magic manga.

Dominion: Tank Police manga
(this page and over).

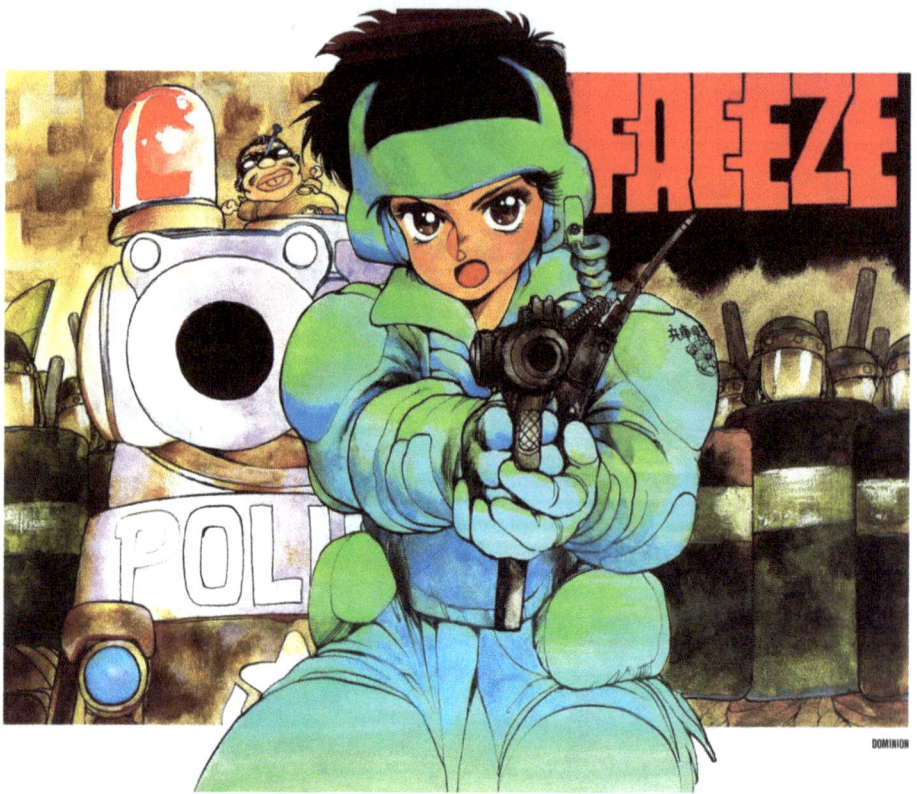

FREEZE

DOMINION

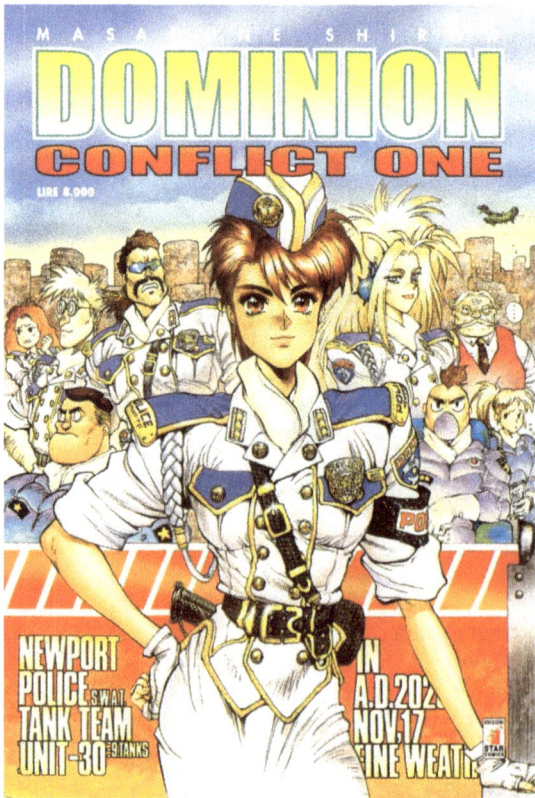

MASAMUNE SHIROW

DOMINION
CONFLICT ONE

LIRE 8.000

NEWPORT
POLICE SWAT
TANK TEAM
UNIT-30 9 TANKS

IN
A.D.202?
NOV.17
FINE WEATHER

Orion manga (1991)
(this page and over).

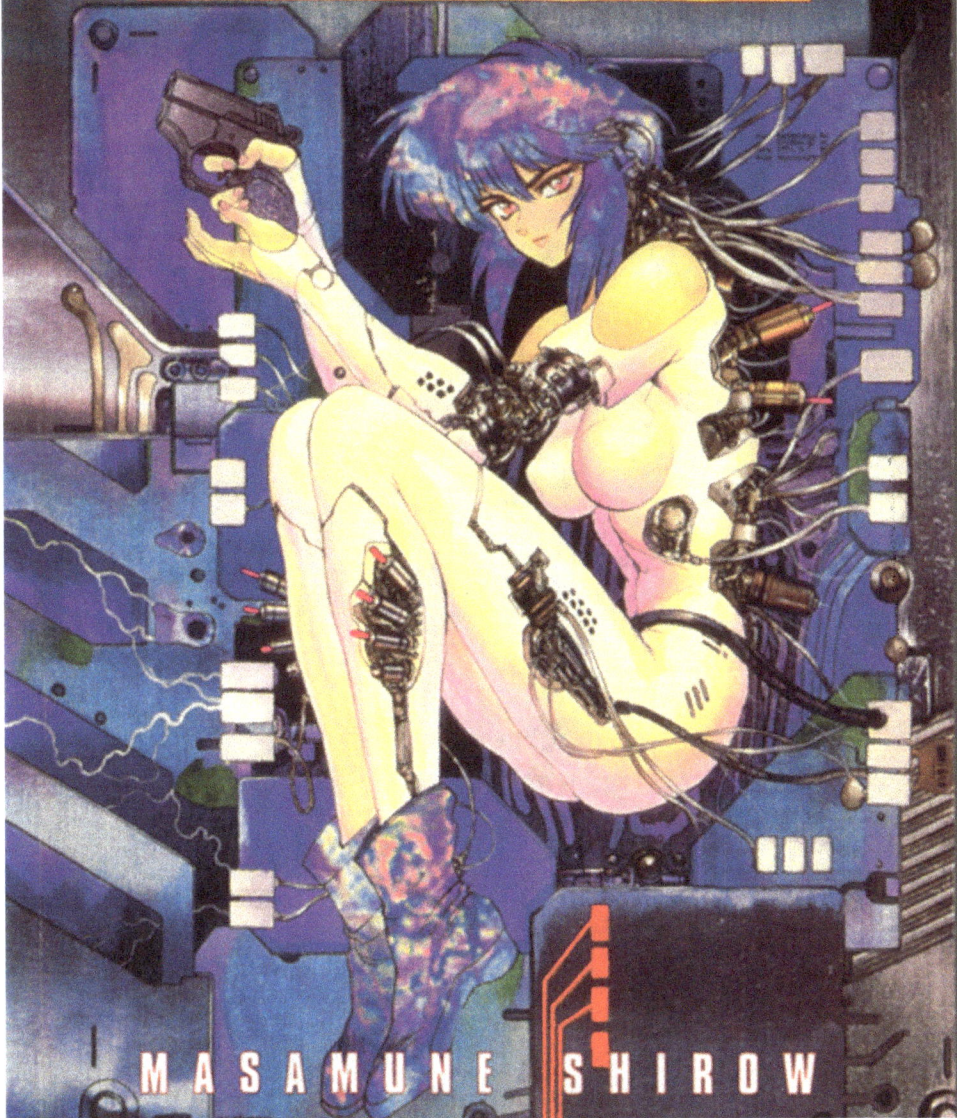

Masamune Shirow's first Ghost In the Shell manga
(on this page and the following pages)

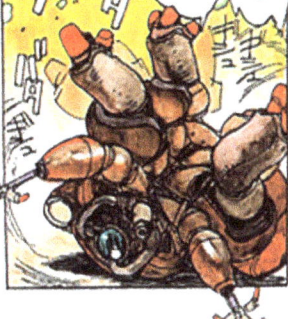

This page and over: pages from Masamune Shirow's follow-up
to Ghost In the Shell, Man-Machine Interface

Cyberworld

見つけたのはいいけどよ
充電してもどうせまた
命令無視して何処かで
作動停止するまで
夕陽を眺めてるんだろ
このロボットは

気に入ったぜ
依頼主にゃ悪いが
電脳コア頂戴して
太陽観測カメラにでも
繋いでやるか？

それとも面倒を
終わらせて
やるべきかな？

Dead Drive (2012-13)

From the Classical Fantasy Within novels (2007-10), in Newtype Ace magazine

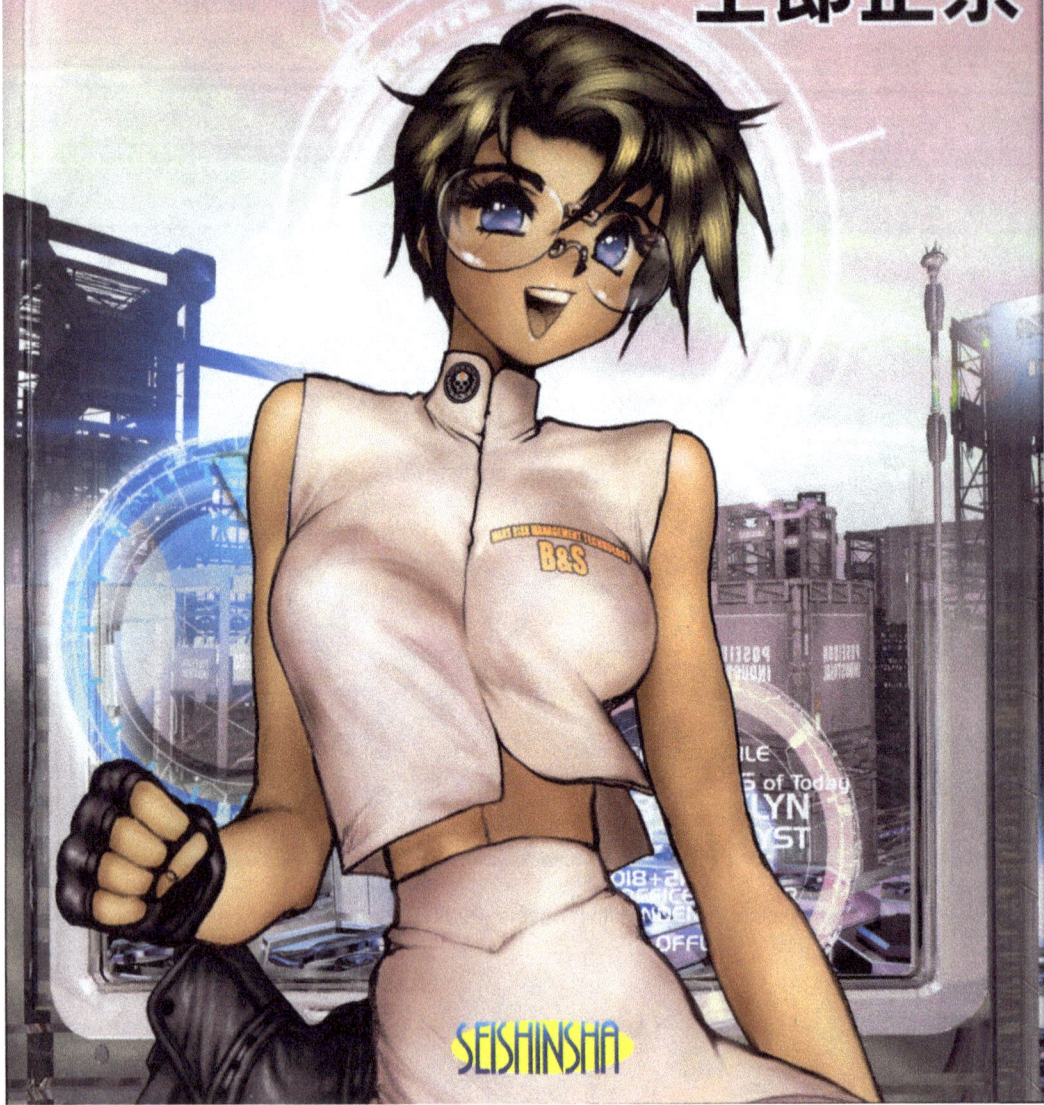

Pieces 2: Phantom Cats (2010)

Pieces 5: Hellhound 2 (2011)

Greaseberries 1 (2014)

Greaseberries 4 (2019)

Canopri Comic cover

023

Examples of variations in the artwork used by Masamune Shirow:
it's the same model in different settings. (This page and over).

Appleseed costume play: Anime Expo, 2007 and Sakura Con, 2009.
Dominion: Tank Police costume play: the Musson Sisters, London Film and Comic Con, 2014 and South Africa, 2010.

Ghost In the Shell costume play: from top left, clockwise: Makiron • Edra Lena • Crystal Graziano • Omi Gibson , 2011 • Rosie Cupcakes, 2014.

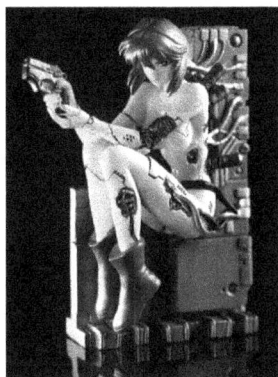

Some toys, games and merchandize based on the
work of Masamune Shirow.

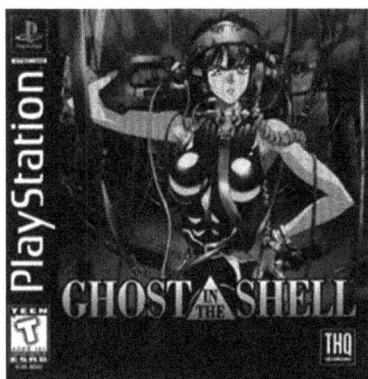
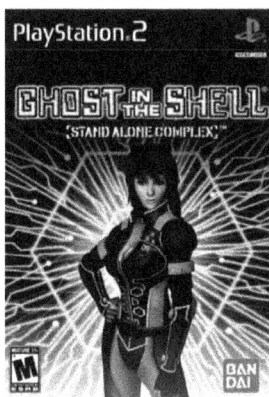

03

THE *INTRON DEPOT* SERIES AND OTHER WORKS

INTRON DEPOT

It's worth considering the *Intron Depot* series, as the books contain plenty of *Appleseed* material. Many famous *mangakas* publish collections of their artworks. Masamune Shirow has published calendars, posterbooks, pin-up collections and art books. 'Intron' is Shirow's term for 'introductory element'. *Intron Depot* (1992), for example, contains some marvellous posters, *manga* book covers, sketches, proposals, video covers and the like, many in colour (clearly aimed at the people who bought the *manga* of *Appleseed*, *Dominion* and *Ghost In the Shell*). Further installments (1998-2019) have included

- *Intron Depot 2: Blades* (fantasy)
- *Intron Depot 3: Ballistics* (military)
- *Intron Depot 4: Bullets*
- *Intron Depot 5: Battalion* (video games and animation artwork)
- *Intron Depot 6: Barbwire* (artwork for the *Classical Fantasy Within* novels)
- *Intron Depot 7: Barbwire 2* (more *Classical Fantasy Within* art)
- *Intron Depot 8: Bomb Bay*
- and *Intron Depot 9: Barrage Fire.*

✳

Intron Depot 1: Trading Figure. Particularly impressive are the many illustrations (30+ pages) that Masamune Shirow collected in *Intron Depot 1: Trading Figure* from his *Appleseed* years. If you're a fan of *Appleseed*, you will want to buy *Intron Depot*, for its images of Deunan and Briareos in a multitude of poses (nearly always wielding guns, and often clambering in and out of Guges mobile suits).

As well as *Appleseed*, *Intron Depot 1* features extra material created for Shirow's signature comics: *Black Magic*, *Orion*, *Dominion* and *Ghost In the Shell*, and for items such as telephone cards, magazine covers (such as *Dragon* and *B-Club*), posters, CD covers, video games, R.P.G. games, and pages from different editions of *Ghost In the Shell*. Shirow provides cutaway illustrations of the mobile suits.

Some of the artwork collected in *Intron Depot 1* goes back to Shirow-sensei's early days as an artist, to the time of *dojinshi* and fanzines (some of these images, featuring space girls and robots, are derivative works in the sci-fi and sword-and-sorcery genres). Part of the charm of the pieces from the Eighties and Nineties is the colour – achieved with gouache, acrylics and watercolour paints. Yes, *paint*. Real paint that you wiggle a brush in and make marks on paper.

The confident and bold use of colour in the works of the 1980s-1990s period reminds us that Masamune Shirow was a master of colour as well as design from early on in his artistic career. Scarlet body armour for the Puma Twins and Motoko Kusanagi, or Leona in a bright green uniform, and mobile power suits in every colour you like (blue, grey, beige, yellow, green, red, silver).

Artbooks like the *Intron Depot* series and the calendars allow the art to shine – printed in full colour, and with a single image per page, where it can breathe, taken out of the context of a story (where it's competing with other material). One of the beauties of Shirow's art is that it operates very well as single images, without needing a narrative context. That is, even in the early days, Shirow was already moving towards the format of the pin-up, the stand-alone artwork. Or, maybe Shirow was always an artist of one-shot images, and was distracted into writing long-form comics. After all, most artists throughout history have worked with single, stand-alone images.

Intron Depot also contains numerous sidenotes by Masamune Shirow, explaining, as he always does, the intricacies of weaponry, high technology, power suits, tanks, and cops. (Shirow, a gun nut like so many artists in the sci-fi, action and fantasy side of the *manga* industry, could've had a second career as a military ideas man, or advising on the PR of the military machine. Shirow could tell you which machine gun looks coolest, and which would be most effective in any given situation).

✳

Intron Depot 2: Blades collects many of Masamune Shirow's illustrations with a magical or fantasy element (usually of the heroic, sword-and-sorcery or dungeons-and-dragons kind). Shirow's vision of fantasy art is unashamedly retro – these images of the 1990s and 2000s might have adorned magazine or paperback book covers or rock albums of the 1970s: angry, young warrior babes wielding swords and axes; wistful, dreamy princesses in floaty dresses; witches holding a book of spells and an *athame* (a witch's ceremonial knife); a dark-hued Amazon in dreads and a leopard skin; and the full complement of beasts from the world of fantasy: griffons, dinosaurs, giant squids and of course dragons.

Once again, one is struck by Masamune Shirow's genius for designing costumes: leather belts buckled over the torso to form a vest; leggings held up by chunky straps; violently scarlet dresses edged with silver; shiny armour with impossibly pointy attachments; white robes so skin-tight they *become* skin; highly eccentric armour that's cut away to reveal corsets and thong panties; and crimson, thigh-high boots with gold buckles.

These women are riding in the sky on griffons; flashing ornate swords and smiling at the viewer; punching the air in joy or triumph; slaying dragons and cutting out their teeth; soaring thru pearlescent skies on angels' wings; or summoning spirits from magical circles drawn on the ground.[1]

In *Intron Depot 2: Blades,* it's all about the look, the attitude, the atmosphere, the colours, the costumes and the accessories. Nearly every character is a young woman with perfect skin, a bright grin, a skinny body and an immaculate costume. Full nudity doesn't interest Masamune Shirow in *Intron Depot 2: Blades* – everyone is adorned to the max with tattoos, jewellery, straps, swords, cloaks, belts, and bandages (they're not nude, but they're highly eroticized). *Intron Depot 2: Blades* is a riot of intricate forms and complex compositions, with the digital technology layering the elements on top of each other, continually enhancing the images, and changing their colour, or their backgrounds, or their beastly familiars.

✳

Intron Depot 3: Ballistics (mainly featuring late 1990s and early 2000s illustrations) shifts the focus into hardware, technology, and the military – but the characters are the same Shirowian women, sleek and blemish-free and enigmatic and aggressive and confident and dynamic. They don't keep still, and they never pose in a straightforward manner.

These women are cops, soldiers, S.W.A.T. agents and guards, and many of them seem to work for Poseidon Industrial, Shirow's super-capitalist corporation that will go anywhere to make money. In many of the images in *Intro 3: Ballistics,* women pose against hi-tech backgrounds, or complicated interiors of glass, metal girders, suspended chains, and lights (part-warehouse, part-laboratory, part-cybernetic centre).

Deunan Knute is here from *Appleseed,* as is Motoko Kusanagi from *Ghost In the Shell* – abseiling down walls in full combat gear, riding motorcycles, and of course brandishing guns. Girls point pistols in cascades of bullet cases; their legs bend in the midst of leaps; they grin at the viewer sometimes, or they're levelling their muzzle towards the viewer. The costumes are remarkable creations of grey or black rubberized material (always form-fitting, usually revealing bare skin around the hips and thighs), supplemented by a matchless array of accessories: fingerless gloves, wrist guards, comms in headgear, handcuffs, chains, straps, shields, elbow protectors, belts, pouches, etc. Every girl wears chunky boots, and many carry glass capsules of precious liquids and cybernetic comms devices on their wrists. (As it's Poseidon Industrial as a chief locale, many images have spider platforms or robots lurking in the background. Some of the images are from the *Galhound* story about a terraformed Mars, where Poseidon Industrial has set up

---

1 Reminiscent of *Fullmetal Alchemist.*

shop. In Uncle Shirow's view, a mega corporation such as Poseidon wouldn't hire burly cyborgs to defend its holdings and semi-nefarious labs, but cute, skinny, smiling young women in part-combat-part-fetish gear).

Certainly Shirow Masamune is one of the kings of girls-with-guns art – and not just any weapons, of course, but very particular snub-nosed pistols, or automatic rifles. These girls know when to pack armour-piercing ammunition, and when a pistol hidden under a pencil skirt will do instead.

Feminists loathe this kind of eroticization of women, where women are linked to weaponry, aggression and warfare (combined with titillating, fetishized costumes and partial nudity). But (male) chauvinists could counter that the women are also depicted as in control: they're the ones with the guns, they are not going to be pushed around.

✳

Intron Depot 5: Battalion focussed on video games and animation artwork created between 2001 and 2009: it's often forgotten that Masamune Shirow has been involved with the computer games based on his *manga* (and must be a lucrative sideline for him – there's plenty of loot in the video gaming industry). Here, Shirow-sensei can produce wholly digital art for a wholly digital environment, whether it's on a PlayStation, a family computer (famicom), or online.

Intron Depot 5: Battalion features page after page of drawings and digital images of *robotto/* cyborgs, monsters, heroines – and all of the accessories that Shirow gets sidetracked by: catsuits, body armour, weapons, swords, tattoos, boots…

✳

Intron Depot 6: Barbwire was a collection of material that Masamune Shirow produced for the *Classical Fantasy Within* novels between 2007 and 2010. Published by Kodansha, and written by Soji Shimada, *Classical Fantasy Within* allowed Shirow to create artwork that wasn't in his usual artistic province, such as mediæval castles and warfare, images of World War Two combat scenes, and fairy tale imagery.

Some of the artwork was published in *Newtype Ace* magazine – including a spider platform from *Appleseed* (an 'A.F.F.V.-M.T.-1'), done in a chunky, computer-aided manner, a tank, the Patrol Light Tank (driven by a young woman, of course!), and more futuristic air battles (this time featuring hanggliders designed like butterflies.)

Among the striking images in *Intron Depot 6: Barbwire* is a rare, unashamedly political outing for Shirow-sensei: Japanese fighters attacking a squadron of North American bombers.

A princess getting ready for bed, aided by a maid, in a Middle Ages castle bedroom, is a gentler image from *Classical Fantasy Within*. Several images take up steam-punk culture of the late 19th century, British sort (the 'classic' era of steam-punk art) – a bath-house, for ex, with elegant wrought ironwork reminiscent of London's Crystal Palace, and sleek steam-punk versions of motorcycles and a steam-car.

＊

Exon Depot features a short sci-fi yarn which mixes familiar Shirowian elements – religious iconography (Biblical imagery, messiahs, gods), super-detailed *mecha* (spacecraft), and mock heroic fantasy motifs. But the real reason for the existence of *Exon Depot* is so that Shirow-sensei can draw near-naked young women (including one who resembles Deunan Knute from *Appleseed*).

Another story in *Exon Depot* (1991) has another Deunan Knute-ish character exploring a post-apocalyptic city (it's overgrown with jungle). For this tough assignment, the heroine wears nowt but a skin-tight, one-piece suit leaving most of her body naked.

OTHER *MANGA* AND ART BY MASAMUNE SHIROW

ARMS.

Arms (1998) is a short (5 or so pages) story featuring the ninja warrior Toguihime from *Hellhound* (it was collected in *Pieces*). The story is simple: thar be a monster in the woods which needs taking care of. So call the neighbourhood ghost hunter/ ogre killer, the kinda girl that goes into battle wearing a bikini and thong combo, a hairband, a bow, and a host of weaponry. During the exorcism, the heroine has to leap and twirl like a circus acrobat, and inevitably she has to reveal her charms with every lunge. *Arms* was published in magazines, and was also included in the *Pieces 1 tankobon*.

＊

PIECES 1: PREMIUM GALLERY.

Pieces 1 (2008) is a collection of Masamune Shirow's fantasy and sci-fi artwork, featuring some well-known icons in the Shirowworld, such as Leona Ozaki, the Twins, Brenten and the gang from *Dominion: Tank Police*, and many of Shirow's fantasy/ sword-and-sorcery outings, such as *Arms*, and some of the pirate women from *Hellcats*.

Some of the material from *Arms* turned up in the *Hellhound* series, collected in the *Pieces* artbooks, numbers 4, 5, 7 and 9. *Pieces 1* also includes the artwork collected together as *Exon Depot* (which goes back to 1991). Some of the pin-up images in *Pieces 1* were also published in Shirow's calendars.

＊

Pandora In the Crimson Shell: Ghost Urn (2012, Kadokawa Shoten) was a *manga* illustrated by Koshi Rikudo based on a story by Masamune Shirow (a film and TV series appeared in 2015 and 2016). *Pandora in the Crimson Shell: Ghost Urn* is about the adventures of a cyborg girl (Nene Nanakorobi) who visits her relatives on an artificial island (which has echoes of *Real Drive*). Nene and her pals fight off terrorists who attack the island.

◆

Dead Drive (2012-13) was published in Kodansha's *Newtype A* magazine. It comprises digital art of an alternative modern era, in the steam-punk manner, and features a group of misfits, including a cyborg muscle-man in a grey suit, brandishing a giant gun; a *bishonen* boffin in glasses and white robes; a spaced, *lolicon* girl in a Christmassy-red outfit; and a stern-looking *femme fatale* in black fur.

ILLUSTRATIONS FOR NOVELS

Among Masamune Shirow's many commercial assignments are illustrations for novels, including the covers. As Shirow put it, 'a novel doesn't seem complete without illustrations'. Shirow, working in full colour, has said he's looking forward to a time when *manga* can be in full colour:

> I like to do full color illustrations for novels because I regard such illustrations as laying the groundwork for full color manga in Japan some day. Of course, for this to happen, there first of all has to be a *demand* for full color manga.

Taima Keisatsu (*Warding-off-evil Police*) was published by Cosmo Engineering (1998). The illustrations for *Warding-off-evil Police* were included in *Intro Depot 2: Blades*. *Valeria File 1* and *2* were novels by Koshu Tani, published by Chuokoron Shinsha (C. Novels - Fantasia) in 1999, for which Shirow provided 20 illustrations (including the book covers).

For the *Classical Fantasy Within* series of (about 8) novels by Soji Shimada (Kodansha, 2008), Masamune Shirow contributed several fascinating illustrations (again in full colour, achieved with software) in the steam-punk and fantasy vein. These were collected in *Intron Depot: Barbwire* (2007-10) – see above.

◆

Shirow-sensei has produced artwork for tie-in novels from his *manga*, and from the books spun off the *anime* adapted from his *manga*, including *Dominion: Tank Police, Ghost In the Shell, Ghost In the Shell: Stand Alone Complex, Black Magic, Real Drive* and *Appleseed*. Shirow has also created art for novels based on *Gundress, Land Lock* and *The Cthulhu Mythos*.

Several tie-in stories, comics and novels have been produced from the movie and TV versions of Shirow's work (principally the *Ghost In the Shell* franchise). Each incarnation in animation has included spin-off comics; collections of short stories and also light novels have been published.

If Masamune Shirow isn't going to write new stories for *Ghost In the Shell* or *Appleseed*, publishers (with Kodansha leading the way) will find other ways of exploiting his brand name in print works. The comics tying in with the Shirow franchises tend to be re-tellings of the movies or TV shows, akin to novelizations of movies. They were published in magazines first (typically Kodansha's *Young Magazine*, where *Ghost In the Shell* first appeared), and later collected in *tankobons*. They are shortish (3-6 volumes), and stick closely to the agreed templates.

The *manga* spun off the works of Masamune Shirow include *Ghost In the Shell* by Akinori Endo (1995, 1998); *Black Magic* by Hideki Kakinuma (2005-08); *Real Drive* by Yoshinobu Akita (2008); two *Ghost In the Shell: Stand Alone Complex* tie-in comics (by Yu Kinutani, 2009, and Yoshiki Sakurai and Mayasuki Yamamoto, 2009); an origins story about Batou and Motoko to tie-in with the *Arise* animated series (2013); *Appleseed XIII* by Yoshiki Sakurai (2012); *Appleseed: Alpha* by Iou Kuroda (2014); and *Ghost In the Shell: The Human Alogorithm* by Yuki Yoshitomo and Junichi Fujisaku (2019). A tribute to *Ghost In the Shell* from a group of contemporary *mangaka* appeared in 2017 as well as a history of the *animé* adaptations of *Ghost In the Shell*, to tie-in with the release of the live-action movie.

Three novelizations of the *Ghost In the Shell: Stand Alone Complex* series were penned by Junichi Fujisaku, appearing in 2004-05.

The two *Ghost In the Shell: Stand Alone Complex* tie-in comics re-told the story in the TV shows. They included a comic by Yu Kinutani (2009), and a series of comic skits called *Tachikoma na Hibi* (*Tachikomatic Days*, also 2009) by one of the writers of the show, Yoshiki Sakurai, and illustrated by Mayasuki Yamamoto. The tie-in comics were published in *Young Magazine*.

Ghost In the Shell: The Human Alogorithm by Yuki Yoshitomo and Junichi Fujisaku was an original *Ghost* story, which first appeared in Sept, 2019 (again in *Young Magazine*). As Fujisaku put it, *Ghost In the Shell: The Human Alogorithm* was a '1.75' version of *Ghost In the Shell* – i.e., it was set between the '1.5' of the *Human-Error Processor* comic and the '2.0' of the *Man-Machine Interface* sequel.

GHOST IN THE SHELL: ARISE: SLEEPLESS EYE.

Let's have a look at one of the tie-in *manga*. The *Arise* animated show of *Ghost In the Shell* of 2013-15 included a spin-off comic series written by Junichi Fujisaku and illustrated by Takumi Ooyama. Published in *Young Magazine* (from April, 2013, and later collected in 4 vols.), *Kokaku Kidotai*

Arise – Nemuranai Me no Otoko Sleepless Eye (= *The Man With Eyes That Do Not Sleep*) was an extended flashback to the early days of Batou and the Major.

Did they meet at an arthouse cinema showing a retrospective of Ozu, where they bonded over coffee in a café? Did they bump into each other while browsing for vintage electronics in a store in Akihabara? No: they encountered each other during a ferocious, chaotic conflict in the Central Asian country of Kuran, where Batou was leading a team of Rangers to guard a local politico.

Yes, *Ghost In the Shell: Arise: Sleepless Eye* is a tough, gritty men-on-a-mission yarn, told from Batou's viewpoint (his are the sleepless eyes of the title). So it's a men-on-a-mission tale, yes, but it also includes a woman – a very powerful woman: Motoko Kusanagi (thus, we see the Major from Batou's perspective).

The *Ghost In the Shell: Arise: Sleepless Eye manga* takes up one of the motifs of the *Stand Alone Complex* TV series: the former military life of Batou and the Major, and Batou's links with former buddies in the military.[2] This provides the link between the present tense and the past, as one of Batou's former cohorts, Norosh, acts as a terrorist bomber wreaking revenge against the military chiefs: dealing with Noroshi in the present tense leads to Batou remembering his past.

Ghost In the Shell: Arise: Sleepless Eye is delivered in the usual tough, macho style of a *Young Magazine* story (aimed at young men): it's soldiers in intense fire-fights with guerillas and other soldiers, caught in a civil war somewhere in the Middle East or Central Asia. The art by Takumi Ooyama is grimy and 'realistic': skin is dirty, walls are pock-marked with bullet holes, and everybody wears pained grimaces.

The design of the Major draws on the *Arise* TV show (this is a younger, slimmer Major, with the same horrible hair-do). But, once again, it's not Shirow's Motoko. For example, the Major has a nihilistic attitude towards her job and the political situation in Kuran (she's been sent by Kurtz and the 501 Squad, who are a prominent ingredient in the *Arise* TV series). Inevitably, Batou and the Major butt heads (and arms and legs) the instant they meet (with the customary Mexican stand-offs of weapons aimed at each other in close combat).

---

2 In the *Arise* series, this involved Colonel Kazuya Soga and his war crimes, and in the *Stand Alone Complex* series one of Batou's cronies, Marco Amoretti, was continuing his own war with obscene serial killings.

Images from Intron Depot 1
(this page and over)

Appleseed –
Deunan in her
mobile suit

Semi-naked, young women in mobile suits is
a favourite motif for Masamune Shirow
(this page and over).

TARGET
MARINA HAYAMI
QUEEN OF POOL
CORE OF PROMISCUITY
SYSTEM ONLINE

Poster for Dragon Magazine

Masamune Shirow

<Darumal>

From Exon Depot (1992)

Intron Depot 2: Blades
(this page and over).

From Intron Depot 3: Ballistics
(this page and over)

Intro Depot 5: Battalion (this page and over).

Player Character Cyborg

Intron Depot 7: Barbwire.
(This page and over)

これは表紙候補だったが分冊再編成に伴い
ボツになった絵の作業途中（手前に主人公
が入るプラン）だったもの。

010

PART TWO

THE APPLESEED MANGA

APPURUSHIDO

01

APPLESEED: THE MANGA

INTRODUCTION.
Appleseed (*Appurushido*, 1985-1989) was one of Masamune Shirow's first big successes in *manga*; it began as a *dojinshi* (fan) publication. It first appeared in *Comicborne* in 1985 (from Seishinsha). Harumichi Aoki, the president of Seishinsha, and one of Shirow's regular editors, was vital in encouraging the young artist to finish the *Appleseed manga*. *Appleseed* is Shirow's most significant success in the world of *manga* after the *Ghost In the Shell* series, and has led to many animated outings (including recent, state-of-the-art computer-aided animations). Shirow is fonder and prouder of *Appleseed* than *Ghost In the Shell*.

Appleseed was published from 1985 to 1989 by Seishinsha (and by Eclipse Comics/ Studio Proteus and later Dark Horse in North America – the second edition was published in 1995).[1] It has been re-published in a large format collector's edition (in four volumes in the West). Books of artwork from *Appleseed* have also appeared: *Appleseed Databook* (1990/ 1995 in the West, serialized in *Comic Gaia*, and in *Super Manga Blast* in English), a reader's guide, and *Appleseed: Illustration and Data* (a.k.a. *Hypernotes,* 2007), plus further volumes. There are more supplementary books for *Appleseed* than for *Ghost* from this era.

There are 25 chapters of *Appleseed*, collected into four volumes:

* *The Promethean Challenge* (*Purometeusu no chosen*), published 1985.2.15
* *Prometheus Unbound* (*Purometeusu no kaih*), 1985.11.10
* *The Scales Of Prometheus* (*Purometeusu no ko tenbini*), 1987.7.31

---

1 Studio Proteus, overseen by Toren Smith, is one of the prominent translators and packagers of *manga* in the United States of America. Among their translations are *Legend of Kamui, Domu* and *Nausicaä.* Studio Proteus has translated most of Masamune Shirow's key works, including *Ghost In the Shell, Orion, Dominion* and *Appleseed.* Shirow may have been more well-known overseas, thru the translations of his work, than in Japan.
    Toren Smith (of Studio Proteus), one of the translators of Masamune Shirow's work in the West (along with Fred Schodt and Diana Lewis), remarked in the first *Appleseed tankobon* that Shirow's 'clipped, highly stylised and literate Japanese is unusually difficult to render into English'. It was also 'a real nightmare' having to rework the heavy use of screen tone in *Appleseed,* Smith recalled.

• *The Promethean Balance* (*Purometeusu no dai tenbin*), 1989.4.15
There are also other *Appleseed* stories:

• *Called Game/ Game* in *Appleseed: Illustration and Data*
• *Hypernotes/ Appleseed Hypernotes* in *Appleseed: Hypernotes*

There are *Appleseed* video games: an R.P.G. in 1988, an action game in 1994, a PlayStation game (*Appleseed EX*, 2007), and online games (2005, 2009). There are three computer-aided animated features (2004, 2007, 2014), a cel animation O.A.V. (1988), and a 13-part TV series (2011).

Masamune Shirow has probably lost count of the number of times that fans have asked about more *Appleseed* installments. Every time a new adaptation of *Appleseed* is produced, no doubt Masa-kun gets questioned (begged) yet again. And, twenty and more years later, he has always answered, yes, more *Appleseed* is possible, but then he lists all of the other things he's doing. (At the time of the 2004 *Appleseed* movie, Shirow stated: 'Currently there are no plans to publish. The situation is such that there are decidedly no plans or even intentions to produce').

In short: Masamune Shirow has moved on to other projects. He has also probably been self-sufficient economically since the late 1980s, and doesn't need to be chained to a desk by a magazine editor to create 20 pages (= one chapter) of comics each week.

However, *Appleseed* didn't completely end with volume four and the fragments of volume five: Shirow-sensei continued to draw Deunan Knute from time to time for his calendars and posterbooks (though not Briareos so much). Thus, Deunan pops up occasionally (firing guns in the 2005 calendar, for instance), and the calendars and later art include Deunan-ish girls doing Deunanian things (like abseiling down a building, or wearing mediæval armour). And anyway, what are most of Shirow's later women, in his digital art from the mid-1990s onwards, but Deunan Knute (or Motoko Kusanagi) in slightly different guises?

Appleseed is a classic Masamune Shirow work: futuristic setting, a giant, technological city, cops vs. terrorists, the battle for control of the society, cyborgs (here called 'biodroids' or 'bioroids'), lots of guns, helicopters, computers, and robots (here, the familiar exoskeletons or giant, metallic, mobile suits of *animé*, called Guges, Landmates, and Protectors), big shoot-outs, sneaky, slippery villains, an authoritarian society, a giant computer network (called Gaia),² some goofy humour, some 'fan service' touches (including lots of nudity), Greek mythology, fetishized hardware and weaponry, references to *Blade Runner,* and that all-important understated romance/ relationship between a human and a cyborg – *Appleseed* has all the usual Shirowian ingredients.

Appleseed is an overly-designed, indeed, obsessively designed story: every vehicle, every machine, every computer interface – and of course every mobile suit and every weapon – has been worked over by

2 Gaia the super-computer of course has an enormous central control room which's filled pipes, terminals, and machinery (using circular motifs).

Masamune Shirow at the drawing board[3] until it's stuffed with details. So Athena and Nike don't climb into just any old car – it's a sleek buggy with doors that hinge upwards, and enormous rear wheels. And Hitomi and Yoshi travel on funky motorbikes. (And Uncle Shirow has worked out the back-stories for everything, too, which appear in either the sidenotes or in the supplementary publications about *Appleseed*).

Deunan's weaponry includes a Gong gun (which fires rubber stun bullets), a single-shot pistol, a Seburo 10-mil pistol, and of course her treasured pistol given to her by her Daddy, Karl (called a Government = 'Gover').

The *manga* of *Appleseed* is very appealing, and very entertaining, with an atmosphere that none of the *animé* versions have captured. It's basically a future society being explored thru the eyes of a young couple, who happen to have enlisted as cops, so they get to see aspects of this new society that regular folk can't see (which's one of the fundamental aspects of a cop show, and the benefits of having cop charas, who have a legitimate reason for visiting many areas of life).

The *Appleseed manga* has a terrific *mix* of elements – it's got action, *mecha*,[4] sci-fi and issues, yes, but also plenty of pages portraying characterization, relationships and humour. (Also, the *manga* isn't bogged down, like some of Masamune Shirow's later *manga*, by numerous footnotes and sidenotes, where Shirow-sensei muses on many topics. Actually, there *is* plenty of additional material in the *Appleseed* universe – it was collected in books such as *Appleseed: Illustration and Data*).

'Since this isn't a novel, all this stuff I've gone on and on about probably really isn't all that important, and I probably don't need to go into it in such detail anyway,' Masamune Shirow admitted in *Appleseed Illustration and Data*. But he did go into it anyway (the form of a novel would allow Shirow to digress and meander and footnote his stories to a far greater degree).

There are plenty of political machinations, principally involving the power-dressing, ambitious leader Athena, her assistant Nike and her bioroid followers. I have to admit when the *Appleseed manga* drifts away from Deunan and Briareos and spends too much time with Athena, Nike, the Director, the Council and Hitomi, or some of the minor charas among the security services (who're somewhat interchangeable), it loses some of its appeal for me. Partly because Athena and the other politicos are rather routine and dull characters (or, rather, the way that they intersect with the themes and issues are routine), whereas you don't always know what Deunan or Briareos are going to say or do. (Athena, for instance, is portrayed in almost all of her scenes standing at a window, staring out over Olympus,[5] and pontificating on how to run Olympus/ Aegis, and on the bioroid vs. human problem).

And also, the most appealing scenes in the *Appleseed manga* are often

---

3 *Appleseed* was created by going straight to layouts, Shirow said, rather than working out the story using thumbnails (1994).
4 Motorcycles, cars, trucks, helicopters – *Appleseed* is jammed with transportation.
5 She is thus literally like the gods and goddesses on Mount Olympus in Greek mythology (or how they have been depicted in popular culture).

those simple conversations between Deunan and Briareos, when they're horsing around, or bickering. (Shirow says he can't draw in the *shojo* style, but parts of *Appleseed* might be produced like a girls' *manga*, and it would be easy for a decent *shojo mangaka* to re-tell and re-design all of *Appleseed* as a *shojo manga*. *Escaflowne*, for instance, was published in editions for boys and for girls).

In the *Appleseed manga*, the relationship of Deunan and Briareos has an innocence and sweetness about it. The *animé* versions don't capture that. A great pity. In the *manga*, for example, Briareos carries Deunan about on his shoulder (that's on the cover of the first *Appleseed tankobon*, for ex. So cute!). And in the first action sequence in the *manga* he leaps from roof to roof carrying Deunan.[6]

Appleseed was successful from the outset: it won the Seiun Sho in 1986. It's a work of youth, of a young man: Masamune Shirow was 24 when it was first published. The *Appleseed manga* has a charm about it, and that charm coalesces in the main around the personality of Deunan Knute, and in the relationship between Deunan and the cyborg Briareos Hecatonchires. *Appleseed* is thus a *manga* with a couple at its centre: a girl and a cyborg. It's a relationship of companionship and romance as well as working for a living and battling terrorists and *mecha*.

Appleseed is Masamune Shirow's power suit/ mobile suit *manga*. The first power suit with a pilot was introduced in *Mazinger Z* by Go Nagai. *Mazinger Z* (Toei Animation/ 3B Production/ T.E.N.) was the first adaptation, in 1972 (in the West it was called *TranZor Z*). The first *Gundam* series was animated in 1979.

As to design, the *Appleseed manga* follows the familiar format of most Japanese *manga*: chapters open with double-page spreads or big drawings; there's a splash or title page; most pages're four, five or six panels; some drawings are highly detailed (the *mecha*, the cityscapes, the computers); many drawings are filled with darker tones (Masamune Shirow admits to using a lot of shading devices); comical scenes are in cartoony or deformed style (and much lighter in tone); there's speech on almost every page; occasionally abstract or stylized compositions're used (heads are placed off-centre, for ex, or against white space); for the action scenes Shirow employs the usual speed lines, tilted angles, exaggerated perspectives, and of course loud sound effects. Chapters sometimes run beyond the standard 19-20 pages of *manga*, so *Appleseed* is longer than a conventional 25-chapter story. Many of the forms in *Appleseed* use Shirow's beloved organic shapes – the buildings often have rounded or elliptical forms (tho' not as extreme as those in *Dominion: Tank Police*).

Appleseed, for Jason Thompson,

> starts out as a fascinating sci-fi exegesis on planned societies but gradually degenerates into combat porn; volume 4 is little more than a you-are-there gunplay reality show punctuated by obsessive footnotes. (15)

---

6 The later *animés* included a *hommage* to that scene.

DEUNAN AND BRIAREOS.

Deunan Knute is one of a number of marvellous female heroines that Masamune Shirow has created, taking her place alongside spunky, independent Leona in *Dominion: Tank Police* and of course, the totally extraordinary Motoko Kusanagi in *Ghost In the Shell.*

The central buddy cop relationship/ romance in *Appleseed* of young, female Deunan Knute and hulking, rabbit-eared cyborg Briareos Hecatonchires is clearly a forerunner of the Kusanagi-Batou relationship in *Ghost In the Shell* (both Deunan and Briareos are tough cops in a Special Weapons and Tactics team who've worked together for years). In the *Appleseed manga*, far more's made of the erotic relation between the two (just as the 1995 *Ghost In the Shell* movie also toned down the Kusanagi-Batou relationship from the *manga*). In Shirow-sensei's *Appleseed* comic, Deunan and Briareos are portrayed in an affectionate, loving manner, including being in bed. None of the *animé* versions have gone that far (they have Deu pecking Bri on the cheek, for instance).

In the *Appleseed manga*, Masamune Shirow offers brief biographies of the charas: Deunan Knute ('Dunan Nut' in Japanese) we learn is a young (23 year-old) former employee of a Special Weapons and Tactics team in L.A. Briareos Hecatonchires (= 'one hundred hands') is 31, was in a bad accident (hence his cyborgization), and feels indebted to Deunan's father Karl. (Of course Briareos is older than Deunan, as in most *manga* of this kind – yes, we know that all of Shirow's female characters have father complexes! In *Appleseed*, the couple were dating when Deunan was only 17, in 2122).

Although I always think of Deunan and Briareos as Japanese (as with all of the Masamune Shirow's heroes), Deunan's parentage is 'complex', Shirow-sensei says (in *Appleseed: Illustration and Data*), tho' he doesn't give her Japanese forebears. Briareos is a 'Mediterranean black' (I'm not sure what that is – an Algerian, perhaps? An Arab? In his pictures of Bri before his accident, he is dark-skinned, and might pass as African or Arabian). Intriguingly, the back-story of Deunan and Briareos (including where they meet) takes place partly in the United States of North America (and Deunan has N. American in her racial mix).

In the *manga* of *Appleseed*, Deunan Knute is cute, blonde, small, slim, (but strong), with the customary *manga* big eyes and button nose (Shirow jokingly says that he's withholding her vital statistics, but she can't be more'n 5′ 4″). She's a classic, Shirowian heroine: determined, stubborn, feisty, athletic, fierce, a warrior, an independent woman yet completely devoted to her cyborg lover Briareos Hecatonchires. Great with a gun (hell, with any *mecha*), Deunan's a fighter, but also somewhat naïve and sweet. She is the 'heart' of the *Appleseed* franchise.

Deunan Knute is also, like so many of Masamune Shirow's heroines, a girl in amongst loads of guys.[7] (Some of the men, Deunan is told, wonder if she is a man in disguise, or if she's taking hormones. Like Motoko Kusanagi, the 'female gorilla' of *Ghost In the Shell* (as the guys

---

7 Pani is a later female addition to the E.S.W.A.T. team.

like Ishikawa who fear her dub her), Deunan is a very masculine, tomboyish woman. She's one of the boys and is completely comfortable being one of the boys).

Briareos Hecatonchires, meanwhile, is the more sedate, restrained, and sanguine member in the Deunan-Briareos partnership. He's another of Masamune Shirow's giant, hulking guys, gruff, macho, a terrific soldier, always prepared, warier than Deunan, and less idealistic. And Briareos has the extraordinary addition of rabbit ears atop a cyborg head (which features a giant, central eye). Those rabbit ears! The animators of the film versions of *Appleseed* must've cursed Shirow! But you've gotta include 'em, no matter how much you tweak Shirow-sensei's original design: it isn't Briareos unless he's got rabbit ears![8]

In the timeline in the *Appleseed Illustration and Data* book we find out that Deunan Knute was born in 2105 (and Briareos in 2096 – so he's nine years older);[9] Deu's mom was murdered in 2115; she met Bri in 2116 (aged 11); Bri joins Deunan's father's team in 2116; Bri is cyborgized in 2122; Deunan starts training in 2123 (at the Special Training Center). Deunan and Briareos were dating when she was 17 years-old (in 2122). The couple moved to Olympus in Sept, 2127.

Briareos, however, suffers his 'accident' not from injuries sustained during combat, but possibly from his former life: we learn in *Appleseed: Illustration and Data* that Briareos killed his commanding officer, and this may be related to the 'accident' that leads to him becoming a Hecatonchires-type cyborg (the movie adaptations changed the origins stories of both charas).

In *Appleseed Illustration and Data*, Masamune Shirow calls Deunan and Briareos 'near-geniuses in their mastery of technique and in the senses they possess' and 'highly trained professionals'. But he insists that they aren't superheroes: 'they are simply highly trained professionals' (but they are portrayed as superheroes several times – even more so in the *Appleseed animé* adaptations).

❊

In *Appleseed Illustration and Data*, Masamune Shirow explained that he chose to tell the story from Deunan Knute's point-of-view because it was about continuity of life, and survival, and existing with the 'other' (in this case represented by science, technology and the bioroids, and perhaps even Briareos, as a woman living with a cyborg. It's an intriguing question: could you live with a cyborg or love a cyborg if you *hadn't* known them before their cyborgization? In *Appleseed*, the relationship of Deunan and Briareos is no different when he's a cyborg; they act exactly like a flesh-and-blood couple. As do Yoshi and Hitomi the bioroid).

Deunan and Briareos are devoted to each other – indeed, their loyalty is one of the endearing aspects of the *Appleseed* stories. There is no suggestion in the *manga* of Deunan or Briareos looking elsewhere for love (however, one of the *Appleseed* movies (the 2007 one) includes hints of a

---

8 On the plus side, the rabbit ears offer a distinctive silhouette, which animators're always looking for.
9 Sometimes Shirow says 6 years older.

romantic triangle, with Deunan and another guy, Tereus. But we don't buy it – we *know* that the *only* guy for Deu is Bri!).

Are they a couple or not? The *animé* versions of *Appleseed* seem reluctant to put Deunan and Briareos together romantically (movies have many reasons for doing that). The *Appleseed manga* is very clear: Deunan and Briareos are *very definitely* a couple (in the 4th *tankobon* they're depicted in bed together). Not only that, they are devoted to each other completely (but, oh no, that's just *not* juicy enuf for movie-makers, who continually set Deunan and Bri against each other in the *Appleseed* adaptations, and introduce cheesy love triangles, or have Briareos acting like a jealous stalker, etc).

THE POST-WAR SETTING.

Appleseed begins with establishing Deunan Knute and Briareos Hecatonchires before any other characters're introduced.[10] They're living in a post-World War world,[11] yet another post-apocalyptic scenario, in 'Badside' (an Americanism for the 'bad side' of town, but it's the 'bad side' of anywhere – most of the planet is now 'bad side'). The global conflict has re-arranged the political landscape – there's an Amerikan Empire (as in *Akira*), new Middle Eastern territories (such as the Mumma Holy Republic), a Soviet Federation, Oz is virtually a new superpower, etc (all familiar stuff in many futuristic fictions, with *Appleseed* reflecting its origins in the political climate of the mid-Eighties).

'This story is set "on Earth soon after a major war". And, because of that, I must admit that drawing or writing it was sometimes a truly unpleasant experience,' Masamune Shirow noted in the *Appleseed Illustration and Data* book.

For Masamune Shirow, war doesn't always mean a nuclear war: in the *Appleseed* timeline, there is a nuclear war, but soon weapons're depleted, and people go back to fighting the old-fashioned way. (There have been two World Wars, which have seriously exhausted everything that humanity had built; the first war, a nuclear war, occurred in the 1990s; the second was conflict using traditional means).

War in the *Appleseed* cosmos is chiefly in the form of terrorism, Masamune Shirow explained in *Appleseed Illustration and Data*. Partly because if there's an all-out nuclear war, it's the End of Everything, and there'd be no story. Also, Shirow reckons that nuclear weapons stocks would be depleted in the 22nd century, and societies would've reverted to more traditional forms of warfare (i.e., bash the hell out of each other).

Middle Eastern politics lurk behind parts of *Appleseed* (as also parts of *Ghost In the Shell*) – Arabic/ Islamic and Israeli politics (and the fictional 'Munma' nation), secret services (Mossad), and weaponry (Israeli mobile suits and guns, fr'instance). Shirow was extrapolating from the geopolitics of the 1980s, when these *manga* were written. But

---

10 Yes, they have unusual names: Deunan said she was teased at school about it. Some of *Appleseed* draws on Ancient Greek culture.
11 There's been a major war, Masamune Shirow noted, which probably led to climate changes.

again, you could say that he was prophetic again, with Middle Eastern unrest continuing in the Iraq War, the Gulf War, 9/11 and the 'War on Terror' (and in picking terrorism as a key political element, Shirow chose something that hasn't gone out of style yet).

The first action sequence in *Appleseed* involves a bunch of renegades (in a tank, of course!) who've been sent to find Deunan Knute and Briareos Hecatonchires and bring them to the man-made island and metropolis of Olympus or to kill them (the ambiguity of the warring groups in *Appleseed* is essential). Doesn't matter – what counts for the *manga* reader is to see Deunan and Briareos in action. The arrival of bioroid Hitomi occurs just before this (in the first chapter of *Appleseed,* entitled "Triple Hound Hunting"), and Hitomi plays her part in helping in the fight against the invaders in the tank (by blowing it up).

When we first meet Deunan and Briareos, they are portrayed as military professionals who can assess a situation instantly, make decisions and react quickly and efficiently to it. Fr'instance, when the tank is some way off, Briareos has heard it (using those distinctive rabbit ears!), and judges its speed, direction and type. Deunan and Briareos are arming themselves within seconds, and have already come up with a plan – they have dealt with scenarios like this before.

❀

OLYMPUS.

Later, during the trip to the capital of the possibly utopian community of Olympus, the socio-political landscape of the *Appleseed manga* is unfolded: a futuristic society, a kind of utopia, but with rivalries, problems and crises bubbling underneath. A world where 80% of the population is artificial (or people who're now artificially-created lifeforms, linked to clones, called 'bioroids'). The irony of the utopias postulated in Masamune Shirow's fiction is that only robots or cyborgs or artificial lifeforms can thrive in them. Humans might dream of such futuristic realms, but only manufactured beings can live there. (The bioroid Hitomi delivers some of the exposition, introducing our heroes to Olympus).

Exactly what bioroids are, compared to clones, cyborgs, robots and the like, is defined by a cop at the police station, where Briareos goes to apply for a job:

> A human artificially created from a genetic pattern from a specific donor. We call clones with genetic material from multiple mother-sources *hybrids*. When they go through special processing, we call them *bioroids*.

Athena is one of the leaders of Olympus (big hair, power-dresser – an *Aliens*-era Sigourney Weaver lookalike – this is the mid-1980s, remember!). The other characters include: a cluster of old coots called the Council. A hierarchy of para-military types, and the cops, and Extra Special Weapons and Tactics. A Mayor. A central city called Olympus with its distinctive Arcology structures, semi-circles 2,000 feet tall (with panels or 'heliostats' used for solar power). A place with apparently no crime, but it's not the utopia it should be (what human community ever has been? None!). Here, the utopia is disturbed by the inequalities between the bioroids and the humans. (In *Appleseed*, Shirow creates the notion that a utopia would only be possible with bioroids, but not with humans. Shirow doesn't go along with that: 'The Council and Gaia believe that an all-bioroid society is the only hope for utopia. I don't', he remarked in a 1994 interview. Instead, Shirow personally advocated tolerance and negotiation. But for the purposes of fiction, the conflicts between the bioroids and humans suit the project, like humans and replicants in *Blade Runner*).

The anti-terrorist team in *Appleseed* is called Extra Special Weapons and Tactics = E.S.W.A.T. Masamune Shirow said he was concerned that readers wouldn't confuse E.S.W.A.T. with American Special Weapons and Tactics teams (in which case, *duh*, why not give the E.S.W.A.T. team a completely different name?! How about R.O.B.O.T.? Or H.U.M.A.N.?).

It's charming, too, in *Appleseed* that Deunan Knute and Briareos Hecatonchires are not already working for the police force, but have come to Olympus City partly to get work (the alternative is farming, which Briareos would be useless at, Deunan teases. Yes, from time to time, Deunan muses about 'settling down', maybe having a family, but never takes it seriously).

In the *animé* versions of *Appleseed*, Deunan and Briareos are already employed by E.S.W.A.T. In the *Appleseed manga*, we see Deunan and Briareos wondering what they're going to do for work as they stay with other people (such as Hitomi). Deunan has her eye on a mobile suit, dubbed a 'Guges' or 'Landmate'. She buys one so that she has a better chance of gaining employment (somehow, in the world of *Appleseed*, powered suits don't cost tens of million$, which they would do in our world). Briareos is dubious (Bri often gets exasperated about Deunan spending $$$$[12]). It's Briareos who first twigs that all is not right in the apparent utopia of Olympus City. A city with no crime, yet they're companies manufacturing and selling power suits? And they have these colossal, spider-shaped, gun platforms?

❄

OTHER CHARACTERS.

The *Appleseed* world contains a *lot* of secondary characters: there are Presidents (Athena) and their assistants (Nike), the seven Elders, Hitomi (the bioroid helper), Ministry of Justice agents (Arugess, Brontes), senators (Boyle), mercenaries, residents of Olympus (Artemis, Dr Matthew, Chiffon, Yoshi), and the Extra Special Weapons and Tactics teams (Sudo, Magnus, Fang, Doric, Barney, Lance and the Colonel).

There are certainly too many minor cop characters in *Appleseed* – having such a large ensemble is appealing to an artist creating a long-running *manga*, of course. But their personalities (and designs) tend to

---

12 Shouldn't the Ministry of Internal Affairs fork out for the mobile suit?

merge together. (Magnus and Morton are the only irritating characters in *Appleseed*: Magnus (sometimes 'Magus') sports a perpetual smug, cheesy grin on an out-dated design which evokes a soldier in a right-wing, Western, military comic of the 1940s).

Yoshitsune Miyamoto is the resident *otaku* and tech-head in the *Appleseed* universe: he works at a garage (Akechi Motors) that services Landmates (mobile suits): naturally, it's not long before Deunan and Briareos pay him a visit (he is recommended by Hitomi, his girlfriend). Yoshi is one of the more everyday characters in *Appleseed* – he's not a kick-ass superhero, or a high-ranking official. Yoshi's comparable with Keiichi in *Oh! My Goddess* or Takumi in *Initial D* (boys working on cars and motorcycles is a common motif in *manga*. Some charas, like Joker in *Akira*, fix motorbikes in their living rooms).

Yoshitsune Miyamoto is also significant among the secondary characters in *Appleseed*: there are many scenes featuring Yoshi (which the *animé* adaptations have mostly ignored). Also, for the chapter headers, the splash pages, and the ads and posters for *Appleseed*, Masamune Shirow often includes Yoshi, coupled with Hitomi, in pictures of Deunan and Briareos. So the four of 'em will be depicted in swimwear at the beach, or in overalls (with Deu and Bri in their E.S.W.A.T. gear), or in pyjamas and a flight suit.

Point is, Yoshi and Hitomi are the closest thing that Deunan and Briareos have to friends in the Olympus utopia. They are already a couple by the time the story starts (they are the ideal of what a bioroid couple would be like, altho' it's not totally certain that Yoshi is a bioroid. I always think of him as human). Bioroid or not, the four friends are unusual: they include a cyborg cop, a brilliant female, human cop, a female bioroid, and a male bioroid or human mechanic. (There's another chara that Deunan and Hitomi hang around with – Chiffon. When Bri asks Deunan to leave their *aparto*, for safety reasons, she goes to stay with Chiffon, without saying why. Hitomi assumes it's because the couple have had a domestic spat. No. In fact, Chiffon turns to be one o' the people involved in the assassination attempt on Briareos, and in her encounter with Deunan, Deunan kills her).

ASPECTS OF *APPLESEED*.

One of the intriguing concepts in *Appurushido* and other Shirow *manga*, including *Ghost In the Shell*, is that Japan is not a country anymore so much as a giant corporation: Shirow created a mirror corporate-country to Japan and called it Poseidon Industrial (and Olympus is also a vision of Japan of the future). As the opening page of the *Ghost In the Shell tankobon* has it: 'on the edge of Asia, in a strange corporate conglomerate-state called "Japan"'. Shirow also links Poseidon and the corporate-conglomerate-state to the phrase 'Made In Japan' (the phrase and the concept of 'Made In Japan' crops up many times in Shirow's *manga*.[13] There's a great pride in 'Made In Japan'). (In the *Appleseed Illustration and*

---

13 Sometimes in Shirow's art it's branded on an android (on a maid's butt, for example).

Data book, Shirow defines Poseidon as 'a force rivalling Olympus. Possesses powerful business skills and will go anywhere, do anything for profit'. Which is capitalism in a nutshell, or any capitalist state). Poseidon is located near Japan, on a man-made island.

That countries in the future will no longer be states or nations but huge corporations (or corporate states) is interesting – maybe it's one end-point/ destination of a super-capitalist nation like Japan[14] – but also very depressing. In a Disney-CocaCola-Sony-Time-Warner corporate country, the individual will become just part of the advanced capitalist machine – just another microchip or nano-machine, so to speak, in the cyborg body of super-capitalism.

Bezekric is where our heroes live, the main city of Olympus: the Arcology structures and the Gaia computer are housed in Gaia City. Altho' they are separate cities – Hitomi's house is further along the coast – urbanization has spread in between each place, so it looks like one big city. (All of the key areas in Olympus plot-wise are near the ocean, reflecting, again, modern Japan – Tokyo, Osaka, and Shirow's home town of Kobe).

❊

The *Appleseed manga* opens with its heroine in the kitchen! Cooking! And she hails her man from the window, welcoming him home! (And, no, no *animé* adaptation of *Appleseed* starts like that! A rock-and-rolling, chicks-with-guns movie starting with the heroine in the kitchen cooking! While Bri hollers, 'Honey, I'm home!' *No way!*).

It's a cliché of a TV sit-com scenario, of domestic femininity. But it is soon sent-up and junked, when Deunan Knute and Briareos Hecatonchires hear an approaching mobile suit in the distance (it's Hitomi the bioroid), followed by a tank, and they're under attack. (That Deunan isn't a great cook is a running gag in the *manga*, a bone of contention between Deunan and Briareos. It's a standard joke with tomboys and action girls: great at kicking ass, rubbish at making omelettes).

There's a lesbian undercurrent in *Appleseed* – Hitomi might be bisexual or just curious (there's a scene when Hitomi, drunk, joins Deunan in the shower, only to be angrily rejected after making a pass at her – Deunan doesn't swing that way!). There's also plenty of 'fan service' nudity in *Appleseed*, far, far more than dramatically or narratively necessary: a lengthy conversation scene between Hitomi and Deunan, for example, takes place at a sauna, where they have a massage, soak in the tub, take a shower, etc – and all – of course! – totally naked. Masamune Shirow makes no apologies for including this very long nude scene in *Appleseed* (none of the animated adaptations have gone there).

❊

The *manga* of *Appleseed* depicts the battle for a futuristic society, with Deunan Knute and Briareos Hecatonchires caught in the middle. Masamune Shirow creates a bunch of conflicting interests and groups: humans vs. bioroids (the primary conflict), humans vs. technology,

14 The notion of a Poseidon or giant corporation-state comes out of the ideology and politics of the 1980s, and the late 1980s in particular, just before Japan's Bubble Economy burst.

computers vs. organic life, Athena vs. the council, and Olympus/ Japan vs. the rest of the world. Ecology is a theme, too, with humanity's massive consumption being criticized (this was conceived in the late 1980s, when ecological themes were big news). Policing society is central, too – how much should law enforcement infringe on people's privacy and their rights? And super-capitalism – all of Shirow's work is a critique of contemporary Japan and its super-capitalist society. *Appleseed* asks, like other Shirow works (such as *Ghost In the Shell*): how much should a free market be regulated?

Masamune Shirow has published several commentaries on the *Appleseed* universe – monologues about the rise of terrorism; a pro-ecology piece exalting the family; a lengthy survey of the guns and weaponry in *Appleseed*; and another piece, about knives.

But there is an irony here that surely Masamune Shirow himself recognizes: that he is publishing essays about weapons and ammo and knives right next to treatises about anti-terrorism and ecology! Similarly, it's all very well Deu and Bri hankering after paradise and peace, while they and Extra Special Weapons and Tactics are armed to the teeth, employ extreme force, and are agents of the State.

❁

The *Appleseed manga* contains an extended action sequence set in Paris, France (not in any of the *animé* versions),[15] in which the E.S.W.A.T. team raid a political meeting, uncovering nefarious elements – such as the sinister image of a room of children and women being used in what is essentially slave-trading (where humans're reduced to playthings or toys, as a chara remarks).

The Extra Special Weapons and Tactics team go up against a bunch-a cyborgs, including some that're much bigger'n them (but of course they've got Briareos, who's no slouch when it comes to punching out robots and cyborgs so that their brains and brain stems're ripped from their shells). Here Briareos' rabbit ears are useful for the reader (and the artist) – in distinguishing him in amongst a bunch of characters in mobile, armoured suits (Deunan becomes just another member of the team, and requires further marks of identification).[16] Some of the characters in *Appleseed*, particularly the young, male ones, are somewhat indistinguishable from each other. They're not individualized enough (Shirow probably included too many charas for what is quite a short *manga*, compared to some long-running *manga*).

But we know that it has to be Deunan Knute who riskily calls the bluff of the 'borgs holding the women and children hostage (tho' her team aren't so sure – it wasn't part of the plan!). But it works, and renders the E.S.W.A.T. mission successful.

The French episode is a by-the-book, para-military operation, running to around 55 pages (including the canteen scene); it's the kinda scenario

15 The *animé* versions of *Appleseed* stayed within Olympus (a.k.a. 'Made In Japan'), but the *manga* ventured to France in one lengthy section, and to North America (Gotham), in another (at the time, Masamune Shirow hadn't been outside Japan. And I don't think he has done since). Only the 2014 *Appleseed* movie ventured outside Olympus (to the U.S.A.).
16 For ex, Shirow employs close-ups of Deunan inside her suit.

which Masamune Shirow seems to really enjoy writing and drawing. Shirow-sensei likes to indulge himself in exploring tactics and strategy – how to negotiate land mines, booby traps and even barbed wire.

In *Appleseed Illustration and Data*, Masamune Shirow goes into detail about the tactics that Deunan Knute employs in combat scenarios – how she fires her gun sometimes to pin down her opponents, not necessarily to kill them, and how she is thinking ahead all the time. (Part of Shirow's personality is a frustrated combat training commander – he's Lance, barking orders to his grunts in the training arena).

❖

In the *Appleseed manga*, the society of Olympus has affinities with the United Nations – thus, partly because it is one of the powerful communities that developed following the World Wars, it intervenes in trouble spots around the world (and is thus resented by other, weaker political powers).

Appleseed attempts to step away from the usual Japan-centred *milieu*, by placing the setting (Olympus) near Africa and the Azores (however, Poseidon is still situated near Japan). Further, Uncle Shirow makes Deunan Knute of mixed race (with some African in there), and Briareos is dark-skinned and a 'Medieterranea black', Shirow calls him. However, there's no doubt that, in the end, *Appleseed* is a thoroughly Japanese story with Japanese characters and Japanese scenarios.

Briareos Hecatonchires voices his concerns in the first *Appleseed tankobon* about being a pawn in the political game, about being used by the rulers of Olympus for their own ends. Deunan Knute is more practical (and more compassionate): she sees even the bioroids (such as Hitomi) as other people, and isn't so bothered about the larger, political landscape.

As Briareos points out, if the Olympus state is so peaceful, with little crime, why are they selling hi-tech weaponry like the Landmates power suits? If it's utopia, why doesn't it feel quite right?

❖

The *Appleseed manga* climaxes with – what else?! – giant combat scenes. In some sections, admittedly, you get one set of guys in mobile suits fighting against cyborgs with very similar-looking suits (or bodies). So it's not only difficult to distinguish who's who, the action is also confusing.

The finest section of the finale of *Appleseed*, however, concerns the heroine, of course: Deunan Knute has a terrific knife fight with three guys in a small, enclosed space. It's choreographed with the precision of a Hong Kong action flick, and displays Deunan at her best. And the *Appleseed manga* is always at its best, too, when Deunan is in the centre of the story (preferrably kicking ass, as she does here). And Masamune Shirow makes sure that Deunan is placed inside the compositions to show off her body to the maximum – so there are always drawings where Deunan's rear and hips are presented to the viewer.

❖

Masamune Shirow concocts several forms of body armour and

exoskeletons for his *Appleseed manga*. There is the K-2 power-assisted Protector[17] suit that Deunan wears in book four; the chunky Orcs body armour; there are Protectors as well as Landmates or mobile suits (they usually have a power-assisted system in them, and are a form of body armour). The Landmates include the Guges, the Guges-D (in book four), the Guges-MM (in book three), the Pan, and the Greyhound (made in Israel). Hitoshi Hayami has produced a detailed (30-page) guide to the *mecha* in Shirow-sensei's *Appleseed manga* (*Mecha World,* published in *Appleseed Databook*), which discusses the *mecha* and hardware of *Appleseed*. And in case you wanted to know how the mobile suits work, Shirow has drawn cutaway guides for them (collected in *Intron Depot 1*).

❋

Some of the action does become a little samey and repetitive in the *Appleseed manga* – the Extra Special Weapons and Tactics team're hurtling into yet another dangerous situation (usually a warehouse), to take out the hoods. It's a staple of the cop show genre, a'course (*Ghost In the Shell: Stand Alone Complex* is full of such scenarios), but it can get a little predictable.

However, the action in *Appleseed* is also highly entertaining, with some terrific duels: about the finest occurs in the fourth *Appleseed tankobon*, when feisty Deunan Knute (now with a black eyepatch!),[18] takes on a bunch of heavies armed with a knife. (How do you show movement and action in static drawings? There are numerous solutions, and Masamune Shirow uses all of the familiar ones. And the result is very effective in the hand-to-hand combat scenes).

---

17 Most of the mobile suits in *Appleseed* are Protectors.
18 In later installments in the *Appleseed manga*, Deunan Knute is injured in the eye, so she takes to wearing a black eyepatch (this is a nod to the character of Snake in the *Escape From New York* movie).

SHIROW. M

Appleseed manga – one of many 'fan service' moments,
when the girls visit a sauna (this page and over).

YOU LOOK ABSOLUTELY *EXHAUSTED.*

AND HERE I THOUGHT YOU WERE THE EFFORTLESS HEROINE.

HI, HITOMI, DEAR. THIS ISN'T YOUR PROGRAMMED DAY, IS IT?

HEY! YOU SKIPPING WORK AGAIN? MUST BE NICE!

I'M JUST GETTING A LIGHT TREATMENT, ANYWAY!

IT'S BETTER NOT TO DO ANYTHING THAT ISN'T ON YOUR PATIENT CHART.

yawn

I WONDERED WHAT THE DEVIL WAS GOING ON...A MASSAGE, hmm?

WHAT DID YOU THINK IT WAS?

YOSHINO, WILL YOU TAKE CARE OF THIS OTHER LADY?

YES, MA'AM.

YOU'RE NEW... HUMAN, AREN'T YOU?

ARE YOU...?

BEEP

YES, I AM.

MY GOODNESS ...YOUR SKIN IS IN TERRIBLE CONDITION...

HITOMI, HOW COULD YOU TELL? WHAT GIVES US AWAY?

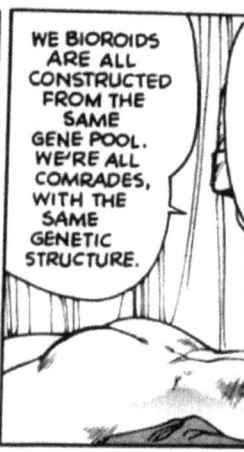

WE BIOROIDS ARE ALL CONSTRUCTED FROM THE SAME GENE POOL. WE'RE ALL COMRADES, WITH THE SAME GENETIC STRUCTURE.

SO WE CAN PICK OUT OUR OWN KIND, LIKE TWINS... OR CLONES.

IF A BUNCH OF US DIE SOMEWHERE IN THE WORLD, WE CAN ALL FEEL IT. THAT SHOULD COME IN REAL HANDY IN THE SPACE AGE.

THE VULCAN GUY ON THAT OLD SF VID-PROGRAM "STAR TREK"--DIDN'T HE HAVE SOMETHING LIKE THAT? PRETTY USEFUL, I GUESS.

IN ONE SENSE, THOUGH, IT CAN BE DANGEROUS.

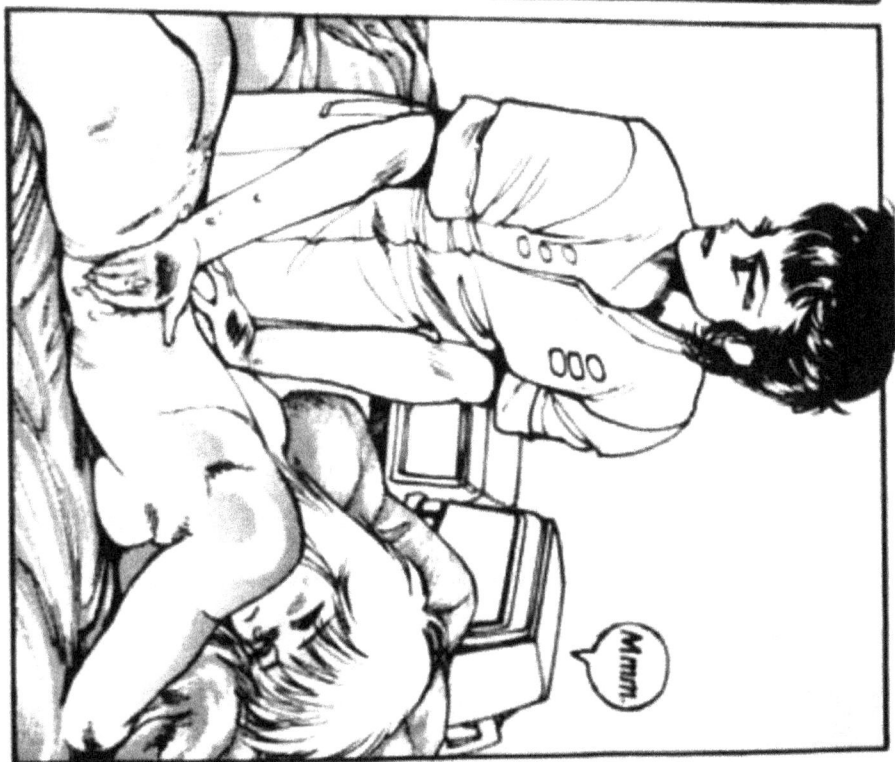

02

OTHER *APPLESEED* STORIES

CALLED GAME

Most valuable (and enjoyable) of all in *Appleseed: Illustration and Data* was the 48-page side story from *Appleseed* entitled *Called Game* (1989; or is the title *Game*?). It counts as chapter 26 in the *Appleseed manga*. It featured the golden couple of *Appleseed* embarking on another hunt-the-terrorist mission. Again, it's smaller, intimate scenes exploring the relationship of Deunan Knute and Briareos Hecatonchires that appeal most in *Called Game* (which is not the most memorable *Appleseed* story, tho' anything featuring Deu' 'n' Bri' is worth reading).

The first page of *Called Game* is a classic Masamune Shirow image: a pin-up of bioroid Hitomi leaning against a motorbike and clad in flesh-revealing swimwear. *Called Game* has elements of a Raymond Chandler detective narrative, or a procedural cop show, as Deunan and Briareos investigate the threat of terrorism (yet again) in Olympus. There is plenty of action (battling cyborgs, an explosion at a packed restaurant, and running down a mob's gunner in an apartment block), to spice up the scenes of driving in cars, talking in rooms, and more talk of how the case is unfolding.

Called Game opens with the discovery of a bomb, which sets off Deunan and Briareos on the quest for who planted it.[1] Deunan acts as bait (on a motorcycle), while Briareos visits the secretary Mary Butler in a restaurant[2] (the only person in the room when the bomb was planted). The terrorists hit the restaurant, but luckily Briareos is able to protect Mary (Deunan is nearby, frantically trying to get in touch with her man; she ends up going flying in a car crash, and runs into the idiotic Kotus cop, who delay

Doric pops up (as a spy, in disguise),[3] there's an E.S.W.A.T. training exercise on a plane, and other bits of business before the story continues.

1 Bri and Deu are also being tapped, as the authorities don't seem to trust them. (Bri tells Deu to be careful about what she says).
2 Susano and Princess Kushinata from Shirow's *Orion manga* make a guest appearance in the restaurant.
3 Doric's involved in a car jostle with Deunan – she too is tailing someone.

During the training exercise, on a jet liner that's been hijacked, Lance happily sits in the passenger cabin, and doesn't move a muscle when a dummy is shot to bits right next to him. And afterwards, Lance gives the customary cry of all military leaders: faster, better.

The stand-out action sequence in *Called Game* involves Deunan and Briareos visiting a shipping company, where they encounter several thugs who want to fight rather than talk or co-operate. These guys take one look at li'l Deunan and think she'll be easy to dominate. No! Oh, no she won't! Deunan fires a stun round to floor one, and tussles with another, in one of Masamune Shirow's short but intense, hand-to-hand combat scenes (one of his specialities). An enormous guy in a cowboy hat who sidles in to gloat before launching himself at Deu is simply punched to the floor by Briareos ('hee hee', giggles Deunan).

As Deunan and Briareos visit the gun runner's *aparto*, and turn it over, they are bantering all the time. Briareos teases Deunan about his past 'experience' with illegal activities like carrying guns onto planes, or going undercover for months on end, and Deunan shakes her head in disbelief. Briareos reckons they should go back one more time to the apartment ('your dad taught me this one', he tells Deunan). Sure enough, the fresh corpse of Kitamura is discovered;[4] in the foyer, Deunan nobbles the female gun runner. At the end of *Called Game*, however, it's revealed that this has been a trap, a delaying tactic so that the real crooks can flee the country (a hijacking occurs at the airport, which pays off the training exercise earlier; however, Lance orders Deu and Bri to go to ground with the gun runner. Which they do – at a place by the sea – the villa with the view and the wine cellar).

Throughout *Called Game*, as throughout the *Appleseed* franchise, Deunan and Briareos are dreaming of finding paradise. Or, failing that, at least having a vacation (reflecting harassed, over-worked salarymen in Japan – and also the stressed-out, under-paid *manga* artist!). Their dream is to sit in the sun under the palm trees on some exotic beach (with Deunan being partial to a glass of wine. The same imagery crops up in the *Ghost In the Shell* TV series, when Batou and Motoko are seen sitting on a beach faked with a hologram).

So the quest for utopia on a grand, metaphysical and political scale in the *Appleseed* franchise, embodied in the communities of Olympus and Poseidon, is mirrored on an individual level by Deunan and Briareos hoping for a vacation somewhere warm and sunny, if they can't find paradise.

---

4 The gun runner berrates him as a coward in a scene where the threat is bubbling just beneath the surface.

Appleseed Hypernotes (a.k.a. *Illustration and Data*) contains a short *Appleseed* story of 4 chapters published in *Comic Gaia* and in collected form in 1996.

Appleseed Hypernotes opens with evocations of several groups of charas before we meet the star duo of Deunan Knute and Briareos Hecatonchires: Hitomi is looking after/ cooking for three mini-Artemises, while their mom, Artemis the cat-girl, is wandering the streets, and the gang of cyborg crooks seen in *Appleseed* volume 3 are gathered, discussing a smuggling operation. Which leads us to a scene of a cyborg approaching a container ship at sea on a jet-ski (Shirow is fond of using jet-skis – they also turn up in *Ghost In the Shell;* maybe he sees them when he strolls down to the ocean in Kobe?).

On page ten of *Appleseed Hypernotes*, we finally meet Deunan and Briareos – they're introduced in the air, in an E.S.W.A.T. aircraft, surrounded by their fellow teammates, on their way to the ship: so it's another mission story, this time with Briareos taking command. They are flying to the container vessel to nobble the criminal cyborg we've just seen.

And that's all that Masamune Shirow needs to produce an *Appleseed* narrative: a crook, a ship and the Extra Special Weapons and Tactics team mobilized to nab him. So we have the usual briefing scenes, the usual joshing between the team members, the usual bit where Deunan jokes and doesn't seem to be takin' the operation seriously (and is cautioned by Briareos in his fatherly role), the usual suiting-up (in Guges – now painted in camouflage – 'looks like a walking billboard!' Deu quips), and the usual salivating over weaponry (*oooh*, look, Deunan has got herself a Seburo 'Woodpecker' gun – 5mm rounds, and 7mm x 35mm x 42 rounds).

For the detractors of Masamune Shirow, a mission like this in *Appleseed* is 'battle porn', where hardware, weaponry, military tactics and banter in a men-on-a-mission story (plus of course shooting and violence), becomes an offensive exaltation of all of the things that nice, liberal people don't like: the aggressive, colonizing, militaristic aspects of being human. But then, *Appleseed is* a cop genre comic, and it *is* about a bunch of E.S.W.A.T. guys (and a girl) who are the protectors of the quasi-utopia of Olympus.

It's true, tho', that by the time of this story, *Appleseed Hypernotes*, Shirow-sensei could create comics like this in his sleep. Or is it that he makes it look so easy? Anyway, the artwork of *Appleseed Hypernotes* is very fine, and the set-pieces are handled confidently: the Extra Special Weapons and Tactics team flying down to the ship in their Guges suits; and cat-and-mouse games on the ship (with the villain seemingly everywhere and nowhere, and always one step ahead of our heroes).

After sending out a bunch-a decoy boats to keep the E.S.W.A.T. team busy, the villain sinks the vessel. Mass panic. Deunan is trapped in the ship as it sinks, and is rescued by her Prince Charming, Briareos. Masamune Shirow even includes a beat where Bri kisses Deu. (Part of this was used in the *Appleseed* TV series).

There's always time for 'fan service' in *Appleseed*, even in the middle of an action scene – and Masamune Shirow duly supplies several drawings eroticizing Deunan (one of the E.S.W.A.T. guys wonders if he could cop a feel as Deu climbs into a dinghy with her ••• on display).

❋

Appleseed Hypernotes continues with our heroes in hot pursuit of their quarry (yes, it's cops and robbers all the way here). They fly to the shore, battle with the robot, cut off its limbs, and beat it about. (At this point, the robot is revealed as designed as an imposing but creepy female with cat eyes. Yes, Shirow loves cats, but why would a robot, which could look like anything, want to have a scary appearance with cat's eyes, which stands out a mile?).

To Briareos' disgust (he hates martyrs), the robot opts to sacrifice itself to the cause (it's another robot from the Middle East) – using electrical whips, it slices itself to pieces. Ugh! What a mess. Meanwhile, nearby, viewing the suicide thru binos, are the robot's cohorts. They are portrayed like the Puma Twins from *Appleseed* – ridiculously bushy hair atop lithe bodies, cleavage and – again – cat's eyes (also observing the fight nearby are Sokaku and co. – so he also survived). Thus, our heroes managed to secure the loot (weaponry) that the smugglers were hiding in the boat.

The last chapter of *Appleseed Hypernotes* switches the scene back to Olympus, with Deunan and Briareos in a car on a freeway. They are being tailed, and the bulk of the chapter involves Deu and Bri chasing down their quarry once more (there also brief scenes featuring Lance, who's overseeing security at the Islamic Federation Conference).

So where do Briareos and Deunan lead their quarry to? Only another harbour, another warehouse, complete with piles of steel containers (it's the scene of ten million action movies, where shoot-outs can take place and stuff can be blown up by film crews). With a bit of *James Bond* flashiness, it turns out that Extra Special Weapons and Tactics squad have built a safe house behind the layers of containers. While Deunan and Briareos josh about food as they switch vehicles[5] (Deu is bringing along armfuls of tinned food), the cyborg, Deinoa, who's been tailing them, is keen to reverse the situation. So she hitches a ride with a stereotypical Yankie trucker (complete with beard, moustache, stetson, fat belly and granny glasses).

And then, just as Deinoa gives Deunan and Briareos the slip, and enters a shopping mall, *Appleseed Hypernotes* comes to an abrupt end. This is part of the unfinished volume five of the *Appleseed* saga.

The storming of the ship at sea is certainly an exciting piece of *manga*, delivered with Masamune Shirow's customary zeal for techie details, and his fetishizing of military operations (it's also the longest sequence – about 40 pages long, up to the moment when the robot cuts itself to ribbons). But the other elements, such as the criminal cyborgs, don't quite

5 And Deunan changes outfits – now her Master (Shirow) has put her in a baggy Tee shirt and even baggier, harem pants.

compel. And, you have to admit, some of the story elements repeat things we've already seen in *Appleseed*: Deunan and Briareos hunting down quarry, cat-like crooks or cyborgs slipping into crowded shopping malls, cat-and-mouse chases on freeways, arguments with boss Lance, etc. Even the joshing btn Deu and Bri, which's the emotional core of *Appleseed*, has been seen before (and better).

What would *Appleseed 5* be building towards, story-wise? Maybe a grander plot, or maybe something about cyborg crooks and arms smuggling. The four chapters published as *Appleseed Hypernotes* offer a terrific opening act for a story, but frustratingly stop halfway thru the chase. And when you add the *Called Game* story, you get the feeling that Shirow was no longer fascinated by *Appleseed*, and had already moved on to other things.

APPLESEED: ILLUSTRATION AND DATA

Appleseed: Illustration and Data (a.k.a. *Appleseed I.D./ Hypernotes*, 2007) was a collection of miscellanea and background info to the *Appleseed manga* series (there are several other books which contain some of the same material, such as the *Databook*).[6] A chapter of colour illustrations and another of b/w illustrations (including some images rejected from the *Appleseed manga*) • a timeline of the *Appleseed* universe • a map of the world of *Appleseed* (Olympus, a man-made island the size of England (!), is near the Azores, off the coast of Africa) • guides to the characters (and their costumes) • guides to the weaponry[7] (a big deal for Masamune Shirow! – this guy is *scary* how much he fetishizes guns and ammo!) • and some fun, *chibi* versions of Deunan and Briareos.

Masamune Shirow created a potted history for his *Appleseed* world – right from 1992[8] and real-world events like the unification of the European Union, to fictional, futuristic incidents like missions to Mars and Venus, wars, the formation of new nations, etc.

In the *Appleseed* timelines, we learn that Olympus has been a long time in the making, and the bioroid experiment is a key to its success. This is the 'Appleseed' of the title – the Appleseed Plan is the name for the bioroid programme (which starts up in 2030). (One little fact in the *Appleseed* timeline doesn't make much an impression in the *manga* and its stories, and that is the reappearance of Jesus Christ. In China! Yep, the messiah returns at the millennium.)

The galleries of illustrations from the *Appleseed* world in *Appleseed: Illustration and Data* included many using watercolours and gouache (so much softer on the eye than the Photoshop and digital work of Masamune

---

6 Beautifully designed by Tina Alessi.
7 There are four pages of info on guns and ammunition in *Appleseed: Illustration and Data*.
8 Shirow said that *Appleseed* was set 130 years hence.

Shirow's more recent artwork). Deunan and Briareos in Army fatigues •
Deunan and Briareos holding their guns and looking mean an' moody at
the viewer • Deunan and Briareos in combat gear in amongst barbed
wire • Deunan and Briareos hurrying thru the Olympian night • Deunan
and Briareos relaxing on the beach in the sun • Deunan near-nude in a
bikini • Deunan semi-naked in her Landmate mobile suit • and even
Deunan and Briareos dressed up in evening wear (!).

Many of the images in *Appleseed: Illustration and Data* are the
Shirowian equivalent of nudie pin-ups, with Deunan Knute smiling at the
viewer with a come-on smile as she flaunts her slinky body that's nude
bar the adornments of Shirowian, hi-tech accessories (and this is the
default configuration for a Shirow woman: naked with gadgets and
weapons). The attention to detail is striking in *Appleseed: Illustration and
Data*, as Masamune Shirow's pencil draws every part of bodies – but also
body armour, weapons, shells, the whole schmeer.

In one illustration, Deunan and Briareos sit behind an array of their
weaponry and ammo spread out on the floor – Masamune Shirow
includes every single item the E.S.W.A.T.s pack for a mission: shells of all
kinds, hand grenades, knuckle dusters, razor wire, penknives, etc. In many
illustrations in *Intron Depot,* there are spent shells flying all over the place
as Deunan or Briareos fire their weapon[9] (years b4 *Saving Private Ryan*
made it fashionable). In his later pin-ups and calendars, Shirow includes
many images of girls amidst showers of bullet cartridges.

For Masamune Shirow, there's a pornography of weaponry, but also,
conversely, a mechanization/ cyborgization/ weaponization of the
human body. Shirow turns guns into the objects of erotic desire just as
strongly as he fetishizes the human body. The beautiful contours of a real
body (here, one of his chief heroines, Deunan Knute), merge with the curves
of a 9 millimetre Seburo bullet or the sleek form of body armour or a
mobile suit (in Shirow's art, it's all curves). Bodies become machines, and
machines become organic. Cyborgization/ technology is the process of
transforming one form into another.

In the end, in the far future, in Masamune Shirow's view, we will all
become cyborgs, machines that can be replaced/ replicated infinitely, with
death a thing of the past (which's what the Puppet Master thinks it's
achieved in *Kokaku Kidotai*), and everyone can have the gorgeous body they
desire. Deunan Knute, like Motoko Kusanagi in *Ghost In the Shell*, is an
ideal, a fantasy, who is part-way to becoming cyborgized[10] (Motoko is
further along the path, and Hitomi in *Appleseed* is already there: she's a
'bioroid', and has been for decades).

The question in Masamune Shirow's futuristic fiction is not: *do you
want to become a robot?*, but: *how can you* not *want to be a robot?* Like Donna
Haraway, the Queen of Cyborg Theory in the West, Shirow would be first
in line if genuine cyborgization was on offer. (Haraway boasted that she
was already partly a cyborg).

---

9 Shirow has drawn and deliberately not drawn shell catchers.
10 Deunan has some implants, Shirow explains in his guidebook.

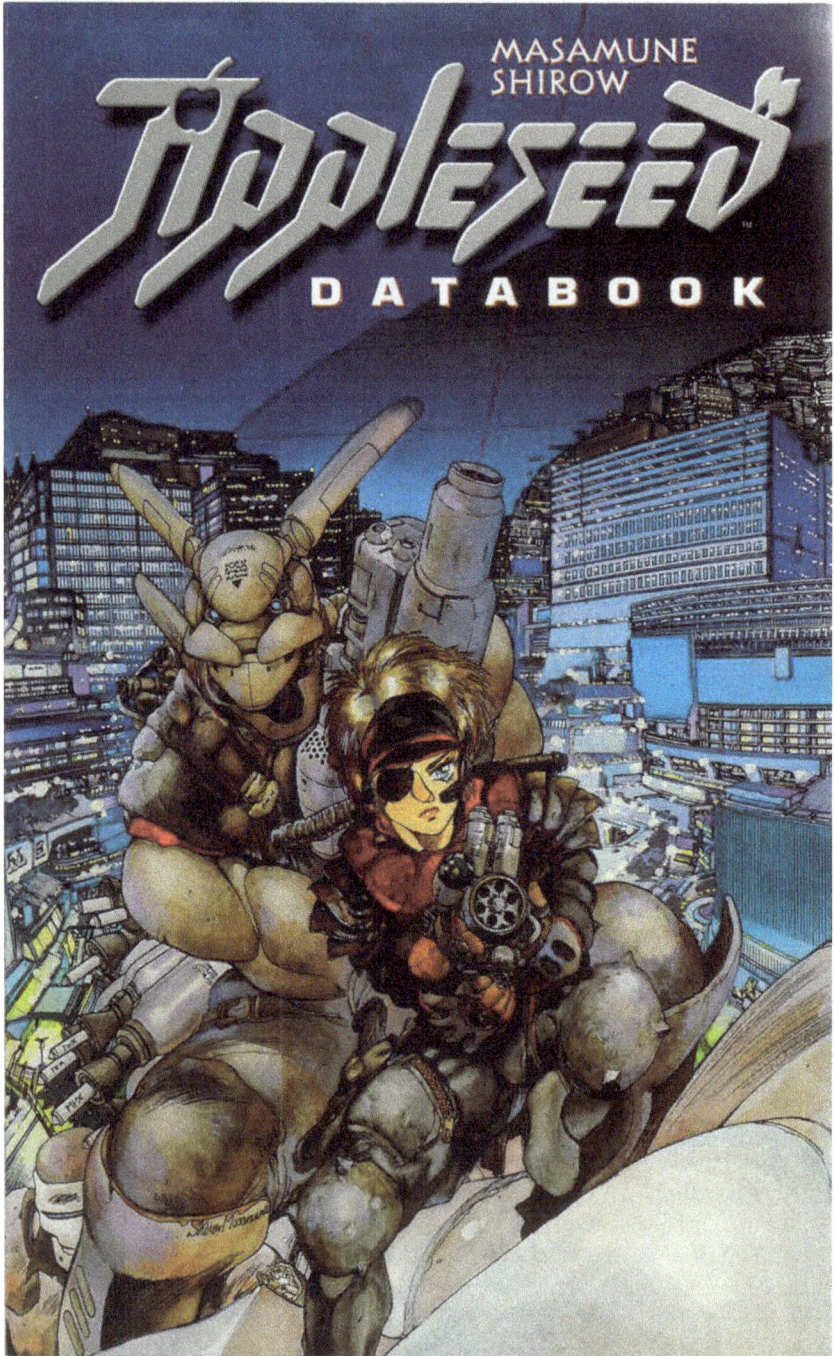

Appleseed Databook (this page and over).

VREEEEEEE

SHHH

TINGG

HUH?!

EXIT

802

KLIK

W-WAIT A MINUTE...

802

SHEESH...

NO, I'M OK... I'M JUST A BIT DIZZY.

802

802

GO! WHRAK

802

OK!

huff

APPLESEED HYPERNOTES

story & art by MASAMUNE SHIROW

translation by DANA LEWIS & TOREN SMITH
lettering & retouch by TOMOKO SAITO executive editor TOREN SMITH

Appleseed Hypernotes (this page and over).

SAY...!

GCHAK

BLBEB

The present JSDF Steinke Hood submarine escape device surfaces at 400FPM, so...it would take about 30 seconds from a depth of 165FSW. Actually, she should extend one arm over her head, and rotate to check for obstacles as she ascends.

KCHAK
WHSKK

DAMN...MY INDEX FINGER'S TINGLING, CLEAR TO THE WRIST.

SPLSSH

COULDN'T BE THE *BENDS*... NOT DOWN LONG ENOUGH.

SQUEEZE..?

FWHOOOSHH

YEEK!!

POLICE OLYMPUS

POLICE

03

THE STORY OF
THE *APPLESEED MANGA*

Here is a brief summary of the story of the *Appleseed manga* by Masamune Shirow:

Chapter 1: *Triple Hound Hunting,* of book one of *Appleseed, The Promethean Challenge* (*Purometeusu no chosen* 1985), introduces the star of *Appleseed*, the brilliant cop Deunan Knute, in a guise seldom seen in the rest of the *manga* (and nowhere in the animations): she's cooking! On page one, there's a medium close-up of Deunan: wearing a pinafore, she possesses many classic *manga* attributes: she has bushy, blonde hair, very large eyes, an elfin nose, a tiny mouth, a triangular face (and her head's over-large).

Putting his kick-ass, gun-totin' heroine in an apron[1] in the kitchen cooking for her man is an amusing mis-direction by *mangaka* Masamune Shirow – because for most of the rest of the *Appleseed manga*, Deunan sports combat gear, hi-tech weaponry, military pants, helmets, caps, body armour, and mobile suits. (But Deu also has an impressive array of civvy clothes, and she changes 'em everyday, Shirow explains).

But the introduction of Deunan Knute like this is important: it emphasizes that these out-size characters in a post-apocalyptic, futuristic sci-fi/ fantasy *manga* value domesticity and modest living. In fact, it's the everyday, domestic scenes which ground *Appleseed* in a recognizable reality: even after World Wars and global catastrophes, people will still need to eat, keep warm, and even live with each other as couples.

Yes, that's also important in *Appleseed*: Deunan Knute and Briareos Hecatonchires are established from the outset as a couple that've been together for years. So, no, there's no angst or strife, there're no 'other men' or 'other women', no marital upsets (about the only thing that Deu and Bri argue over is money: she spends too much (on wine and mobile suits), while he complains and yearns for some time off). But the *animé* adaptations found it necessary to add numerous conflicts within the

1 Apron scenes are a minor category of Japanese porn.

couple.

'We're the only living things around here, aren't we?' Deunan muses, as she looks out of the window: the double-page drawing that opens the *Appleseed manga* depicts a war-torn city (with nary a soul in sight – neither human, cyborg, bioroid or a robot box on wheels). Briareos is in his customary position – relaxing in an armchair (again, this is seldom seen in the cartoon versions). Bri likes to take it easy when he can: when he's home, he's chilling, he's not sitting at a desk drawing *manga* all day, fr'instance.

Briareos Hecatonchires's design in *Appleseed* is a big, burly guy with sort of utility clothing, and chunky boots. His cyborgization isn't explained for some time: what pops out instantly, of course, are the multiple eyes and the rabbit ears on Briareos's noggin (as if Masamune Shirow was acutely conscious of pop culture being full of robots and androids (Japanese pop culture especially), and so he aimed to do something distinctive and unique with his *manga*).[2]

Oh, and Deunan's cooking is not something that Briareos is crazy about – but the food is swiftly forgotten when we see Briareos using his famous rabbit ears for the first time, picking up the sound of an approaching mobile suit. In a flash, the couple become professional soldiers, ready to defend their patch (they have a keen disaster mentality, where everyone is a potential threat), arming themselves (using high explosive squash heads, as Shirow-sensei explains). This is where the story starts in *Appleseed*.

Looming out of the gloom is a mobile suit – the first of many (!) in the *Appleseed manga*. It turns out to be Hitomi,[3] a small, svelte bioroid who's been sent to 'Badside' to retrieve Deunan and Briareos and bring them to Olympus. The first shot (of many!) that Deunan fires in *Appleseed* occurs here: she shoots Hitomi in the chest (with a stun shell), knocking her out (so the first bit of action in *Appleseed* features a woman shooting at another woman, altho' she's a bioroid. Not long after this, Deunan kills a woman – Chiffon). After some brief exchanges (with our heroes treating Hitomi as an annoying intrusion who has to be manacled to a pipe), the first major action sequence in *Appleseed* starts up: our heroes versus a tank.

And that, of course, is all many *manga* artists require in terms of dramatic ingredients to produce a chapter or two of comics art: two heroes and a tank intent on killing 'em. This is where Deunan and Briareos really show off their stuff, out-manoeuvring their opponents in a marvellous cat-and-mouse episode. (One of the cutest images in *Appleseed* occurs here: Briareos carrying Deunan in his arms as he leaps from building to building. It was also the subject of one of the many images that Shirow created for the supplementary material of *Appleseed*. Alas, the adaptations have only briefly included this image).

Chapter 1: *Triple Hound Hunting* is Masamune Shirow in full flight,

2 Indeed, if you set out to design a new robot in Japan, you might be better off *not* looking at everything that's been done before. Because it has.
3 That Hitomi travels on her own isn't convincing – and it doesn't fit Hitomi's character-ization. But this was early in the making of *Appleseed*, before everything was developed to its final state.

staging several wild action beats filled with his customary fanatical attention to detail. And it displays Shirow's heroes at their best: Deunan, for instance, is a girl who can drive a jeep at high speed, skid, turn and shoot a machine gun, nailing her prey. (There's no question that our heroes kill several people, whether they're bioroids, cyborgs or humans).

Each of the three heroes are given their mini-set-pieces, and Masamune Shirow gives bioroid Hitomi a role, too – having escaped from the handcuffs, she hurls her last grenade into the hatch of the tank. BOOM!... End of the heavies... Cue the *dénouement* scene of chapter one of *Appleseed*: Hitomi delivers the exposition about the state of the world following the war: a kind of United Nations for Earth, called the Central Management Bureau or Aegis, has been established (the HQ is in Olympus). Hitomi invites our heroes to the new utopia.

✻

Chapter 2: *Civvy Street* takes us immediately into the air-space above Olympus by chopper, for the customary big, impressive views of Olympus, the semi-circular Arcology structures (800 metres high!), and vistas of the parks, freeways, skyscrapers, etc, all the way down to street level. (So our heroes've already decided to accept Hitomi's offer).

But into this approach-and-landing sequence, Masamune Shirow inserts the first flashback to Deunan Knute's past: a training session, where the teenage Deu is being instructed in the tough, macho world of combat. The subtext? Loud and clear: the father-daughter complex, with Briareos arguing with Deunan's father Karl the whole time, complaining that he is putting his daughter through hell (the *animé* versions used the concept of Deunan training several times. But they *didn't* use the beat right afterwards, when Deunan wakes up and snarls at busy-body Hitomi when she interrupts her rest: 'GET OUT!').

As our heroes're put into quarantine in Olympus, the *Appleseed manga* shifts the focus to introduce two secondary but significant characters: Athena and Nike. Athena is a striking version of the assertive, bitchy, 1980s businesswoman, with her bushy hair and Jackie Collins-meets-*Dynasty* wardrobe (plus some Ellen Ripley-isms from *Aliens*).4 Athena, as head of Olympus's administration, tends to pose proudly or strut boldly about (most of her scenes're spent gazing out of windows at Olympus and ruminating, typing her as a god-like observer). Nike, incidentally, is portrayed in the *animé* adaptations as the sulky, dutiful secretary or bosomy sidekick to Athena, but in fact she is the Minister of Internal Affairs in Olympus.

The introduction of Athena and Nike (two women, note), is the first real inkling that *Appleseed* is going to be more than the adventures of a young couple in a futuristic society. It's going to depict the hierarchy of a society, up to the top people who run it.

In the next sequence in chapter 2: *Civvy Street* of *Appleseed*, Hitomi is used by Masamune Shirow once again to act as the tour guide (and

---

4 Athena's introduced smoking a small pipe – actually quite common in *manga* (inc. for older, female charas, like the witchy Yuko in *xxxHolic*). Of course, none of the *animés* have shown that!

exposition service) for Olympus: she arrives to pick up Deunan and Briareos (who're sitting in the sun on some steps, finding their bearings, after the bureaucratic processing thru quarantine).

The motorcycle drive thru Olympus allows Hitomi to deliver more exposition (Briareos has a car to take him). Much more interesting, tho', is the stop-off at the Akechi Motors garage, where we meet a new character, Yoshitsune Miyamoto, a mechanic who services Landmates (mobile suits or exoskeletons). Yoshi, permanently clad in overalls (except in the posters, covers and splash pages of *Appleseed*), is a delightfully 'ordinary' character in *Appleseed* – the tech-head/ gear-head/ *mecha*-nut, and boyfriend of Hitomi. Shunted aside in the *animé* adaptations of *Appleseed*, Yoshi is vital among the secondary charas in *Appleseed* – partly for what he *isn't* – he's not an Elder, an administrator, a villainous cyborg, a terrorist or an Extra Special Weapons and Tactics agent. He's a guy who fixes things. (Shirow stated in *Appleseed: Illustration and Data* that Yoshi is 'really a fairly insignificant figure, but he has some mysterious quality that makes me always have fairly high expectations for him'. Yet Shirow includes Yoshi in many scenes, and in much of the additional imagery for the *Appleseed* series).

The other element introduced in the garage scene in chapter 2: *Civvy Street* is the mobile suit, the Landmate, an icon of the *Appleseed* universe (E.S.W.A.T. use one called 'Guges'). As soon as she lays eyes on it, Deunan Knute is smitten (it's a bit like Leona and her beloved Buonaparte tank in *Dominion: Tank Police*). Deunan simply *must* have one!

In our world, a piece of hi-tech gear like a mobile suit/ exoskeleton would cost – what? – million$ and million$! But in the Fantasy Land of *Appleseed*, Deunan is able to buy one (even tho' Briareos keeps insisting in the background that they're broke: 'we're flat broke so don't even *think* about it!' But Briareos looks at Deunan, and knows that she's got an idea in her head).

However, Deunan Knute is already thinking that she will apply to work for Extra Special Weapons and Tactics (what else can we do, she asks her man, be farmers?). And just look at the level of *detail* that Masamune Shirow has lavished on the Landmate suit that Yoshi shows our heroes! You could probably build one from the illustrations that Shirow has drawn (which're almost as detailed as blueprints. No doubt Shirow could also draw a blueprint if he wanted). There's one drawing, then another, then another, then another, then another – oh, Shirow-sensei *loves* that mobile suit even more than Deunan does (and that's *a lot*).[5]

So that's work/ money sorted out for our heroes. Next is accommodation: Hitomi takes the couple to her place to stay until they find a home of their own. It's built above an *ominal* (coffee shop), where Hitomi has plenty of friends. (This minor detail is seldom revisited, and doesn't appear in the *animé* adaptations).

In their *aparto*, Briareos and Deunan kick back: some of the most enjoyable scenes in Masamune Shirow's *Appleseed* saga are those where

---

5 Hitomi complains to Yoshi, 'I think you like *them* more than *me!*'

Deu and Bri do nothing but sit around and talk. Item: working for E.S.W.A.T. Item: Deunan's smuggled in a knife[6] and bottles of wine thru quarantine (one of the running gags of *Appleseed* is Deunan being partial to wine: 'don't guzzle it! You have no idea how many ruins I crawled through looking for those!').

And now for some 'fan service': what's a good way of having your heroine justifiably naked? Why, a shower, of course! So Deunan duly takes a shower. At which point, Hitomi calls. And tries the wine. And gets drunk (on Deunan's precious wine!). And staggers off to the shower, to join Deu under the spray.

Deunan, like Faye Valentine in *Cowboy Bebop*, takes weapons into the shower (!), and Hitomi is repelled first (with a knife) when Deu thinks she's an intruder. Both girls are nude. Hitomi collapses into Deunan's arms, which Deunan interprets as Hitomi making a pass at her: 'you... YOU IDIOT! I'm not into that! Leggo!' yells Deunan, but Hitomi is already passed out cold. (Nope, none of the film/ TV adaptations have attempted that scene, or any like it; tho' they have, of course, included 'fan service' partial nudity. But lesbianism? Nah!).

✳

Chapter 3: *Even Bets* develops the upper levels of the administrative organizations of Olympus: Athena meets the bearded, imposing, middle-aged Director, and they argue about how to run Olympus (Athena is more of a peacekeeper here), and we meet the seven Elders, who spend pretty much the entire *Appleseed manga* debating the future of humanity (whom they call *homo sapiens*), of bioroids, of the troubled relations btn bioroids and humanity, of Olympus, and of the world (intriguingly, the Elders are bioroids). The Elders act like the gods on Mount Olympus in Ancient Greek mythology, observing all, weighing, judging, and of course pontificating at length (why use one word when you can use three hundred?). This is a non-Deu 'n' Bri chapter (tho' they're mentioned in the dialogue).

✳

Chapter 4: *Hospitality*: the girls are hanging out in the park: Hitomi, Deunan and a new chara, Chiffon (who appears at first to be Hitomi Mark 2; she's isn't given much of a personality). Deunan checks up on her new Guges at Akechi Motors (and Yoshitsune wishes he'd never shown her the catalogue). Deunan is so techno-savvy, she can argue about the pros and cons of outer joints, drive trains, torque dampers, sensoring and so on with the engineer. Deunan has eyes for a particular model of Guges, and buys it.

Over drinks in a café in chapter 5: *Hot Potato,* Deunan and Chiffon discuss the would-be utopia of Olympus. Chiffon, who doesn't seem to like Olympus, either, says an odd thing:

> It's a zoo. A zoo for those weird animals that build their own cages and hide inside of them.

6 A girl's gotta look after herself, Deunan explains. She keeps the knife close by at all times.

Chiffon preferred life back in Oahu (she has a surfboard in her bedroom). Meanwhile, Athena and Nike plot and scheme, as politicos tend to do.

And, in another park, Deunan and Briareos contemplate the possibility of the snakes in the grass of Olympus (so it's not only Briareos who expresses doubts). Briareos's worrying is compounded by the concept of cloning – when he meets a guy called Arugess, who used to work with him in the military (but who doesn't recognize him now; this is later revealed to be a lie). To enhance the irony of the discussion about serpents in Eden, mini *tableaux* of paradise are trotted out (children're depicted frolicking in the park, ice cream, smiling couples, etc).

Chapter 5: *Hot Potato* climaxes with an important scene in *Appleseed*, where Briareos decides they need to do something about the possibility of Olympus being more than a zoo, but a dangerous experiment (with themselves caught in a trap).

The scene, comprising an argument/ discussion btn the heroes, is set up via contrasts: first some humour (Deunan sneaks up on Briareos in their apartment, to show off her new Guges mobile suit – how could something that big take Briareos with his rabbit ears by surprise?! – he can hear a mobile suit miles off!), followed by a disagreement: Deunan thinks the best of people (until proven otherwise), while Briareos is much more suspicious and cautious.

In a clever piece of storytelling, it's the Guges mobile suit itself which's part of Briareos's argument: he reckons that the very existence of machines like Landmates proves that Olympus is not the crime-free utopia it's being promoted as (a direct comment on the low crime rate in Japan coupled with its hyper-capitalism).

While Deunan and Briareos disagree, she leaves anyway, as he tells her to (for her protection). To Hitomi and Chiffon, this is portrayed by Deunan as lovers falling out – but Briareos is proved dead right in the next chapter.

✳

Chapter 6: *The Battle of Titan* intensifies the narrative in *Appleseed* now, with the first Big, Dramatic Event: an attempt on the life of Briareos, which's witnessed by his lover, Deunan. This leads directly into the first Big Action Sequence in *Appleseed*, an attack on the super-computer Gaia by a cluster of terrorists. (Athena and her office have been instrumental in encouraging this with the use of a war drug. It helps her to get the jump on the Director and his team, and on the Elders).

The preamble scenes depict Deunan sleeping on Chiffon's couch, but jumpy enough to grab a knife and investigate a noise next door, where Chiffon seems to be checking her mobile suit machinery. Chiffon, it turns out, is one of the terrorists who attack Briareos. (Deunan has a knife in a leg holster which she always carries – in the supplementary material, Shirow-sensei goes into detail about all the weaponry and gadgets that Deunan has).

Masamune Shirow can't resist putting his heroine into panties and a cutaway Tee shirt (plus boots!) for the scene where Deunan rises, checks if Chiffon is around, and goes downstairs. Deunan is just in time to hide round a corner when the mobile suits appear: she's armed with a knife, but it's not enough to stop the Landmates firing on Briareos as he climbs the stairs outside their apartment.

When Briareos gets shot in the *Appleseed manga,* he bleeds: he doesn't have the super-tough shell of the *animé* adaptations. Kneeling beside him, Deunan has his blood on her hands and face. Typically for ever-the-professional cop, Bri commands her to pursue the criminals, and not to stay with him. Hitomi is soon on the scene, fretting, summoning an ambulance. And our heroine dashes away full-pelt (in undies and a croptop) – straight to her new Guges mobile suit.

Exactly what's going on in chapter 6: *The Battle of Titan* isn't clear at first, who's doing what, and why: instead, it's a non-stop action sequence: the police're mobilized; exoskeleton suits burst into the Director's apartment, demanding to know where Gaia is; the police are rapidly mobilized; and Deunan, now in her new Guges suit, is in amongst the chaos as an individual.

It's a *mecha*-rich installment of *Appleseed,* with Shirow-sensei orchestrating the full arsenal: tanks, armoured personnel carriers, helicopters, guns, Landmates, etc. And it's one of the finest sequences in the *Appleseed* franchise, full of high speed action (plenty of speed lines), and Shirow's customary attention to detail. Best of all, it has Deunan at the centre of the *melée* (with cutaway views inside her Guges suit).

Athena has the police on her side, and the Director also has a police squad. The Air Police are in the skies, too. The rivalry btn the Director and Athena is crucial, and swiftly emerges. Earlier, there was a scene where Athena orders Nike to stir up the people staying at Hitomi's place with drugs – thus, Athena is strengthening her powerbase by artificially creating conflicts (unfortunately, none of the *Appleseed* adaptations, including the 2011 TV series, have really got to grips with this aspect of Masamune Shirow's *manga*).

In one memorable scene, Deunan Knute, having got the better of her mobile suit opponent, discovers that it's Chiffon facing her. 'N-No, wait!' Chiffon cries. But Deunan has her gun trained on Chiffon. Whether Deunan kills Chiffon or not is left a little ambiguous (the *manga* cuts to a side view of Deunan at this point). But on the next page, yes, it does seem as if Chiffon has been shot, with blood dripping down.[7] Indeed, earlier, a cop kills a terrorist who's already been over-powered, and is lying on the ground; there is no need to kill the guy and not take him in (also, the cop chuckles as he pulls the trigger, which further damns him). The chapter closes with the Elders and Athena and Nike discussing the events (the Elders guess that Athena is behind it all).

In *Appleseed: Illustration and Data,* Uncle Shirow explains that, yes, Deunan does kill Chiffon:

---

7 Deunan offers her some advice which villains in movies would do well to heed: 'If you're going to use force, don't talk until you *win*' (which villains always ignore! They haveta deliver their big speeches).

Deunan shoots Chiffon, but it's because Chiffon's flamethrower nozzles are pointed straight toward her; it's not because she wants revenge for Bri, although it's true that she's angry.

✳

Chapter 7: *Rest* opens with a scene used several times in the *Appleseed* adaptations: Briareos injured, and recovering in hospital. As Briareos observes, Deunan is now 'smack dab in the middle of their power struggles'. Book one of *Appleseed* ends with a kiss btn Deunan and Briareos. (There's a short, jokey appendix to the first book, featuring Hitomi and Yoshi, depicting their relationship: he is, as ever, working on his machines, and Hitomi is trying to civilize him. Hitomi is exasperated by Yoshi, who remains a devoted *mecha*-nut. None of the adaptations have used this scene).

▼

Chapter 8: *Alien* opens *Appleseed*'s book two, *Prometheus Unbound* (*Purometeusu no kaih*, 1985): several days or more have passed, and Deunan is now working for Extra Special Weapons and Tactics. The first half of the chapter portrays a terrorist and hostage scenario (which was used for the 1988 *animé* of *Appleseed*). Deunan is right in there amongst the boys – and she gets in through a window in a manner that Masamune Shirow is keen to demonstrate (he explains it in the notes): not by crashing thru the window (which looks good, but is dangerous), but by cutting a hole in the glass near the latch.

Well, shoot, a hostage scenario is something that Masamune Shirow can write and draw in his sleep (that's how easy he makes it look!). In ch. 8: *Alien*, all goes by the book, except for the doofus robot cop Kotus working alongside the Extra Special Weapons and Tactics team (it squashes and kills one of the criminals. Public Security Section 9 killing their targets is a recurring motif in *Ghost In the Shell*. Even the Major makes that boob; in one instance, it lands her in court).

Deunan is so good at her job, she is soon head-hunted. In another park scene (there are many of these in *Appleseed* – well, it is supposed to depicting a utopia, where people can sit about in the sun in parks), Deunan and Briareos discuss her new job (but they are both being followed).

Dr Matthew pop ups in this scene – he's a quirky medicine man, who revels in the prospect of repairing Briareos H. after his injury (the doctor's unusual characterization was established in the aftermath of the shooting). Matthew offers a sceptical, leftfield view of the human vs. bioroid issue of Olympus. For him, the possible utopia offers some intriguing scientific prospects – such as the fact that 'we're only a step away from immortality'.

It's the Minister of the Interior herself, Nike, who picks up Deunan Knute and takes her to meet Athena (Deu is surprised). There's another lengthy conversation in a car (mirroring the motorcycle ride in chapter 2: *Civvy Street*), as Nike adds more exposition about the warring factions in Olympus (both Dr Matthew and Nike are sort of lecturing Deunan).

There's a long stop-off at an E.S.W.A.T. training ground (to shake off the people following them, Nike says), in which tiny Deunan Knute plays the innocent, young girl in amongst squads of burly men who just happens to be a brilliant soldier herself. Deunan can act sweet, polite and girlie when needs be (while she takes the measure of the people Nike's introducing her to), but she can also be tough and uncompromising when she finds out she's been followed (and she swiftly brings the stalker down to the ground, taking his gun).

Subsequent scenes of Deunan meeting Athena, of the Elders talking with Hitomi, and of Deunan with the Extra Special Weapons and Tactics officer, develop the themes, and set up the next action sequence, featuring the spider platforms.

▼

Chapter 9: *Dominate the Mind* opens with the squabbles and wrangling among the politicos of Olympus (set in a large, circular conference room). The Elders introduce their Hope programme 'for the optimization of the human race': that gets everyone's attention (cries of outrage echo round the floor). The Elders, who're bioroids, reckon that humanity is getting out of hand: altho' the bioroid scheme has only been in operation for, what, 50 years, a 100 years, the Elders take it upon themselves to pontificate about humans – despite humans having survived for between one and three million years already. This leads to the Elders being put behind bars (which none of the *animé* adaptations have shown).

Some of the speeches by the Elders come across as the rants of a liberal griping about the selfish consumerism of the 1980s, where people only think of their own material gain, fostering the isolation of modern society. *Appleseed* reflects the ideological and political environment of its time, espousing the liberal, peacenik views which promoted alternative, ecological solutions to social problems.

The political debates at the high level are contrasted with two small-scale, domestic scenes: Briareos chats with his eccentric doctor, Matthew (who's still fixing the cyborg), and Deunan talks to Yoshitsune Miyamoto, her Landmate mechanic (who's servicing her mobile suit – Deunan doesn't go easy on it, to Yoshi's irritation).

In chapter 10: *Hide and Seek*, the political disputes continue: Athena and Nike have a lengthy discussion during a car journey about what they're going to do, and the Elders, in their (rather pleasant) prison admit that they expected too much of humans and the legislators.

▼

There are many pages of dialogue in this part of *Appleseed*, with each group putting forth its viewpoint on the would-be utopia of Olympus. Both the Director and his flunkies and Athena, Nike and their assistants visit the super-computer Gaia (at different times). The computer techs try to hide the fact that Gaia is operating largely independently, and doing things its way.

Realizing that the *Appleseed manga* has continued for many pages without much action (and also without Deu or Bri in evidence), Masamune Shirow delivers some at the end of chapter 10: *Hide and Seek*. It involves Hitomi and Yoshi sneaking up to the detention cell where the Elders are being held captive, using mobile suits, and clambering around the outside of the building. Hitomi has a special relationship with the Elders, and is going to pick up a memory bank which the Elders hope to slip thru the window to her.

Hitomi and Yoshi, however, are not professional operators when it comes to snooping around the outside of the Arcology structures (in daylight, too, where they're easy to spot). So it's nothing for the E.S.W.A.T. team, led by Deunan Knute, to capture them. It's a surprise to see Deunan face-to-face with her friends, and siding here with the law (none of the *animés* used this twist, but none of the *animés* filmed this sequence anyway). Deunan strongly advises Hitomi and Yoshi to co-operate (and the comic opened with Deu firing on Hitomi, so we know it's not an idle threat).

In part 2 of chapter 10: *Hide and Seek,* three techs checking on Gaia via a monitor are possessed by the super-computer (or someone or something who might be working thru the computer). As if hypnotized,[8] the techs enter the hangar where the enormous spider platforms are kept, and order them to be fitted with live rounds (for the street parade). That the mechanics duly comply with barely checking anything is ridiculous – who needs live ammunition for a public display?! (And who organized this parade, ignoring the public's safety with spider machines that're too big for the streets?).

The black, imposing police platforms are one of Masamune Shirow's iconic creations – with the Tachikoma robots in *Ghost In the Shell,* their spidery forms are instantly recognizable as a Shirowian construct. No one else designs *mecha* quite like this (tho' Shirow is not the only *mangaka* to take up insect forms). The *animé* version of *Appleseed* paid *hommage* to this sequence, including using the same low angles.

The *Appleseed manga* is building up to one of its most impressive action sequences – indeed, for many, this would be the stand-out sequence in the whole *Appleseed* franchise (it isn't bettered elsewhere in the *manga*). Giant spider robots going nuts in a futuristic city – it's pure pulp sci-fi, and pure Masamune Shirow!

▼

Chapter 11: *Zero Hour* opens with festive scenes of the parade: it's a lovely day in Olympus, people are out, jets're soaring overhead in acrobatic displays, Athena and the Director're on a balcony, wavin' 'n' smilin' at the crowds, and the spider platforms join the procession in the streets. This is how utopia is meant to be, you could say. The ærial view of Olympus at its happiest and most relaxed have a curious affinity with photographs of processions in Moscow or Peking during the Cold War: rows of military vehicles, and cops marching in blocks (in which case, no, this isn't utopia, merely More of the Same, politically and ideologically).

The first inkling that something ain't right with the central computer Gaia occurs in modest scenes around the city: bath water isn't hot

8 In the 2007 *Appleseed,* Briareos was possessed.

(complains a naked girl), an old man gripes that the Arcology towers aren't reflecting any sunlight, etc. (But this also neatly demonstrates how silly the idea of a super-computer controlling everything is, if you need it for providing hot water or sunlight).

Seems like the heliostats (the mirrors on the Arcology structures used for power in Olympus) are being controlled by Gaia. They're turning towards Tartarus, the bioroid facility. Also, Gaia has a signalling device on the top of the complex, for sending messages to the spider platforms. 'Vreee!' go the spider platforms, answering the computer's call, beginning their riot. 'BBOOM' – now the spiders're shelling the Tartarus building, the opening salvos in the chaotic parade-gone-mad sequence.

▼

Chapter 12: *The Battle of Typhon* of *Appleseed* is a long (40-page) chapter depicting the war between Gaia and everybody else. (When will humans learn *not* to give god-like powers to bleedin' computers?!).

Deu and Bri are down on the street, watching the procession. Everybody is getting mobilized – Athena and Nike in a chopper, the cops on the ground, the Director yelling for his S.W.A.T. teams. Nobody knows exactly what's going on, or why Gaia is attacking Tartarus, or how to stop the spider platforms.

The drawings are black outlines on white, with only pale screen tones: Masamune Shirow saves full black tones for the spider robots, which enhances their menace. The images of the 200-foot machines stalking thru the city, crashing thru skyscrapers, throwing cars aside, are Masamune Shirow's version of a 1950s sci-fi B-movie, Shirow's *Godzilla* or a Ray Harryhausen movie.

The overriding goal for Athena and the authorities is to shut down Gaia at all costs (we kind of guessed that). Deunan and Briareos are struggling through the crowded streets and traffic jams. In the sky, the Air Police are trying to stop the spider platforms (using missiles).

The action in chapter 12: *The Battle of Typhon* comes thick and fast, one action beat after another. In one, a spider platform smashes up the streets right next to Deunan and Briareos, sending them flying. Bri races to Deu to pull her from the wreckage (she's in her Landmate, but that isn't enough to stop her from being battered). Deunan and Briareos are thrown into a group with Kotus and Hitomi: they're tryin' to get to Gaia's control centre, but the spider platform seems intent on blocking their path (by stomping everywhere with those colossal legs).

Ducts – yes, that old staple of the action-adventure genre is employed by Shirow-sensei to sneak our heroes into Gaia's control room. At Briareos wisecracks, 'at least it's cleaner than a sewer!' Yup, a fibre optic duct is preferrable (altho' it seems way too small to squeeze a Landmate through[9]). Hitomi is their guide (she has the eyes for the retinal scans of security, fr'instance), and she knows how to sneak into Gaia.

Our heroes manage to get the spider platforms shut down, but then Gaia trains the heliostats of the Arcology towers to attack the nuclear

---

9 Mobile suits are not made for sneaky work.

plant (like a magnifying glass and an ant).

In part two of chapter 12: *The Battle of Typhon*, our heroes're storming the Gaia complex, to shut down the out-of-control machine. They're getting closer to their target. Bri and Deu are in full combat mode, but Hitomi is scared and doesn't want to hold a gun (she would probably rather be shopping for new shoes; she's satirized as a woman who bases her life around consumer magazines). In true 'fan service' style, Shirow-sensei has Hitomi clad in only panties and a croptop, for no particular reason – in the middle of the biggest action sequence in *Appleseed*.

◉

Chapter 13: *Appleseed* depicts the group of heroes reaching Gaia's central nervous system (an impressive, shadowy array of machines – Yoshi goes, I don't what it is, but, wow!). Protecting Gaia are several robots, which Deunan and Briareos fight in crunching, punchy action drawings.

One of the intriguing ingredients added to the Shut-Down-Gaia sequence in *Appleseed* is that Deunan Knute is having a crisis of conscience: are they doing the right thing?[10] Are they going to destroy bioroids in the process? What if they set back the utopia in Olympus many years?

It's not like Deu Knute to have such a major moral wobbly in the midst of an action sequence – afterwards, or before, yes, but seldom during. So it's up to Bri Hecatonchires to convince his lover that, yes, they are Doing The Right Thing: 'Gaia can be a *weapon* against us! …This may be our *only* chance to show that *we* control our destiny, not her!'

What does 'Appleseed' actually mean? Anything – but Masamune Shirow actually includes a scene where real apple seeds are employed. As bullets, of course! Briareos decides that apple seeds will be perfect for putting inside bullets to plug up the circuit connector hole in Gaia (it's typical that the heroes havta use a gun and a bullet to shut down a computer, a weapon to control or shut down a weapon!). Yes, apples have all of the familiar connotations with the Garden of Eden and the Tree of Knowledge (altho', with all of its Ancient Greek mythological influences in *Appleseed*, maybe Shirow-sensei was thinking of the apples of immortality?).

While Briareos prepares the new ammo, it's Deunan who has to take the shot, because Bri's fingers are wrecked from the many fights. There's an urgency here, because they don't have much time (the clock is ticking), but Deu really isn't sure they are Doing The Right Thing. She's arguing with Briareos even tho' there are barely seconds to go (and Hitomi is jumping up and down and screaming at her: '50 seconds! Deunan! The time!'). In Deunan's mindscreen, we see her moral confusion: 'what should I do? It's a utopia, like a perfectly constructed toy, 'to what end? for *who*?'

But then Deunan Knute swivels up the gun, sights it, and takes a shot, in one of the strongest drawings of *Appleseed*'s heroine, a classic Deunan

---

10 Deu's hesitation creates some problems during the fist fights, as cyborgs attack both Bri and Deu.

image – on one knee, arms raised, two hands on the pistol, eyes glaring, with speed lines flared behind her.

▼

Chapter 14: *Cybernetics* begins with the Mission Accomplished: over the break in the chapters, Masamune Shirow has the shot firing and hitting the mechanisms to shut down Gaia's rampage. Outside in Olympus, environmental drawings depict the spider platforms sinking to the ground. It's all over. Deunan hugs Briareos; she's in tears. She apologizes for hesitating, but 'whether Gaia's right or wrong, I can't let her destroy this city'.

Ch. 14: *Cybernetics* shifts to aftermath scenes, with Athena and her coterie discussing what happened, Hitomi and Yoshi wonder if they'll be sent back to jail, and Briareos carries Deunan on his shoulder (a pity none of the *animé* adaptations used this gesture, it's so cute!).

Prometheus Unbound, book two of *Appleseed* (and chapter 14), closes with some sweet scenes of Deunan and Briareos together: as they walk away thru the wreckage around the Gaia facility and the Arcology structures, they discuss taking a long vacation (as they usually do when they have time to think about such things). They joke about Deunan's cooking. Deunan's holds Briareos's arm, and they walk off into the sunset.

The light-hearted appendix to *Appleseed*'s book two features the foursome (Yoshi, Hitomi, Deu and Bri) visiting a gun store. They look at guns: 'Briareos! They've got a custom Steyr GB like the one my Dad used in that crime prevention poster!! I've got to get it!' There's some joshing about guns, and motorcycles (Yoshi's fetish), and bioroid-human differences. We also discover that Briareos's surname, Hecatonchires, comes from the 100-headed giants in Greek mythology (not, as Deu thinks, from the Goddess Hecate).

▼

Book three of *Appleseed*, *The Scales Of Prometheus* (*Purometeusu no ko tenbini*, 1987), opens with chapter 15: *Point Man*, and a new story in a new setting: New York City, and a killer, cannibal bioroid.

Appleseed vol. 3 is notable for its increased 'fan service' ingredients – such as even more *mecha* and action than ever, and a huge amount of nudity (chiefly from Deunan and Hitomi), nudity which is pretty much completely gratuitous. The artwork seems heavier, greyer, with more screentone – it appears like the denser images in the *Ghost In the Shell* manga.

Post-apocalyptic Gotham opens chapter 15: *Point Man*, a city that's been blown to bits more times in Western fantasy and sci-fi literature and cinema than any other (tho' maybe not as many times as Tokyo in Japanese pop culture!). So, yes, here are the smashed skyscrapers, the littered streets, with grizzled survivors hunkering down around fires in oil barrels, or sleeping on chairs ripped out of cars.

Like many artists, Masamune Shirow has a field day when it comes to portraying post-apocalyptic ruins: there's nothing more satisfying than seeing hyper-capitalist societies toppling into anarchy and chaos. Here, it's a bunch-a guys from Extra Special Weapons and Tactics (led by Magnus an' Morton), who've come to find and capture a fearsomely powerful (and feral) bioroid, by the name of Artemis.

This scenario draws of course on part of Masamune Shirow's *Black Magic manga* – and hunting a killer cyborg has been re-used several times in the *Ghost In the Shell manga*, TV and movies.

She's short, she has cat ears and cat eyes (Masamune Shirow adores cat-women!), but, wow, she is a ferocious fighter! It takes all of the ingenuity (and guts) of the E.S.W.A.T. team to pin down and quell Artemis – and even then it's not enough, because on the voyage back to Olympus, Artemis wakes from her drugged suppression and creates hell in the flying craft (it's the bringing-back-a-monster-to-civilization motif of *King Kong*).

Deunan and Briareos don't go to Gotham; they remain in Olympus.[11] They are attending a swanky party (even Deunan has donned an evening dress). But parties and schmoozing are not Deunan and Briareos's scene: she's outside on the balcony,[12] looking out over nighttime Olympus. Bri joins her. Deunan has turned wistful and pensive again: 'I wish we were still back in Badside'.

The story kicks in with a classic device: Briareos hears a distress signal[13] from the stricken aircraft returning to Olympus (well, sure, this is a 1950s-style, B-movie plot, but what the hey?! 99% of science fiction literature is B-movie plots!). So of course, Bri has to answer the call (it's a cyborg's ethical duty, you understand), but Deu could stay at the party. No way! – Deunan was just looking for an excuse to cut loose. (The computer-aided remakes of *Appleseed* used a swanky party scenario several times, but never the hunt-the-feral-cat-woman plot).

So our heroic couple're hurrying down to the lobby to commandeer a ride to follow the May Day signal. Here Masamune Shirow introduces a sassy, black woman who's totally happy that her sporty car's been requisitioned by Extra Special Weapons and Tactics for a high speed chase ('All right! I've been waitin' for something like this to happen!' Which's who you need in an action scene. But she gets more than she expected, as her vehicle's inevitably smashed up).

Shirow-sensei mines some comedy from the woman's exhilaration in being part of an E.S.W.A.T. operation, her dismay when her car's beaten up, and Deunan's antsy jibes and rapid commands (Deunan dislikes the woman from the outset – especially when she says, *pace* Briareos, 'hey! You *sleep* with that guy! That's *mega*!').

High speed chases, sports cars, motorcycles, freeway pursuits, a futuristic megalopolis at night, and killer bioroids dressed as cats on the loose – this is Masamune Shirow in his element.

The scenario in *Seedyapple 3* is as pulpy and simplistic as you can get, but not the way that Masamune Shirow portrays it. The aircraft, for

---

11 Morton and Magnus are far less interesting charas. Actually, their smugness and wise-cracks rapidly become tiresome.
12 With a glass of her favourite tipple – wine.
13 Reprising the moment in ch. 1 when Bri heard the distant mobile suit of Hitomi.

instance, crashes into a skyscraper and tumbles to the streets below (the explosion and smoke handily alerts the heroes to the aircraft's location). Artemis emerges first, of course (and seemingly unscathed). Deunan and Briareos are soon on the scene, dealing with the wounded. They don't know, yet, just what Artemis is or what she's capable of. They take off in hot pursuit. Diagonal speed lines slew across the drawings as the killer flees with Deunan and Briareos behind.

If it's a street chase, there has to be crowds, right? Masamune Shirow follows the North American movie pattern, and places his protagonists in amongst people in a shopping mall. Artemis shoots Briareos in the eye (luckily, he has multiple eyes. So again we have the motif of Briareos being injured).[14]

Deunan is still operating at fever pitch, pursuing the quarry in the sports car. At this point, Masamune Shirow introduces a second chase and a new prey, as a fleet of Landmates appear on the streets. Fang, Brontes and the F.B.I. (not the North American F.B.I., Shirow points out),[15] are searching for a different quarry. Deunan and Briareos meet up, both wounded (Deu was scratched by Artemis). Nothing is resolved, and there's a long argument btn Fang and the F.B.I. and Deunan and Briareos (who have interferred with the F.B.I.'s work).

The new charas in vol. 3 of *Appleseed* merge together somewhat – Fang, Arguess, Brontes, Morton, etc – they're all of a certain age, and a certain character type (gruff, cynical, seen-it-all-before veterans). Their dialogue and sarcastic quips become irritating – this is Shirow in his North American action genre mode (or maybe it's the American English translation that gives some of these scenes that formulaic tone?).

▼

Chapter 16: *Life Point* opens with some shameless 'fan service' from *mangaka* Masamune Shirow: his heroine lying in bed,[16] semi-naked. Her Tee shirt is ruffled up from sleep, revealing her torso, and her panties tease with more skin (much more 'fan service' is on the way at the end of the chapter). In the bed, Deunan finds a computer chip (which is Shirow's excuse for portraying his heroine semi-naked). Briareos examines the chip (with his electronic eyes): it turns out on the following pages that Extra Special Weapons and Tactics is being set up and investigated, and Deunan and Briareos are being tailed (a *lot* of both *Appleseed* and *Ghost In the Shell* comprise scene of charas tailing or being tailed).

In the following sequence, with a change of pace and setting, Masamune Shirow depicts Deunan Knute as a bicycle cop on duty in the local parks and streets. It's the design of Deunan's outfit here, and the architecture (Hitomi's mushroom-like new home), and the cars (a big, American car), that're more significant than the story. Deunan K., for instance, has put on a cute, police woman's uniform just for kicks – it includes very short shorts (with Shirow using his customary low angles

14 But here he can be fixed rapidly, on the spot.
15 Why didn't he choose a different name or acronym?
16 There's a *chibi* toy of Briareos – but why would anybody have a stuffed toy version of their lover?!

to display Deunan's rear).

There're chats with Yoshi, with Hitomi, with her visitor, a black, North American woman (Miss Meranpous, bodyguard to another Russian visitor, Masha Gavilov). Hitomi shows off her new addition to her house – a traditional, Japanese, Zen Buddhist garden. The chat's interrupted by Deunan's ride appearing – Briareos on an *Akira*-cool motorcycle (what is it with Japanese artists and motorbikes?! Yoshi, working outside on a Landmate, is drooling over the bike). And Deunan and Briareos whizz away (much to Hitomi's annoyance – she wants to show Deunan more of her new place. Hitomi is often portrayed as rather superficial).

The second part of the chapter 16: *Life Point* depicts our heroes in uniform as dutiful, attentive members of Olympus's E.S.W.A.T. team. Yup, it's that old staple of cop (and military) shows – the briefing scene (followed by a canteen scene). The only departure, story-wise, is the appearance of 'Doric' (the female spy, who's tailing Deu an' Bri), and Lance is joined by the bug-eyed commander, Argus. They've been picked for a new mission, soon to occur (in France); nukes and drugs are suggested as the real reason for the mission.

OK, who wants to see Deunan Knute nude?

It's Girls Being Girls in the third part of *Appleseed*'s chapter 16, as Hitomi takes Deunan for some girlie-style pampering at a sauna. None of the adaptations of *Appleseed* have touched this sequence, but we've got 9 pages of full nudity of two young women here (in a volume of 220 pages, so it's a significant proportion of the *tankobon*). The dialogue's only one element in this part of *Appleseed* – because Masamune Shirow depicts his heroines in multiple naked poses: there's Deunan lying down, Deunan taking a shower, Deunan on all fours (showing off her butt), Deunan sitting, Deunan walking, and Deunan being massaged.

Masamune Shirow gives the nude Deunan Knute a very muscley body, without an ounce of fat: apart from the usual slender, appealing figure (of all of Shirow's heroines), Deu displays markedly broad, beefy, muscley shoulders and upper arms. This is a girl who *really* works out.[17]

As Shirow-sensei explains in the *Appleseed Databook*, Deunan may not be as strong or as tall as the other Extra Special Weapons and Tactics members, but she is very quick and agile – she is a martial artist, Shirow notes. She knows how to hit pressure points, for instance, in her opponents.

The lesbian subtext is pulled into the foreground of *Appleseed* (using the pretext of the Japanese tradition of bathing in public, which is everywhere in *manga* and *animé*). Not only are Deunan and Hitomi portrayed over nine pages nude and close together, they are massaged by two (older) women. Who's complaining? Masamune Shirow's editors and publishers know exactly who their audience is, and they know how to play to them (*Ghost In the Shell* is *seinen manga*). 'More nudity', 'more 'fan service'', 'more *mecha*' and 'more action' are precisely the sort of requests that *manga* editors make of their artists working for the young, male

17 There are jokes about Deunan being a little too masculine – a recurring sub-theme in fiction that includes physical fitness.

market. (And Shirow is happy to respond to such requests).

Anyhoo, apart from this 100% 'fan service' sequence, there *is* some information exchanged in the conversation: we discover that Deunan's grand-parents were white and black, from Africa (Sudan), and her grandfather was a British-French journo (from the British Broadcasting Corporation). And thus her mom and dad met in Rhodesia (Zimbabwe). Hitomi is suitably impressed: 'Gosh... a white black African'. Deunan's mom was apparently killed by black supremacists (and Deunan ended up in the U.S.A.; she was taken to Frisco aged ten - which's where she met Briareos).

❄

Chapter 17: *Live Drive* introduces a coupla villains: *mecha* scientist Doctor Slade and a scary cyborg from the Middle East, Kainisu, a religious zealot (Kainusu sports that tall, angular, imposing design, with flattop hair, resembling the American singer and model Grace Jones, that Masamune Shirow sometimes uses for his foreign villains. The Arab might be male or female - or neither, or both). What are these bad guys up to? Slade has created a Titan mobile suit take on the authorities[18] (with links back to Munma, the Islamic nation).

✦

The next sequence in the *Seedy Apple manga* is another training exercise: in this one, Deunan Knute is so good, so quick, and so vicious, she runs rings around everybody else (this short but wiry girl gets the better of guys twice her size. In *Appleseed*, Deunan is a natural warrior). She chalks up victims with an 'X' on her biceps, and hands out derisory signs to the losers ('if only I had a brain'). She pokes her tongue out at guys she's tumbled to the ground. She admits, 'I'm a bad, *bad* girl!'

But stern Briareos H. is *not* impressed: he haughtily reminds her that her buddies might have to save her ass in a life-or-death situation, and she shouldn't make fun of 'em. Deu, who never likes to see Bri upset, is suitably repentant (and in the pre-ops canteen scene, she apologies to everyone[19]).

In fact, Deunan Knute is sometimes cocky and self-assured to the point of irritation of those around her: in the next chapter, she sings as she flies into battle with her fellow soldiers (and has time to ask Doric if she has any kids).

The journey to Paris, France is announced with a double-page spread of Olympus Police personnel aircraft flying at night, guarded by jet fighters. Lance orders the E.S.W.A.T. team to suit up (they have chunky body armour called Orcs (it doubles Deunan's size): Masamune Shirow would draw variations on body armour literally hundreds of times in his later work (the posterbooks, calendars, *Pieces* and of course erotic art).)

The pre-ops sequence focusses on Deunan who is... singing! Yes, Deu takes to making up silly songs: 'Oh mammy were a drug lord's whore, he shot her up 'til she were shot'. Daddy Bri silences her. Clearly, our Deu gets high before an operation: she is simply a professional who enjoys her

18 Wait 'til Matthew sees this, he brags.
19 They, in turn, resent Briareos sticking his nose in.

job!

Masamune Shirow isn't going to rush this part of the *Appleseed manga* – he's going to make sure that every stage of the Benandanti operation is covered. So we have (A) the pre-ops canteen chat, (B) the plane journey, (C) the unloading of the aircraft, (D) the trip in police trucks, (E) the surveillance outside (F) the building, (G) the preparations for the storming, etc. The build-up to the mission is explored at length, with movie-like pacing (thus, we get to know the charas in the canteen scene, which will pay off later during the op, exactly like a movie).

In the *Appleseed* notes, Masamune Shirow discusses his research into exactly how to perform this sort of military operation – a secret raid on a building full of military dignitaries. Shirow is an artist who has studied the special operations units of every major government and nation on Earth. This part of *Appleseed* is stuffed with the fruits of that research (for ex, there are all sorts of details in the drawings which you might not notice if you're reading this in the usual *manga* fashion – three seconds per page. Shirow's art encourages more lingering than that! And, just to make sure you catch everything, in the *Databook* of *Appleseed*, Shirow points out some details that you mighta missed. For ex, Deunan's K-2 Protector suit leaves the forefingers bare, so she can have maximum sensitivity on the triggers of her firearms). These are some of Shirow's most heavily-worked *manga* drawings, across all of his output, with costumes, faces, settings and of course *mecha* all portrayed with obsessive detail.

It's a very wet night when the Extra Special Weapons and Tactics team finally reaches gay, old Paree: every exterior drawing has blurred vertical lines of rain added to it. The drawings are so movie-ish and atmospheric, an animated or live-action version of this *manga* is simply superfluous. (Thus, while I have griped that none of the *animé* adaptations have nailed Masamune Shirow's *Appleseed manga,* it doesna matter, because we have the original material. And it's sensational).

The building in Paris where politicos have gathered just happens to have a distinctly Japanese look (it's in the blocky, modernist style of glass and concrete and wood). And it's surrounded by extensive gardens, like a traditional, Japanese teahouse.

It's a textbook operation in the first half, as the E.S.W.A.T. team from Olympus surrounding the building, as well as guarding the sewers (with Shirow's customary jokes about the stench of sewers. You probably would *not* want to be in a French sewer, even in the hi-tech 22nd century!).

The problem with putting every chara in full body armour is that it obscures their faces. So Masamune Shirow resorts to cutaway close-ups, so we can see Deunan, and Doric, and Fang (Briareos, of course, is instantly recognizable by those distinctive rabbit ears!). There're also minor additions to the helmets, at the front, for the eagle-eyed readers (such as a black triangle for Deu).

✳

Chapter 18: *Dead or Alive, Part 2*: all goes well with Operation Benandanti (no casualties, several deaths, most of the targets are captured and tied up on the floor), until a stalemate is reached in another part of the building. Briareos arrives to find two cyborgs in laminated armour who've apparently got 100 hostages to barter with (plus they've rigged the area with claymore mines, bear-traps and booby traps). The stand-off continues, with both sides arguing about what to do, until our Deunan, ballsy as ever, forces the tense situation by demanding that the 'borgs release all of the hostages, or they die. (Other members of the team grumble about Deunan under their breath – she always wants to work outside of the agreed boundaries, and to dive in with guns blazing).

When the giant cyborg appears, seemingly out-matching the E.S.W.A.T. team, Briareos leaps into action, doing what he is very good at: punching the hell out of opponents. Forget guns and ammo and gizmos (which Deunan relies on too much, Briareos complains), all it takes is several well-aimed and full-force punches, and Bri literally decapitates the cyborg (Deunan, tho', is providing back-up by blasting away at the 'borg). The drawings are full of wild, blurry, swinging action, depicting Bri and Deu at their fiercest.

Briareos also guesses where the other cyborg is hiding (under the debris, pretending to be dead) in a room thick with booby traps. Sokaku is one of the very quirky, jokey, clown-like designs[20] that Masamune Shirow gives some of his cyborgs/ robots from time to time (so we don't take Sokaku seriously as an opponent, even tho' he's a pyrotechnic whizz).

However, the terrorists are certainly venal: one of the most disturbing scenes in all of Masamune Shirow's work is the portrayal of the hostages in chapter 18: *Dead or Alive:* they are women and children, most of 'em depicted naked, all are in a sorry state (one is having a miscarriage), and they have no front teeth. They are humans used as toys and slaves, exchanged between people with money and perverted tastes.

No wonder, then, that Deunan Knute launches herself in fury at the politico (the Imperial Navy's Special Agency's assistant director) held captive in the back of a truck (behind a wire mesh, like an animal), when he yells at the Extra Special Weapons and Tactics agents not to touch 'his children' (this particular chara is given a ridiculous shock of wild hair, in another of Shirow's monkey-like caricatures). Deu embodies the outrage of ordinary people when confronted with slave-trading, exploitation and other injustices. (Deunan is also for shooting these guys; in this operation, Deunan is placed alongside Doric, who has a more indifferent, cynical view of things, to contrast with Deunan's high emotions).

Afterwards, Fang (who has it in for both Briareos and Deunan), complains to Briareos about Deunan's undisciplined behaviour. Briareos defends her, and insists that she is the unpredictable, unusual element in the team which makes it work (and if she hadn't acted earlier, he would be dead, and the villains would've got away). Fang doesn't get it: he reckons that Deunan will be the death of Briareos. But Briareos isn't even listening anymore as he an' Deu hunker down in the aircraft after the operation's over, when everybody's exhausted, and they're heading back

20 As with some of the other cyborgs/ robots in the Shirowverse, it could be argued that Sokaku is another negative representation of black culture.

to sunny, ol' Olympus.

✳

Chapter 19: *Dead Point* is a little bitty and underwhelming – at least after the high excitement of the French operation. *Dead Point* opens with a complete change of pace, setting, story and design. After the shoot-em-ups and furious conflicts of *Dead or Alive*, Shirow-sensei has decided that it's time for some 'fan service'. Thus, when Deu visits Hitomi in her mushroom-shaped home, the bioroid is scantily-clad, and in several images Shirow poses Hitomi with her body on display. (Meanwhile, Deunan wears a curious, braided hair-piece, and a pencil skirt).

There's not much story unfolding in the five pages of chapter 19 of *Appleseed* at Hitomi's place, apart from the girls talking about the creature Artemis, the combat cyborg that's gone A.W.O.L. In the next section of 19: *Dead Point*, we're introduced to the cat-girl cyborg Artemis, and the cops who're hunting her.

The chase, in a pleasant park in Olympus, isn't one of Masamune Shirow's most compelling examples of storytelling. The cops – Magnus and Morton – are his dullest characterizations (and they're inter-changeable with many other secondary cop charas in *Appleseed*). And altho' Artemis is an intimidating quarry, the hunt doesn't have any sense of jeopardy (compared to the scenes in Gotham in chapter 15). (At the end of the chase, Artemis covers herself in plaster, which of course dries rapidly (she doesn't know what it is). This seems to be a nod to the movie *After Hours* (1985)).

In fact, this is one of the least compelling chapters in the *Appleseed manga*: for a start, Deu and Bri are not included; second, the cops chasing Artemis are boring (Morton, Magnus and several spiky-haired agents); third, the Artemis-plot is ultimately a side-story; and fourth, thirty pages're expended on this chase (which's far too many). It's no surprise that this chapter hasn't been a part of the animated adaptations.

Once Artemis has been captured, and is under-going examinations in a laboratory in Olympus, there's a brief visit to Athena and Nike (in just one page), followed by an intense training sequence, where Lance is lashing his troops with a whip to do it better, faster: 'Again! From the top! Again! Again!' (The grunts are sick of hearing their commander urging them to do it quicker, better, faster, better).

Time for some more 'fan service' in ch 19: *Dead Point*: it's a post-training shower scene, in the girls' locker room (a favourite location of *otaku* and pervs), with Deunan Knute naked, in amongst her fellow (female) colleagues (Shirow-sensei crams in six eroticized views of Deu nude across two pages, plus more bare skin from the other women).

Meanwhile, the outfit that Deunan has selected to welcome home Briareos at the heliport is bizarre: baggy, Aladdin pants held up by braces (with the customary triangular, Shirowian pouch over the pubic mound), a croptop (with shoulder pads!), and a *Thunderbirds* hat (none of the *animé* adaptations have put Deunan in anything like this!).[21]

---

21 However, *Appleseed XIII* did put Deunan in a sort of baggy pants and braces combo.

Poor Briareos is beaten-up and grouchy (the riots in Russia were the 'worst ever', he says). He's a bag of glum no fun when he exits the returning chopper (with nary a kind word for the glammed-up Deunan come to welcome him home). The bickering btn the heroes is brief, however, and they've soon made up. (Briareos goes off for more maintenance, a regular occurrence in the fiction of Masamune Shirow – Leona polishes her Buonaparte tank in *Dominion*, for instance, and Motoko Kusanagi is forever having her body/ bodies updated or repaired).

At the end of ch. 19, Deunan Knute ponders whether she's wasting her time (or treading water) in E.S.W.A.T. (and she wants to be teamed up with Briareos again). At the end of the chapter, Briareos and Deunan are going to be working together again. (He keeps encouraging her to be flexible, and get used to working with other people. But Deunan is a One-Man Girl).

+

The four-page appendix to book three, *The Scales of Prometheus*, depicts our heroes (Deunan, Briareos, Hitomi, Yoshi, and even Artemis), in a light-hearted setting. The gentle joshing between the charas takes a back seat to the real point of the appendix: to offer views of nude girls in panties climbing into mobile suits. The appendix features three panels of Hitomi entering her Landmate, as she chats to Deunan and Yoshi. Nothing gives Shirow more pleasure, it seems, than spending hours drawing an attractive, young, semi-nude woman messing about with a futuristic mobile suit. (The best Christmas present you could give Shirow-sensei would be a mobile power suit – and the cute cyborg to ride in it!).[22]

✳

OK, so book four of Masamune Shirow's *Appleseed manga*, entitled *Purometeusu no dai tenbin* (*The Promethean Balance*, 1989), opens with the E.S.W.A.T. team[23] in full action mode.

A fifth *tankobon* of *Appleseed* has been rumoured since the building of the Pyramids in Ancient Egypt (part of it appeared in *Appleseed Hypernotes*). Yes, some *manga* fans would prefer it if Shirow-sama directed some of his attention towards drawing a new Deunan and Briareos story, rather than anonymous, inter-changeable babes being gang-raped by tentacled aliens (this seems to be the popular view of Shirow's output from the late 1990s to the present day. Only partially true).

But wait – in chapter 20: *Dry Run*, it's yet another training exercise, not an operation to storm a drug lord's manse in Colombia. Yep, Commander Lance is pushing his boys (and a coupla girls) through the wringer once again. (Some critics have complained that book four of *Appleseed* is 'combat porn', and certainly parts of it, like this long and indulgent training sequence, can come across like that. But then, 'combat porn' describes 90% of Masamune Shirow's art!). Also, training is a key

22 So it wouldn't be a cheap Xmas gift!
23 E.S.W.A.T. has some new aircraft – which of course look even more like bugs. (They're called Autobugs or Bugs).

element of *manga* (and not only *manga* aimed at boys and young men). Sports *manga* are extremely popular, and training is central to them. Training scenes pop up regularly in action *manga* too (*Bleach, Naruto, Vagabond,* etc).

There are superb images of Deunan giving it her all, crouched in low slung poses, legs apart, or diving and firing at the same time. (But the first time that we see Deunan, she's snoozing! And she has to be woken up).

Deunan Knute is teamed up with a black woman, Pani. There is no love lost btn them (Pani derides Deu as 'some tin cyborg's sex doll', and Deu is similarly dismissive of Pani. Everyone is just jealous, Deu reckons, of her relationship with Bri).[24] Unfortunately, this is the sequence where Deu is badly injured in the eye during the exercise, and in fury she blames Pani (thus, Deunan spends the rest of *Appleseed 4* wearing an eyepatch. Which gives her a suitably rough, pirate-like look,[25] but was thankfully rectified in the *Appleseed Hypernotes* story).

So the new story in *Appleseed*'s book four, opening with chapter 20: *Dry Run,* involves stolen Landmate parts, a kidnapping, a Bezekric company, activists working for the Islamic Munma nation, and a giant Landmate. Best of all, Deunan Knute is front and centre in book 4. (Bezekric houses government bldgs and embassies).

There's the usual briefing scene at the top of chapter 20: *Dry Run,* followed by the usual bickering interaction among the Extra Special Weapons and Tactics team (Magnus is dating Pani, Deu is ribbed 'cos she's so good and she's Briareos' pet, Morton's out of the operation, etc). And the usual dry, wry comments from Briareos: 'bribery, corruption, sloth, divorce, alcoholism, drug abuse... the Soviets and both the Americas are going straight down the tubes'.

❊

Chapter 21: *Decoy* starts up the story of book four of *Appleseed* with some rapid and explosive action. One of the villains injects a guy with a drug which compels the man to wake with a jolt and jump into a large Landmate,[26] in order to fight for the Holy Munma Republic (in Masamune Shirow's future vision, the Middle East continues to be a hotbed of political unrest, with powerful nations like Israel, Iran and the new 'Holy Munma Republic' at loggerheads).

So the drugged dupe stages a war on 'the enemies of Munma!!' by going nuts with the over-size mobile suit in downtown Olympus. He's smashing into the cops and their vehicles, evading missiles from the Air Police, and he seems unstoppable (like all out-of-control characters do in Shirow-sensei's *manga*).

Lance decides it's time to send in Deunan and Briareos – which's what we want to see (tho' Deu reckons the guy in the Landmate is a decoy. And she's right. She'd rather nab the whole of the heavies – one

<hr>

24 It must cause some ructions among the E.S.W.A.T. team that two of their high profile members are in a relationship (and deeply in love with each other, to rub it in!). The resentment emerges in characters such as Magnus and Pani.
25 And is possibly a reference to Snake in the 1981 *Escape From New York* movie.
26 This was used in the *Appleseed* movies, when the guy in the construction mobile suit goes A.W.O.L.

rampaging Landmate isn't challenging enough for her). There is plenty of action in chapter 21: *Decoy* – enough to satisfy any action junkie (speed lines race at the back of every drawing, and Shirow blurs trees, roads and buildings to enhance the feeling of speed). Even Hitomi and Yoshi are brought into the mix (as potential victims, tho' Yoshi protects Hitomi).

This latter beat stretches credibility – that the out-of-control Landmate should just happen to run into Hitomi, Yoshi and their chums in the street. (Check out the costumes of the entourage; and Chief Aramaki makes a cameo).

❋

Chapter 22: *Outlet Store* continues directly from chapter 21, with Deunan preparing to torture the captured criminal for information (using a giant knife that's as big as a short sword – Deu is very fond of knives! She carries two knives). We don't see this – it's not something we want to see (tho' we know that Deunan, especially this new, mean, eye-patched Deunan, is capable of it).[27] Instead, after a warning from Briareos – 'don't forget the Red Cross is watching' – the *manga* cuts to the rest of the E.S.W.A.T. team (Lance, Morton, etc). Indeed, this is Deu at her most vicious in the entire *Appleseed* franchise: a mean scowl, an eyepatch, wielding a big weapon, preparing to torture a victim. (Quite a departure from the cute, smiling girl we met in chapter one, cooking for her boyfriend in a kitchen).

The next section of chapter 22: *Outlet Store* depicts Fang and Bolt casing an apartment that belongs to the terrorists (and has been booby-trapped). The clownish robot Sokaku turns up, hoping to bargain with the guys about disarming the booby traps.

Back with Deunan and Briareos flying in the air above nighttime Olympus in their Guges suits: there's a touching piece of characterization, as Deu hovers next to a department store with a display of wedding dresses in the window (well, she *is* the heroine, so she's allowed to dream wistfully about marriage. And it happily contrasts with the previous scene of the Mean, Moody Deunan). Briareos reminds her that they are on duty (they also discuss the geopolitical situation, of Munma, Israel, Imperial Americana, etc, and the relation to Olympus, as they fly past stores and malls).

❋

Chapter 23: *Outlook Envelop* continues the investigation of the terrorists by our heroes: again, Deunan K. is in the forefront of the story. The narrative of pursuit is secondary to the many images of Deunan in her mobile suit, Deunan flying over freeways, Deunan clambering onto motorcycles, etc. This is more Pin-Up-*Appleseed* than Story-*Appleseed*: the drawings exhibit Masamune Shirow's customary obsession with detail and fetishization. Notice, for instance, at least two large-size images of Deunan clambering into or out of her mobile suit: in *Appleseed*, either Deunan or Hitomi are depicted numerous times in power suits.

Oh my, how Shirow-sensei adores his amazing Deunan the Extra

---

27 Shirow depicted Batou torturing a crook for info in *Ghost In the Shell*.

Special Weapons and Tactics warrior, with her shock of bushy, blonde hair, her muscley, athletic body[28] head-to-toe in full body armour, and her big *manga* eyes (and her eyepatch!).

In this part of *Appleseed*, there is plenty of characters standing up on top of buildings surveying the streets below, plenty of Guges flying thru nighttime Olympus, plenty of chat between '109' (Deunan) and '45' (Briareos), and plenty of *mecha* on display: cars, motorbikes, Landmates, guns, and ærial transports in the shape of bugs.

The terrorists discuss their plans in their car in a long scene, as they make their way to the Arcology structure. For a change of pace, Shirow-sensei has Deunan tailin' 'em on a motorcycle she's commandeered for E.S.W.A.T. (much to the owner's bewilderment: 'M-m-my little V-baby!').

Nike talks with Senator Boyle and other bigwigs at a high level meeting (where the issue is the political relations between Imperial American, Munma, Israel and Olympus).

❈

Chapter 24: *Stealth* further explores the pursuit by Deunan of the terrorists. In a bar, Deunan follows the terrorists, and pretends to be a journalist[29] so she can obtain some intel from the bartender (she's not great at play-acting! Tho', in fact, she could exploit her *kawaii* looks more often).

There's more'n more build-up, with scenes of Deunan exploring the warehouse out back. Masamune Shirow indulges himself with many environmental, atmospheric drawings. After quite some time in between action scenes, Deunan finally springs into motion, and she discovers, of all people, the robot Sokaku (who's hiding in the rafters). Both Deunan and Sokaku are lurking in the upper levels, hoping to overhear the meeting of the terrorists down below. Sokaku wants to make a deal with Deunan.

While the story has been stretched out considerably (there are many more pages of Deunan Knute and Sokaku in the warehouse than necessary), Masamune Shirow features Deunan in numerous dynamic poses, as if he's challenging himself to create anything but a standard pose for his heroine. So she's crouching low, she's spread out on her front, she's leaping into the air, she's diving into a headstand (all of these drawings of course highlight Deunan's tough, sleek form – at least a third of the drawings emphasize Deunan's butt. She's wearing close-fitting body armour, called K-2).

Meanwhile, what about Briareos? We haven't seen him for some time: he's outside, on the roof, waiting with Sudo for the action to explode. He has a bad feeling about Deunan taking so long inside the warehouse (Sudo accuses him of being too weak where Deunan is concerned, an echo of Fang's doubting views of the Deu-Bri professional relationship[30]). During operations, Shirow continually exploits conflicts among his comic teams – Azuma and Togusa, Batou and Kim, Motoko and Batou, Leona and

---

28 Now with the torso and legs elongated.
29 From *Pirate* magazine! Hence the eyepatch!
30 There's undoubtedly an undercurrent of jealousy in the repeated sniping about the Deu-Bri relationship from the others in the security forces.

Brenten, etc. The banter btn Sudo an' Briareos is More Of The Same.

When the action begins, as we know it inevitably will when E.S.W.A.T. are casing a joint occupied by terrorists armed with Landmates, Masamune Shirow includes a new addition to the *Appleseed* universe: a giant mobile suit. As big as King Kong. Which means, of course, larger amounts of destruction: out come the speed lines, the explosions, the carnage (these drawings have a Godzilla-like feel to them, as another giant creature smashes up large chunks of a modern city). Soon everybody's involved – Morton, Pani, Fang, Sudo, etc.

❄

Chapter 25: *Shalom* – the last chapter of *Appleseed*'s book four – switches the story back to Deunan and Sokaku in the warehouse. You will notice that Briareos is absent from much of the finale of book 4 of Masamune Shirow's *Appleseed manga*.

Now Deunan Knute is a one-woman army, busting up the meeting of terrorists with her usual bag of tricks (grenades, guns, knives, etc). For several pages, every drawing contains some action (as the building collapses – courtesy of explosives expert Sokaku).

Masamune Shirow has decided to give his heroine a giant action sequence to round off the last of the four *Appleseed* volumes. She is taking on everybody, and winning. Shirow's goal seems to be to explore as many unusual poses for Deunan Knute as possible, and to never repeat himself: he draws Deunan leaping high, legs together, head lowered, like a diver; she's crouching very low on the ground (to avoid an attack); she's flipping over, limbo-style (to land a shot on a rival); she's upside-down and kicking high; and she's falling backwards (while she re-loads her gun – so cool!).

Certainly this is Deunan at her most physically dynamic, turning combat into choreography. She looks like a pixiefied pirate, but she's deadly as all hell. And in full body armour and wielding guns and knives, she's unstoppable (the villains don't know what hit 'em).

Among the stand-out scenes in the finale are a one-on-one duel between Deunan and a guy wielding a piece of pipe[31] like a spear in the manner of Jet Li (tho' he loses to Deu, and Jet Li never loses!).

This is swiftly followed by a stunning knife fight,[32] one of the finest action scenes involving Deunan Knute in Masamune Shirow's *Appleseed manga*. Seeing this five foot four-ish woman taking on a bunch of burly guys armed with knives and besting them is very enjoyable. Especially accomplished is Shirow's control of movement, action, spatial relationships and the like to evoke the speed and power of the fight. And the flow of the action is superb, too, and intricately worked-out. (Indeed, there's no need for Briareos to help out when Deunan is this good!).

Indeed, I'm sure that many *manga* fans would be happy if Masamune Shirow continued to draw installments of *Appleseed* with action this accomplished for years and years, into the 1990s and beyond – if *Appleseed* became a long-running battle *manga* like, say, *Naruto* or *Bleach*.

31 It also looks like bamboo.
32 See the article by Shea Hennum on the This Is Famous website, 2014.

(After all, Masashi Kishimoto (*Naruto*) and Tite Kubo (*Bleach*) have based their whole careers on drawing one fight after another).

Outside, Briareos and co. are battling the giant Landmate, with Briareos thumping it repeatedly with shells from his over-size gun. Eventually the giant's destroyed, and Kainisu dies ('I go now to Paradise'). Briareos is particularly disdainful of Kainisu, and the notiom of religious sacrifice. These are big scenes, with Shirow-sensei throwing in pretty much everything from the *Appleseed* cosmos.

Magnus and an Extra Special Weapons and Tactics team corner one of the remaining terrorists. They realize at the last moment that the quarry is wired with explosives (with the cable in his mouth, a grotesque image also used in *Ghost In the Shell*). Magnus shoots him.

It all turns out well, of course, with E.S.W.A.T. triumphing, as they always do. A series of aftermath and *dénouement* scenes follow, with the customary sarcastic quipping from charas such as Magnus and Pani, the bawling out of Deunan by Lance (because, as usual, she went her own happy way, ignoring orders), Magnus criticizing Deunan, Deunan re-uniting with Briareos (with a kiss), Lance reporting to Minister Nike, etc.

At the end of the 25 chapters and the four books of *Appleseed*, Deunan and Briareos are together, in a humorous mood. Deunan has some unfinished business with the robot Sokaku (she's rigged his car to blow, hoping that it'll cost him 50,000 to fix his body once it's in bits. The same gag is used in *Ghost In the Shell*, with Chief Aramaki).

❄

The appendix to book four of *Appleseed* is sweet, sweet: it begins with Deunan and Briareos asleep in bed together (and having *chibi* dreams), and moves on to depict them relaxing at home. Deunan's happy, drinking wine, and clad in a revealing T-shirt and shorts (they're talking about debts and money again).

Just as Briareos and Deunan are lying on the couch, planning their vacation, and embracing, who should call, but Hitomi, plus Yoshi, plus the cat-girl Artemis's offspring. Deunan is miffed that the mood is spoilt, when she and Bri were seemingly going to make out. Hitomi asks for cake, which's handed out to the kids, who're messing around noisily. The *Appleseed manga* ends on a note of resignation from Deunan: 'bet you there's an emergency call just about the time Hitomi leaves' (meaning, they'll never get to have their longed-for vacation).

Pages from one of Masamune Shirow's finest
works, the Appleseed manga (this page and over).

MASAMUNE SHIROW'S

BOOK 4

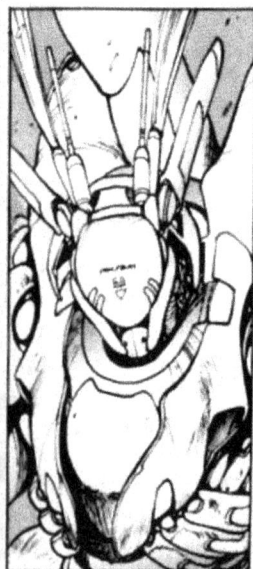

YO!

HEY, Y'ALL! IT'S GOOD OL' HITOMI!

I JUST BROUGHT THOSE MAPS YOU ASKED FOR! THAT'S ALL! JEEZ-- CALM DOWN!

MAPS?

TRAVEL MAPS, WITH ALL THE PLACES WE'RE GOING TO ON OUR VACATION ALREADY MARKED.

SUCH PLANNING! GOSH!

My Hero!

Y'KNOW... I FEEL LIKE WE, mmm, BARGED IN ON SOMETHING...

HEH HEH

OH, DON'T BE SUCH A SILLY! I'M SURE THERE'S A HOMEMADE CAKE JUST WAITING IN THE FRIDGE! RIGHT, DEUNAN?

YUM YUM

....!

IS ANY OF THAT CAKE STILL LEFT FROM YESTER- DAY...?

BET YOU THERE'S AN EMERGENCY CALL JUST ABOUT THE TIME HITOMI LEAVES...

US LOYAL RETAINERS GOT IT ROUGH.

OKAY, OKAY! I'LL GIVE YOU MY PIECE! JUST DON'T BITE!

EEEK!

JUST WHAT DO YOU THINK YOU'RE DOING!!!

WAK WAK WAK WAK

Milk

DESTRUCTION AND BLIND FAITH AND BUREAUCRACY DON'T EQUAL PROGRESS.

RIGHT? OF COURSE NOT.

END: APPLESEED VOLUME FOUR

YAHAHAHA!
YOU DUM-DUM!
The Flight of the Squid
ANIMAL EYES AND SENSORS

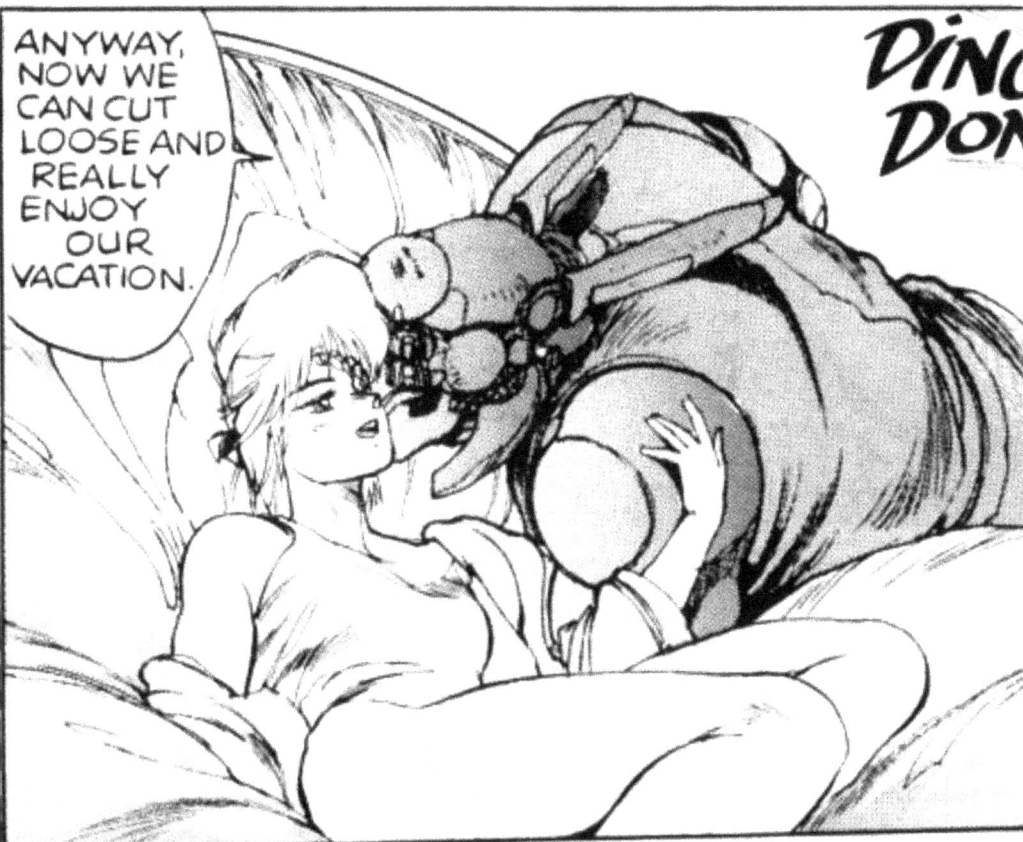

Two double-page spreads from Appleseed, Volume 4.

Deunan at her most fercious, in the knife fight from the final volume.

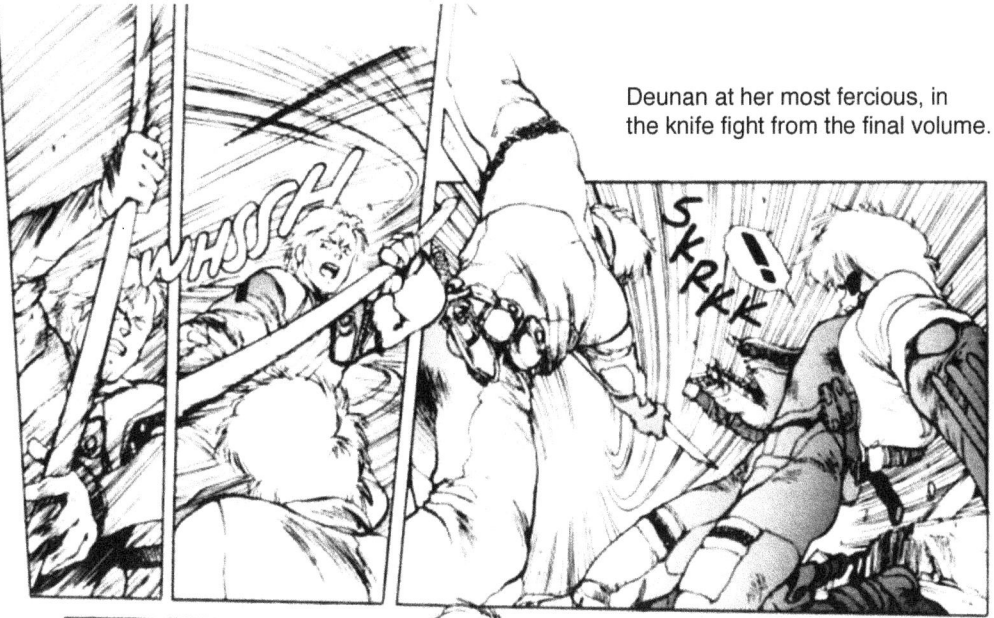

HITOMI

WEAPONRY

Tears are the woman's weapon.

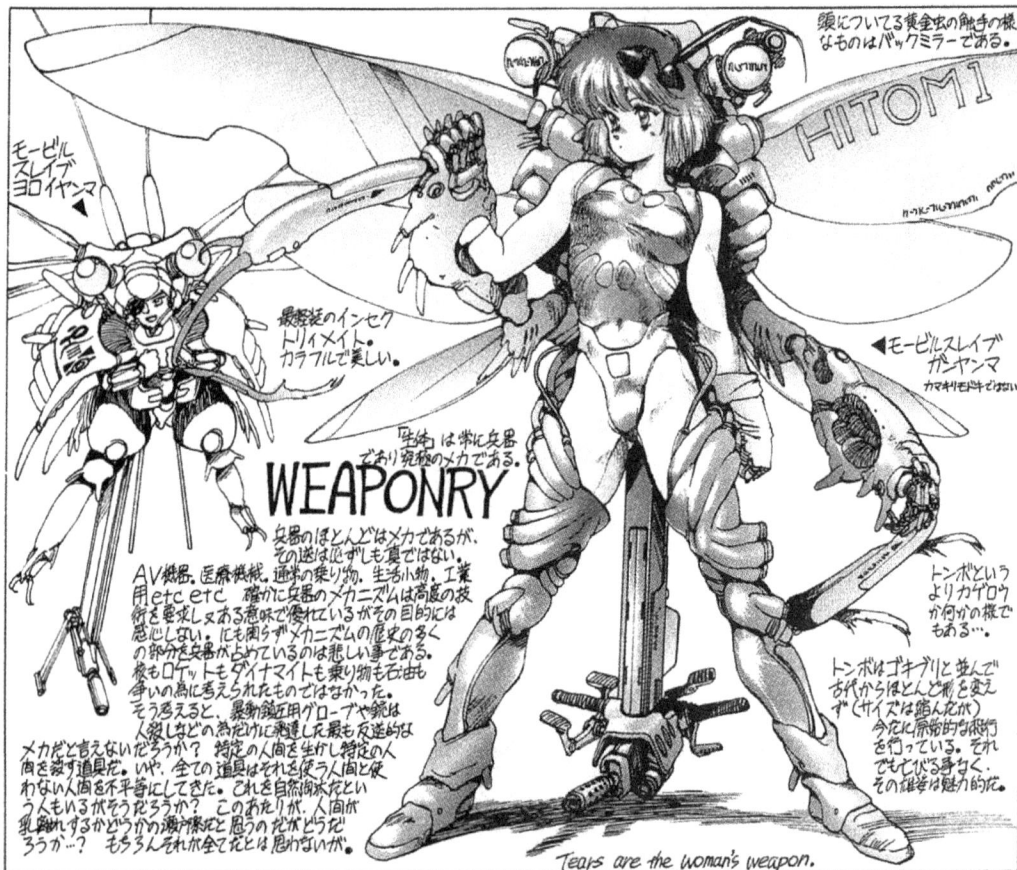

Appleseed – Hitomi (from one of the guides to the series).

Appleseed manga artwork, collected in Intron Depot 1.
(This page and over).

PART THREE

THE APPLESEED ANIMÉ

APPURUSHIDO

01

APPLESEED IN ANIMATION

INTRODUCTION.

The *Appleseed* universe in *manga* has certainly caught the imagination of animation producers – because as well as the three computer-aided animated movies of 2004, 2007 and 2014, and the first animated adaptation of 1988, a further *Appurushido* series has been produced: *Appleseed XIII* (2011) was a 13-episode *animé* series. There are also two video games (plus the usual tie-in merchandizing).

The origins of the characters and the world of *Appleseed* has fascinated filmmakers: an *animé* series was planned in 2005/ 06 (*Appleseed: Genesis*), but became embroiled in lawsuits. One of the latest outings is a prequel movie of 2014, entitled *Appleseed: Alpha* (meanwhile, the 2004 *Appleseed* movie was also known as *Appleseed: The Beginning*).

The theme of *Appleseed* was the notion that a utopia would only be possible with bioroids, but not with humans. However, Shirow himself didn't go along with that: 'The Council and Gaia believe that an all-bioroid society is the only hope for utopia. I don't', he remarked in a 1994 interview. Instead, Shirow personally advocated tolerance and negotiation. But for the purposes of fiction, the conflicts between the bioroids and humans suited the project, like humans and replicants in *Blade Runner*.

The film adaptations of *Appleseed* declined to use numerous characters from Masamune Shirow's *Appleseed*. The bug-eyed, monkey-faced commander Argus, who often works with Lance, wasn't utilized. Nor were many members of the Extra Special Weapons and Tactics team, such as Magus, Morton, and Doric (the female spy), or other cop/ solder/ criminal charas such as Fang, Bernd, Dr Slade, Kainis, or Chiffon, Hitomi's bioroid chum, or the black, American Meranpous, or the cat-woman, assassin cyborg Artemis.

Unfortunately, despite the talent involved, the money shelled out, the hard work undertaken, the adaptations of *Appleseed* have been extremely disappointing, seen as versions of Masamune Shirow's comic. (Somehow, the magic that's blessed the versions of *Ghost In the Shell* has evaporated with *Appleseed* on screen). But I wouldn't be surprised if Shirow is fonder of the *Appleseed* adaptations than the ones of *Ghost In the Shell*.

Every time I decide to watch one of the adaptations of Masamune Shirow's *Appleseed*, I think, maybe this time it'll be better – maybe the 2004 computer-aided *Appleseed* will be better than it was the last time I saw it, as if it could secretly cyborgize (or bioroidize) itself into a great movie. But it doesn't happen.

APPLESEED, 1988

The 75-minute *animé* version of *Appleseed* (*Appurushido*, 1988) was written and directed by Kazuyoshi Katayama, and produced by A.I.C., Bandai Visual, M.O.V.I.C., Tohokushinsha Film Corporation, and the famous Gainax[1] company (Gainax had made their name the year b4 with *Wings of Honneamise*).[2] The executive producers were Hirohiko Sueyoshi, Shinji Nakagawa and Yutaka Takahashi; the producers were Atsushi Sugita, Masaki Sawanobori, Taro Maki and Toru Miura. Norimasa Yamanaka wrote the music, Kiyomi Tanaka designed the *mecha*, Yumiko Horasawa designed the charas and was also animation director, and Hiroaki Ogura was art director. Hideaki Anno (co-founder of Gainax) was also a designer.[3] Masako Katsuki was Deunan Knute and Yoshisada Sakaguchi was Briareos Hecatonchires. Released 1988.4.21.

Helen McCarthy said that 'bad language' was added to the dub of *Appleseed*, 'to make it attractive to teenage boys' (2008, 42). Yes – although there is 'bad language' in the *Appleseed manga*,[4] it's not in the same quantity or harshness of the *animé* versions.

Subtitles and dubs for Western editions of Japanese *animé* are sometimes coarsened, with 'bad language' added to appeal to the target audience (similarly, swearing is included in Hollywood movies that're essentially 'PG', raising them to 'PG-13' or 'R', to persuade the audience they're seeing something cool).[5] In *Appleseed*, the translators (John Volk) have gone to town with rewriting the dialogue.

Thus, 'what?' in Japanese (*nani*), becomes in American English:

1 Gainax Studio was founded in 1982 (by Hideaki Anno, Takami Akai, Yoshiyuki Sadamoto and Hiroyuki Yamaga). Its big successes included *Wings of Honneamise, Mahororomatic, Gunbuster, Nadia: Secret of Blue Water, Appleseed* and *Neon Genesis Evangelion*.
2 H. McCarthy, 2008, 42.
3 Director Hideaki Anno (b. 1960, Yamagata Prefecture), is one of the important figures in contemporary *animé*: he was was co-founder of Gainax Studio in 1982 (in Osaka (where he studied) with Takami Akai, Yoshiyuki Sadamoto and Hiroyuki Yamaga); he married Moyoko Anno, a *mangaka*. Anno later directed *Evangelion, Nadia: Secret of Blue Water, Cutey Honey, His and Her Circumstances, Maho-roromatic* and *Gunbuster*. He designed the opening credits to *Submarine 707R* (2003). He produced a documentary about *Thunderbirds*. He has launched other studios. An early job was animating the Giant Warrior in *Nausicaä of the Valley of the Wind*. Anno has cited Satoru Ozawa (*Blue Submarine No. Six* and *Submarine 707R*) as a significant influence on his love of technology.
4 Also, that might come from the translators – Fred Schodt, Studio Proteus, *et al*.
5 Bad language was added to the foreign versions of some *animé*, to help them appeal to the target audience. So *Patlabor* becomes 'R' rated, when it's really a 'PG' show. This also happened with the *Appleseed animé*, and also with the comic of *Ghost In the Shell*.

'What the fuckin' hell? Oh Christ'
And 'damn' (*kuso*) becomes:
'Fuckin' cocksucker'

Which makes *Appleseed* sound like a bad knock-off movie of the Scorsese/ Tarantino ilk, or one of those cruddy, desperate-to-be-cool thrillers. You hear characters say *kuso* all the time in *animé* (usually it's translated as 'damn'), but the subtitlers don't usually render 'damn' as 'fuckin' cocksucker'!

❖

Ultimately, the 1988 *Appleseed animé* is an average-to-below-average *animé* adaptation from a stellar *manga*, and has since been eclipsed by many other *animé* outings. The animation, design and look of *Appleseed* is not quite distinctive and inventive enough (it's too bright, too straight-forward and plain, and too samey in tone throughout), so the simplistic aspects of the story are exposed (the low budget no doubt contributed). And if you don't see the original language version (a must), the rather clumsy translation and dub gets in the way, too.

It's Deunan and Briareos and their passion to track down the part-cyborg terrorist A.J. Sebastian (yet another *Blade Runner* allusion) that keeps *Appleseed* afloat, as well as oddities such as Athena, the female dictator of the community of Olympus (the Greek elements in *Appleseed* make the city look directly like Cæsar's Palace Casino in Las Vegas – but not as much fun!).

The script of *Appleseed* (by Kazuyoshi Katayama) is poor – which scuppers the entire show. It misrepresents Masamune Shirow's carefully worked-out world of Olympus • it concentrates too much on the troubled cop Karen Mawserus, and the terrorist A.J. Sebastian (both inventions) • it adds psycho-drama elements which don't exist in *Appleseed*, or anywhere in Shirow's output • it doesn't deliver enough exposition to explain how Olympus works • it takes too long to introduce the principal charas, and doesn't give them a decent introduction[6] • and, critically, it doesn't spend enough time with Deunan and Briareos, establishing their characters. (It lacks, for instance, their origins in 'Badside', which're only referenced in dialogue, and one or two glimpses. So it's Hitomi who gets the helicopter trip back from 'Badside', and her efforts to bring back humans is referenced in dialogue btn Athena and Nike).

The look, design and animation of *Appleseed* is far too pedestrian for an adaption of a Masamune Shirow *manga*, which absolutely demands a distinctive vision. This is a major Japanese artist with a highly evolved vision; you can't just trot out the usual, TV-style animation! Regular 1980s-style animation, where every scene is brightly-lit in bland colours, simply *doesn't* do justice to Shirow's *manga*, or his ideas and themes. It's lit like 99% of television shows, with light blasting into every corner of the set. (However, the animation does replicate some of the compositions of Shirow's drawings closely, but not, alas, their vitality).

Take the opening action sequence, the hostage scenario: it's a situation

---

6 Deu and Bri are first seen riding a helicopter, on their way to the hostage situation.

that Masamune Shirow has depicted several times. The *animé* makes the mistake of not giving us the viewpoint of Briareos and Deunan enough,[7] so it comes across as a generic cop show scene. What the terrorists are asking for isn't clarified sufficiently. At a minor level, the tactical ingredients, of exactly how to deal with terrorists and hostages, which Shirow emphasizes so strongly, are cast aside (after reading *Appleseed* and *Ghost In the Shell*, you feel like you could deal with a hostage scenario as either a terrorist or a cop).

The music in *Appleseed* (by Norimasa Yamanaka) sounds like a North American cop show of the 1980s such as *Miami Vice*. Though not as good: it putters on in electro, pseudo-disco/ funk style. Ryuichi Sakamoto and others composed the music for the 2004 *Appleseed*. (And in the finale, the music lets down the proceedings, which could do with some suitably climactic cues).

The nihilism that bubbles underneath 1988's *Appleseed* also seems to be a staple of Masamune Shirow's work in adapted form (it's an important part of *Ghost In the Shell*): *Appleseed* opens with a woman's suicide, falling from a skyscraper, which haunts the traitor cop Karen Mawserus (yes, the translation gives him the name Karen, although the voice actors pronounce it more like 'Caron' – is it from 'Charon', in Greek mythology?): it's the oppressive, authoritarian society of Olympus, Mawserus tells Deunan and Briareos in a peculiar cemetery scene (*animé* is curiously full of graveyard scenes), which puts people in cages and clips their wings, so they're not really living. Karen even suggests that it was murder – that his wife was murdered by utopia!). *What is all this technology for?* is a question often framed within an Existential, philosophical context in Shirow's *œuvre*.

Altho' the cop Karen Mawserus is in cahoots with the terrorist villain, A.J. Sebastian, he is also humanized, and given reasons for his grudges against the would-be utopian society of Olympus (the suicide of his wife, for starters). One of the flaws of the *Appleseed animé* is that Mawserus is also a rather dull personality, and eats up too much precious time which would be better spent with Deunan and Briareos.[8] (Why invent Mawserus, when you've got Deunan and Briareos: we don't read the *Appleseed manga* for the anti-hero cops or the minor charas, but for the heroes!).

❖

On the plus side, to be generous for a moment, the 1988 *Appleseed* Original Video Animation does include 100s of elements of the designs and look of Masamune Shirow's wonderful *Appleseed manga*. Altho' the story in the *animé* is new, and only contains part of the *Appleseed manga*, the look of the 1988 O.A.V. is impressive in sections. If you know the *manga* of *Appleseed*, you'll see aspects of it all over the 1988 *animé*. Gaia, the Arcology structures,[9] downtown Olympus, Deunan's and Briareos's

7 Now they work for 'S.W.A.T.', not 'E.S.W.A.T', despite Masamune Shirow emphasizing the difference.
8 Karen voices some of the doubts about Olympus that Briareos does in the comic.
9 The *animé* cleverly includes a very long shot of the arches of the Arcology buildings end-on, making them look like the Pyramids, which's right there in the *manga*.

apartment, the tanks and *mecha*, and the all-important character designs all draw heavily and closely on Shirow's *manga* (but the O.A.V. lacks the intensity of invention and detail that Shirow put into *Appleseed*).[10]

For fans of the *Appleseed manga*, it was disappointing that the 1988 *animé* adaptation streamlined so much of the *manga*, leaving out some of the finest sections. Inevitable in any adaptation of this sort, of course, but it would've been great to see Deunan and Briareos in 'Badside', and to see them taking on the tank,[11] the action sequence that opens the first *Appleseed tankobon*. Or how about the knife fight, where Deunan tackles a bunch of terrorists single-handed (a masterpiece of depicting action in *manga*. This is the kind of storytelling that many fans wish Shirow would keep creating, instead of dodgy porn).

The filmmakers at Gainax *et al* opted for a terrorist narrative which would absorb some of the key elements of the *Appleseed manga*, and they also invented plenty of elements, too (like the character of the corrupt cop Karen Mawserus, and his suicidal wife). So all of the terrorists are condensed down to one, A.J. Sebastian, with his accomplice, Mawserus; Hitomi the bioroid has a far less important role; now it's Mawserus who visits Yoshi about the Landmate suit; the cop teams become compressed (there's no real interaction among the teams, such a big part of the comic); and Deunan and Briareos are already employed in Olympus City, instead of searching for work (tho' they go for a transfer). Meanwhile, out from the *manga* of *Appleseed* go the council, the director, the F.B.I., the E.S.W.A.T. captain, the rivalry between the different departments, etc.

The terrorist plot in the *Appleseed animé* does involve the giant platforms, however, and the attack on Olympus, from the *manga*, though altered once again. For instance, the multipede gunships are now able to fly (which seems very silly, and ruins the whole point of their spider design. It does, of course, means that the legs don't have to be animated, they just hang limply from the machines).[12] And the 1988 *Appleseed animé* does include Gaia malfunctioning, with everything in Olympus being controlled by the central computer (the 1988 *animé* does demonstrate how preposterous and incredibly dangerous this would be – Gaia controls the traffic signals, and even drinking fountains and the gas in a kitchen cooker). No point introducing a super-computer in a sci-fi show unless it malfunctions. (Now Hitomi is kidnapped by the villains – she's the Princess To Be Rescued, because, for some ditzy reason, her DNA is a key to start up the spider platforms! Whoever created the security system in Olympus should be shot! The concept was revived in the 2014 film *Appleseed: Alpha*).[13]

And the 1988 animated version of the *Appleseed manga* does portray a huge battle in the finale, as the security forces try to stop the runaway spider tanks, which captures some of the incendiary action of Masamune

---

10 There should also be a feeling of awe when Olympus is first encountered.
11 A tank is featured in a single still image.
12 Their design recalls the probe droid from *The Empire Strikes Back*, 1980.
13 There are four consoles dotted around the city that can access the Gaia computer – and they're not even defended!

Shirow's marvellous *manga*.[14]

One of the key themes in the world of *Appleseed* is the over-reliance on technology, on centralizing infrastructures and super-structures, and how if things go wrong, they could go *very* wrong. The 1988 *Appleseed anime* does capture that. But the equally important theme, of bioroids vs. humans, is more sketchily rendered (on this issue, the 2004/ 07 animations of *Appleseed* and the 2011 series were certainly more successful).

The really intriguing thing about the Olympus society in *Appleseed* is that 80% of the population are artificial, are bioroids. It raises all sorts of fascinating issues about what a utopia could be. None of the animated adaptations of *Appleseed* have really got to terms with that issue.

On the whole, the 1988 *Appleseed* animation isn't true to the spirit of Masamune Shirow's *Appleseed manga*, and is very disappointing in portraying the two central characters, Deunan Knute and Briareos Hecatonchires. There's a sloppiness to the conception and scripting and direction of the lead charas, as if all the attention has been given to the *mecha* and the action sequences. But without the main charas, it's just a bunch of sound and movement, not amounting to much. The indifference with which the main characters are conceived and portrayed weakens the piece considerably (but the 2004/ 2007/ 2014 computer-aided *anime* movies of *Appleseed* didn't crack that problem, either). For Peter Evans and Cefn Ridout, the *anime* of *Appleseed* was 'far too naive and 'clean' to really capture the spirit of the original, despite some fairly accurate character designs' (1994).

Also, it's worth noting that the 1988 *anime* of *Appleseed* might have led to more Original Video Animations, or maybe an *Appleseed* theatrical movie, or maybe a TV series or a series of O.A.V.s (in the manner of *Dominion: Tank Police*). Alas, no. Producers and companies didn't come back to the world of *Appleseed* until 2004, when a fresh wave of adaptations of the world of Masamune Shirow broke (*Ghost In the Shell: Stand Alone Complex, Ghost In the Shell 2*, etc).

The quality of the *manga* being very high, ideally the *Appleseed anime* should've been so much more satisfying (and also the filmmaking team is high calibre): it contains all of the elements necessary for a slambang action movie. But the *anime* is simply too tame, and doesn't venture very far – in any direction. The more times you watch the 1988 *Appleseed*, it doesn't get any better.

You get to know Deunan Knute and Briareos Hecatonchires very well if you've read the *Appleseed manga* several times (as I have). Sadly, their characters have yet to appear satisfactorily on screen in any of the five animations (of 1988, 2004, 2007, 2011 and 2014).

---

14 Including a tower collapsing reminiscent of the Twin Towers.

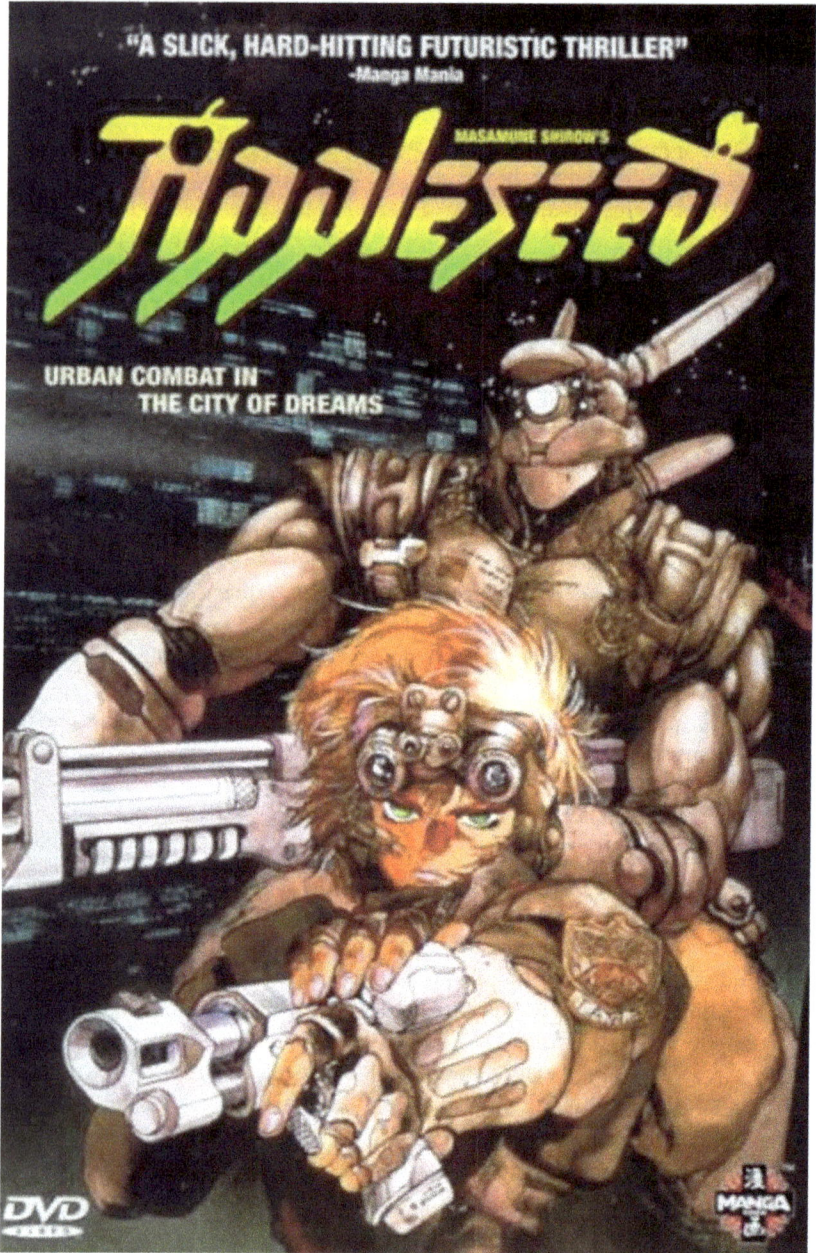

Appleseed (1988)
(This page and over)

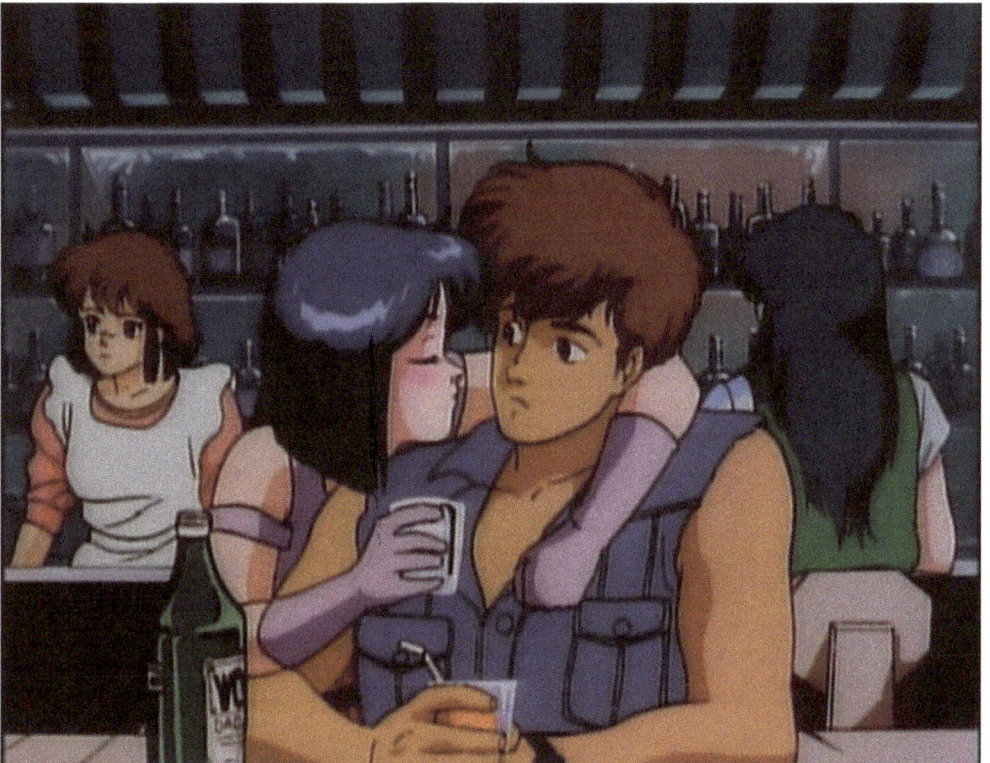

02

APPLESEED (2004)

In 2004, Masamune Shirow's *Appleseed manga* was re-made in animation, in a production from Micott & Basara,[1] S.O.R.I., Geneon Entertainment, Mainichi Broadcasting System, T.B.S., T.Y.O., Toho, Yamato and Digital Frontier, executive producer was Sumiji Miyake, produced by Hidenori Ueki, Fumihiko Sori and Naoko Watanabe, directed by Shinji Aramaki, and written by Haruka Handa and Tsutomu Kamishiro.[2] Music was by Tetsuya Takahashi,[3] sound design by Koji Kasamatsu, sound director was Yota Tsuruoka, prod. des. by Shinji Aramaki, and chara des. by Masaki Yamada. Ai Kobayashi was the voice of Deunan Knute, Jurota Kosugi was Briareos, Mami Koyama[4] (she was Kei in *Akira*)was Athena, Miho Yamada was Nike, and Yuki Matsuoka was Hitomi. Budget: $10 million.[5] 102 minutes. Released by Toho on 2004.4.17.

Born in 1960, director Shinji Aramaki has worked on *Gundam, Armitage, Getiko!, Megazone 23, Buibblegum Crisis, Naruto, Soul Eater, Wolf's Rain, Fullmetal Alchemist*[6] and *Astro Boy* (the remake), usually in *mecha*, conceptual or production design capacities. Aramaki's director credits include *Harlock, Viper's Creed, Metal Skin Panic, Ultraman,* two *Starship Troopers* movies, and the best of the segments in the *Halo: Legends animé* compendium (2010), a shoot-em-up men-on-a-mission tale. There's no doubt that Aramaki was ideally suited to helming the *Appleseed* films, and the later *2045* version of *Ghost In the Shell: Stand Alone Complex.* (Producer Joseph Chou said that 'it was a pretty chaotic production. It was done in under a year from start to finish').

Shirow-sensei didn't sign away the rights to his *Appleseed manga*

---

1 Micott & Basara were involved in the later *Appleseed* adaptations.
2 There is a 'making of' documentary about the live-action version of *Appleseed*, called *Appleseed: Special Prologue.*
3 Also: Paul Oakenfold, Basement Jaxx, Boom Boom Satellites, Akufen, Carl Craig, T. Raumschmiere and Ryuichi Sakamoto. Shin Yasui was music producer.
4 Mami Koyama's credits include: *Sailor Moon, Detective Conan, Dragon Ball, Gundam, Millennium Actress, Metropolis, Lupin III, X, Gunnm, Riding Bean, Urusei Yatsura, Vampire Princess Miyu, City Hunter, The Dagger of Kamui, Doraemon, Lensman, Harmageddon* and *Dr Slump.*
5 $10 million for a movie this complex is a bargain.
6 Aramaki did a brilliant job with the production design of the masterpiece series *Fullmetal Alchemist*, recreating a militaristic, quasi-European nation of the late 19th/ early 20th centuries.

and have nothing more to do with the project. Instead, he was involved with the production, advising on elements such as the mobile suits (getting their design just right was important for Shirow – he's been drawing power suits for most of his career). Shirow commented on the movie at the time:

> This *Appleseed* CG *anime* is different from the original work content-wise, but it is the rare case where I personally feel happy – with the same affection I have for the original work – about points everywhere within it.

The 2004 version of *Appleseed* was given the computer-aided anim-ation treatment (following one of the general drifts in film animation of the 1990s and 2000s towards digitalization), and, in the West, motion capture of actors for reference for animation, alongside toon shading for the visuals.[7] Around this time, too (2008), the first *Ghost In the Shell* movie was revamped with computer-aided (and sonic) additions, and released as *Ghost In the Shell 2.0* (and the second *Ghost In the Shell* movie, *Ghost In the Shell 2: Innocence*, used much computer-aided work, and was also released in 2004).

The look of parts of the 2004 *Appleseed* echoed Shirow's own work in the digital realm – sections such as the spider platforms in the film's finale were very reminiscent of Shirow's artwork in *Intron Depot* and *Pieces*.

The 2004 *Appleseed* was an enjoyable if narratively predictable outing. Action scenes were right out of computer games (in terms of the look, concept, cutting and narrative). Fab hardware, *mecha*, designs, environments and visual effects, but thin characterizations and some very ropey screenwriting (by Haruka Handa and Tsutomu Kamishiro).

The humour, the lighthearted sections, and the digressions of Shirow's comic were also jettisoned; this was a much more 'serious' or straight interpretation (just like the *Ghost In the Shell* adaptations have nearly always dropped the comedy).

Part of the trouble with the 2004 version of *Appleseed* is the use of too many North American action movie plot motifs, right down to the cliff-hanger climax, where Deunan Knute has to hang onto her injured lover Briareos with one hand[8] while trying to reach the button to Save The World with the other hand (all she's gotta do is to type the password: 'HITOMI'!).[9] The 2004 *Appleseed* is very much a hybrid project, technically and cinematically, and also culturally and socially. It brings together Western (North American) and Japanese approaches to storytelling and ends up with technically flashy but narratively clumsy mixtures that don't gel fully.

For Jonathan Clements and Helen MacCarthy, 'the Aramaki *Apple-*

---

7 Digital Frontier were one of the companies involved in producing *Appleseed*: they also worked on *Rayca* and *Zoids*.
8 How heavy would Briareos be?
9 The filmmakers explained that they extended this sequence several times, adding shots of panic, right into the editing process, just to make it more exciting. The last letter – 'I' – is added remotely, perhaps, some wondered, by Dr Gilliam, or the Elders.

seed stumbles with an inept and amateurish script, full of redundancies, technobabble and B-movie motivations', a script 'forced into unending repetition of dull exposition, broken up by perfunctory action sequences' (2006, 26).

A number of actors played Deunan Knute – the reference for the motion capture filming included actors to perform stunts, and to embody Knute. Meanwhile, some actors performed multiple roles for the reference footage. However, it wasn't simply a case of feeding data from the motion capture sessions into a computer and coming out with perfectly animated characters. The animators had to go in and polish and tweak the performances (standard practice in motion capture filmmaking).

The greatest *animé* director of them all, Hayao Miyazaki, despises using photographic reference material – it reduces an animator's pleasure in their work, and the results are hopeless, Miyazaki asserted (citing the figures in Disney cartoons who move like ballet dancers – because they used dancers for reference).

The drive towards using motion capture photography comes from the North American film industry: it's part of the aiming towards 'naturalism' or 'realism' in North American visual effects and animation (an ambition which began way back in the 1930s, at the Walt Disney studio). It is also *very* expensive, demanding costly machinery in a costly process: thus, only heavily resourced and capitalized movie operations can use it.

Motion capture footage also evokes the troubled relationship between Japan and North America: Japan's animation is flat, composed in planes, highly stylized, even abstract, and self-consciously non-realistic and non-naturalistic. All of which works against North American (and Western) animation (and visual effects), which aims for a lifelike, 'realistic' look.

Motion capture photography seems to encourage much more conventional forms of cinema/ television in terms of how the camera is used to tell a story. It's a very sophisticated and complicated process: perhaps that's why so many motion capture scenes are filmed in a traditional manner (often, it's people standing there and talking). The freedom to do anything and try anything seems to vanish when the production relies on motion capture photography.

The use of Toon Shading software was a curious choice: *Appleseed* could've been entirely produced with the computer-aided, 3-D approach. Instead, the filmmakers opted to use Toon Shading for the human and bioroid characters, because they reckoned that audiences would respond better to the flat, 2-D kind of animation (which replicates traditional cel animation). So while the environments and the *mecha* and the buildings and the vehicles and the mobile suits[10] were created with 3-D (and 2-D) computer-aided animation, which took the photorealist approach of Western animation, the faces and characters were flat.[11]

---

10 Much of the time the characters're riding in mobile suits: to get around that visual obstacle, several solutions were employed, such as different coloured suits (pink, red, yellow), and continually cutting to close-ups inside the helmets.

11 The 3-D work on the *Appleseed* movies was overseen by Sori Fumihiko, known for his work in live-action movies and visual effects.

Motion capture photography sometimes creates uneasy collaborations between the live-action actors and how they were directed (on a bare stage, with minimal props), and the (team of) animators and how they animate the characters (add the voice actors to the mix, too). In short, in conventional animation, several groups of talents contribute towards creating a single character, but the motion capture approach adds a whole other team. In the *Appleseed* movies, as in many other movies which employ motion capture material, the movements and gestures don't always fit – not only physically, but also psychologically and dramatically.

There is an interesting 'making of' documentary with the *Appleseed* movie on home releases: in it, one of the producers says he was worried most about the human characters, and if the filmmakers could deliver a computer-assisted animated character who could hold the audience for a whole movie. Unfortunately, despite the enormous amounts of work visible in every single frame of *Appleseed*, it didn't always pay off: the digitally-fashioned human characters, and Deunan Knute in particular, are sometimes as robotic and lifeless as the cyborgs, bioroids and the *mecha*.

❖

There are some really clunky exposition scenes in the first act of the 2004 *Appleseed*, for instance – a knock-on result of opening the movie with a seven-minute action scene, which always pushes back the exposition to later in the piece. In one excruciatingly long scene, our heroine, Deunan Knute, rides in a car[12] with the girlie, annoying, sort-of-buddy bioroid Hitomi,[13] who fills her in on the futuristic world of Olympus. But the bioroid (Yuki Matsuoka) rabbits on and on about the society for pages and pages of the script. This is *animation*, remember, folks! You can have movement and cuts and all sorts of things going on! You don't have to explain a whole bunch of stuff using dialogue alone! (To be fair, tho' we do get to see many views of the apparent utopia of Olympus – people in parks, freeways, skyscrapers, the Arc structures, etc).

Happily, this boring exposition scene (it's two people having a chat in a car) is ended abruptly by the villains making an appearance: a van vs. car chase ensues[14] (which's *very* Shirowian), and act one of *Appleseed* 2004 climaxes with a street fight btn Deunan and three (female) robots/ cyborgs (with Briareos riding in the rescue, as he does several times in this flick). The old ninja favourite of razor wire is employed here, and the robo-guards slice up Briareos's weaponry (these mysterious robots/ cyborgs were reprised for the third computer-aided *Appleseed* movie of 2014).

Unfortunately, the over-writing by Handa and Kamishiro also occurs

12 In the *manga*, it's Nike who drives Deu.
13 Hitomi plays a slightly different role in the *Appleseed manga* – there are the inevitable lesbian scenes, for instance, in a Masamune Shirow *manga*. The 2004 version of *Appleseed* retains only a hint of that, when Hitomi, drunk in a bar, wonders what it's like to experience *lerrrve* (a common scene featuring robots in Japanese culture). In the *manga*, Hitomi's drunk in the shower with Deunan.
14 Deunan wrenches the wheel from Hitomi, sending the car careening away from the pursuer, as if to say, OK, shut up! We've heard enough exposition to sink a battleship!

in the Deunan Meets Gaia scene, where the Elders go on and on about the utopia of Olympus. The producers don't trust the audience to understand this story – they forget that we have seen *thousands* and *thousands* of movies! We've seen *every single possible variation* on a story, on a utopia, on an idealized community! (However, there are one or two visual inserts in this scene, which *show* rather than *tell* us about bioroids and the like).

A later scene with the Elders is also over-written and too long – when Deunan returns with the bioroid reproductive data, the Elders go on and on about the utopia of Olympus, and how they're going to end it all!

There aren't enough characters in the 2004 *Appleseed* – it's an odd view, but look:

Deunan and Briareos – the heroes
Athena (and Nike) – the administrators
Hitomi and Yoshi – the helpers
The Elders – the advisers
Uranos and Hades – the villains/ rivals

And then a bunch of minor charas such as Lance[15] (the Extra Special Weapons and Tactics commander, who barely makes an impression). But it's not enough: gone are the other leaders of Olympus (the legislators, the Ministry of Justice, and the Director), the interaction among the E.S.W.A.T teams, the rival cyborgs, and the terrorists. Missing out the Director and his department, for instance, leaves out the important rivalry for control in Olympus between the Director and Athena. The 2004 *Appleseed* (and the 2007 movie, too), streamlines the charas.

One of the obvious challenges of adapting the *Appleseed manga* into the form of a feature-length movie (not a 50-minute O.A.V., and not a long-running animated series), was the characterization of Deunan Knute: in the story of this movie, for too much of the time Deunan is being dragged along by events. She is not driving them. She is an observer, she is a cog in a machine.

In the 2004 movie, Deunan Knute is our observer figure, witnessing the world of Olympus with us (and for us). Too often, Deunan is barely reacting as events unfold (the filmmakers use the ploy of using blank, neutral reaction shots, so the audience can project emotions onto Deunan. But it doesn't always work). The script doesn't quite solve the problem of combining the Observer Figure with the Action Girl Figure. (And, as she's an observer, Deunan loses her worldly-wise qualities, her tough, seen-it-all-before qualities. In the *manga*, Deunan is much smarter and aware, much quicker to perceive and understand. Deunan is also funnier and cuter in the comic, given to displays of teenage humour.)

Hitomi is an irritating character, with a permanent smug, simpering smirk – she's the sort of character you want to slap. I wish the producers had given Deunan a different buddy. When Hitomi's around, the film becomes simply boring, partly because she's one of the main exposition

---

15 Lance's in the training scene.

figures. (Hitomi's role was bumped up from Shirow's *manga* and the 1988 *Appleseed* presumably to increase the female/ feminine quotient – along with turning Nike and Athena into more prominent characters[16]).

However, Yoshitsune Miyamoto does feature in the 2004 *Appleseed*: he performs one significant function: he appears on the beach and revives Briareos (and gives Deunan a flying suit to get back to Olympus). But, no, Yoshi is nothing like the light-hearted, *mecha* nut of the *manga*. Here, he's a blue-haired youth who tells Deunan that bioroids've got feelings too. (Yoshi also appears in the *otaku* scene, helping Deu trying out a Landmate. Here we see a long *hommage* to mobile suits and how they work).

Olympus is based in the Azores, near Africa (i.e., a *long* way from Japan). Masamune Shirow says that in the end, it doesn't really matter where Olympus is. But of course we know it's really a futuristic/ alternative Japan (as is the rival country/ corporation, Poseidon).

❖

The 2004 *Appleseed* did follow the *manga* by Masamune Shirow in depicting an encounter with a tank in 'Badside' in the first act. This is a stand-alone sequence, a hi-octane action episode of seven minutes in which the filmmakers establish the post-apocalyptic setting, the central character of Deunan Knute, a bunch of bad guys (cyborgs? robots?),[17] and tons of *mecha* and shooting (there's very little dialogue here). Deunan, curiously, is alone in this sequence (which's basically a girl with a gun – something that Japanese animation dines out on all the time!). Briareos appears at the tail end of the sequence, and isn't properly introduced until the hospital scene, where Deunan's being healed (and she's in Olympus). At the end of the shoot-em-up, E.S.W.A.T. agents arrive, nobbling the last of the antagonists, and bringing in Deunan (by shooting her in the back,[18] usually something that only bad guys do).

So Deunan Knute is battling 10,000 baddies in a war-torn city that has every mark of being a computer game scenario. It's a marvellous scene, showing off the computer-aided animation to the full. The slo-mo stunts bear the mark of *The Matrix* (by way of Hong Kong action cinema). If the rest of the 2004 *Appleseed* were up to the quality of the prologue, or the amazing action of the finale, it would be an *animé* masterpiece. But as soon as the talky scenes kick in, as soon as characters start to say something, as soon as someone tries to express something, the 2004 *Appleseed* collapses into sappy stodge. (In which case, you might be better off simply fast-forwarding thru the domestic and talky scenes, and hitting each action beat).

So in the 2004 *Appleseed*, Deunan Knute is coveted by Athena and co. and also by the villainous robots/ cyborgs because she is a great warrior (which sort of justifies the long action sequence), and because she's the daughter of Karl Knute. Which makes her special, right? Yeah. She also possesses the MacGuffin of the bioroid data of her mom, Dr Gilliam.

---

16 And giving Nike a ridiculous cutaway costume that emphasizes her chest.
17 These red-eyed nasties are never really explained in the movie. Are they working for General Uranos?
18 With a tranquilizer.

(Thus, the baddies in the opening action scene kill everybody else but not Deunan, and the Extra Special Weapons and Tactics team sent to retrieve her from 'Badside' stun her and drag her back).

❖

For the 2004 *Appleseed*, producers Miyake, Ueki, Sori *et al* opted to have Deunan and Briareos separated, and, when they're re-united, it's an uneasy encounter. Why? Oh, for the usual reason of using friction and conflict to keep the drama simmering, and to add some personal tension to this bang-bang action movie. Apart from the 1988 O.A.V., each adaptation of *Appleseed* has the central couple falling out over something or other.

Movies often reduce the characters surrounding the hero, to enhance the discord and the drama. Deunan seen alone is deemed more compelling than Deunan in a strong, unquestioned relationship with her lover Briareos. Shirow's comic has Deunan as the main character, yes, but it's also about a couple.

Here, the producers of *Appleseed* altered the back-story of Deunan and Briareos: now Deunan doesn't know that Briareos has been injured (apparently in North Africa), so they're not living in 'Badside' together (Deunan cooks for Briareos, and welcomes him home when he returns from a foraging expedition in Shirow-sensei's comic). They *were* lovers, Deu tells Hitomi in the bar scene, but not anymore (not since he was mechanized).

In the 2004 *Appleseed*, Deunan Knute is eager to be back with her man, but he remains distant, insisting that he's there to protect her only (they are given separate rooms, for instance, by Hitomi and co.). There are one or two flashbacks in act one to reveal the pre-cyborgized Briareos (but we don't really see his face – altho' Shirow-sensei drew him in the *manga*); more importantly, we see the couple working together (Deunan also has a nightmare where she dreams that Briareos becomes a demonic figure; which's very Shirowian – if it was a humorous scene, that is!).

Yes, folks, the humour in Masamune Shirow's *Appleseed* *manga* has been abandoned for the 2004 flick; in the comic, Briareos is a wry, occasionally jaded commentator on the adventures. Briareos likes nothing better'n relaxing at home in a comfy chair with a drink and a magazine. He makes jokes about Deunan's over-spending, her cooking, her crazy ideas.

But not in the movie, where Bri's introduced from the outset as a gloomy, grudgeful, aloof soul. In the key scene in *Appleseed*'s act one, when he and Deu are alone together at last (after the super-irritating Hitomi has finally excused herself), he stands far away, by the window, and soon leaves. (Bri is also involved with Hades, behind the scenes, which further drives a wedge between the couple).

❖

The themes in *Appleseed* of humans vs. artificial intelligence (humans vs. bioroids), the uses of modern technology, and the building of a future utopia are typical Masamune Shirow concerns (the quest for a utopian society, a common motif in science fiction, is mirrored in the personal yearning of Deunan and Briareos for finding a paradise where they can live). They take bizarre trails, though: the third act of the 2004 *Appleseed* has the seven Elders of the Olympus society (grizzled, old coots who float around on anti-gravity chairs and dispense wisdom), opting to unleash a virus[19] to kill humanity because of its 'sins': they'd prefer to leave the world to the robots (the bioroids). So the Gods of Olympus let loose the Titans, in the form of colossal battle tanks – the spider platforms from the *Appleseed manga* (there's a lot of Greek mythology in *Appleseed*), and it's down to our heroes Deunan and Briareos to save the day.

Meanwhile, there is a faction (linked to the Army) which opposes the prevalence of bioroids (it's a 50-50 mix in this movie, but not in Masamune Shirow's *manga*, where it's 80-20, with bioroids in the majority). Heading up the anti-bioroid group are Uranos and Hades. They'd be happy if bioroids were wiped off the face of this cosy, little utopia. They are linked to right-wing, nationalistic ideology; so it's the conservative, right-wing faction versus the liberals (Hitomi and the bioroids). The filmmakers stop short of issuing them with samurai swords and waving Japanese flags or fans, but their leader is addressed as Shogun (Yuzuru Fujimoto – who plays Uranos), and he's given the familiar gruff, must-be-obeyed voice of all commanders in Japanese movies.

❖

The 2004 *Appleseed*, with its use of computer-aided and 3-D animation, and its motion capture photography approach to the characters (actors were also filmed to provide reference material for the animators), with Toon-Shading software being used to move away from 'realism', certainly approached the look and feel of a Masamune Shirow *manga* closely (more so, perhaps, than cel animation – or, at least, the cel animation of the 1988 *Appleseed*; and Shirow has been employing more and more digital material and Photoshop-led artwork in his *manga* – compare the second *Ghost In the Shell tankobon* with the first one). But, despite the technical achievements and the lavish presentation, you wish that the 2004 *Appleseed* amounted to more than it was.

If we leave aside the name Masamune Shirow and the title *Appleseed*, there is much to enjoy in the 2004 version of *Appleseed*. Forgetting the material that this movie is based on (and ignoring the deficiencies of the script), and approaching it purely as entertainment, it does present some cool action scenes, several tons of amazing *mecha*, and raises some fascinating issues. (Approaching it like a Hong Kong action movie – dumb but fun, where you don't angst over the shallow characterizations, or the hackneyed storylines, but thrill to the martial arts action, the silly jokes, the *very* rapid pacing, and the gorgeous cinematography and design (even on budgets of less than $1 million!). I mean, just to see Jet Li or Jackie Chan in full flight is pretty incredible in itself!).[20]

19 The virus is noted in the long Hitomi monologue in the car.
20 In *Appleseed*, though, despite the cartoony acrobatics of Deunan, which clearly draw on Hong Kong action cinema, no one can move like Jet Li or Jackie Chan.

There are scenes and shots in *Appleseed* which delight and amaze – Deunan versus the mean cyborgs in 'Badside', the storming of the Mobile Fortresses on Olympus, Deunan diving off the Arc and clambering into her power suit, and so on.

Aside from the gargantuan tonnage of 'fan service' in the form of *mecha*, the *Appleseed* in its 2004 incarnation features some erotic 'fan service'. Deunan is the focus, as in Masamune Shirow's *manga*: when she recovers in hospital, God forbid that she should be covered up with a blanket to keep her warm! Oh no! She's put in a white sports bra and panties combo! When she's kicking back in her *aparto*, she's in a Tee shirt and short-shorts. When she dresses up to meet Gaia and the Elders, she's in a mini-skirt (a very un-Deunan-like costume, tho' in the *manga* she does glam up occasionally. It's an *hommage* to the *Ghost In the Shell* sequel, where Motoko presents herself as a businesswoman, and also to Cyril Brooklyn and others in Shirow's erotica). At least the designers didn't put Deu in absurd costumes when she goes into battle (as they do in the later *Appleseed* movies): here she's in combat pants and a tight top.

In the *Appleseed manga*, Deunan is sometimes cocky and even arrogant: she knows she's good. For ex, she sings before an operation (in the plane), much to the annoyance of the grunts around her. And she trumps everybody in the training exercises, putting joke labels on them.[21] Needless to say, none of the adaptations have portrayed Deunan like that.

❖

In act two, *Appleseed* 2004 delves into the back-story of Deunan Knute: several elements're added to Shirow-sensei's *manga*, including a holographic flashback to Deunan's mom (Dr Gilliam), who uncovered the secrets of making bioroids able to reproduce (the filmmakers call this 'Appleseed' – Masamune Shirow doesn't really state what 'Appleseed' is in the *manga*). As soon as *that* narrative nugget's been disclosed, of course it's time for Momma Gilliam to bite the dust (right in front of Deunan).

All of this occurs in a Shirowian setting of a disused research facility at night in the wild ocean. The face-off that follows, however, with its sappy, emotional material, is so *not* Masamune Shirow! He doesn't use this sort of Western/ Hollywood mode of drama, with its artificial intensification of dramatic conflicts. The hokey melodrama, the appearance of li'l Deu aged six (as a blonde, *kawaii* moppet in bunches), the MacGuffin of Gilliam's bioroid data being hung around Deunan's neck in a pendant (by her mom – her final act, which's re-discovered by Deunan hidden in the butt of her dad's gun!), the mother's death, and the series of one Mexican stand-off followed by another (everybody is pointing a gun at someone else, too many times) – this is garbage, really. It's lame. It recycles numerous movies, but doesn't come up with anything to add of its own.

And it is, fatally, drastically over-written. Thus, General Uranos has his say, then Hades has his say, then Briareos has his say – and Deunan stands there, listening to it all – as confused as the audience is! (And Briareos seems to have sided with the anti-bioroid faction. Or has he?).

21 Bri carps that Deu is getting too cocky in the training exercise sequence, which he also does in the comic.

So Deunan Knute is backed into a corner – she is standing against the railings on the roof of the research facility, while the rain pours and wind swirls and the men chatter on and on with their pro-bioroid and anti-bioroid arguments. Now, we know that Deunan is going to escape by leaping over the side, the question is: will it happen during this century?

Anyhoo, Deunan and Briareos duly dive off the roof (with Bri shielding her from gunfire), and the only pleasing element of the scene is that, at the last moment, in slo-mo, Deunan manages to land a bullet between the eyes of the whingeing S.O.B. Hades. This climaxes act two.

To be fair to the 2004 *Appleseed*, it *does* employ the issue of the conflict between humans and bioroids, which's a key subtext in Masamune Shirow's *Appleseed manga*. But the *way* that it presents that feud, with so many Hollywood/ Western-style motifs, gestures and lines of dialogue, is almost anti-Shirowian. The 2004 *Appleseed* is mawkish and saccharine, an area of drama where Shirow doesn't venture much.

Also, the 2004 *Appleseed* movie doesn't clarify satisfactorily exactly *what* the bioroids are, and why they are needed. In Masamune Shirow's *manga*, there are panels and side-notes which explain his unusual concept: are they clones? No. Are they cyborgs? No. Are they robots? No. Are they modified humans? No (tho' you could see them as that). Are they slaves? No (or maybe). They are Shirow's way of expressing aspects of humanity (such as the troubled the interactions between humans and technology).

But because the conflict in *Appleseed* pivots around a utopia being compromised because of the struggles between bioroids and humans, we need to know fully and completely just what a bioroid is, why it's needed, how they differ from human beings, etc.

❖

The finale of *Appleseed* Version 2004.0 contains stunning imagery of the spider platforms storming Olympus, smashing up skyscrapers, battling Extra Special Weapons and Tactics teams, and blasting away aircraft. Even the grumpiest of Masamune Shirow fans can't help but be impressed by these shots – the filmmakers have really gone to town. It's a dense, noisy, flashy and very complicated sequence. (And the design of the spiders, by Atsushi Takeuchi,[22] with their little, red eyes swivelling about, is delightful). Yes, it's *Godzilla*, it's monsters terrorizing a city, but what fun!

After all, when it comes to smashing stuff to bits, and blowing stuff up, nobody can match Japanese animators! Oh, how they *love* to blast every darn thing to pieces! When we watch the endings of our favourite animé – *Akira, Bleach, Fullmetal Alchemist, Ghost In the Shell, Laputa: Castle In the Sky, Princess Mononoke, Seven Deadly Sins, Urotsukidoji, Hellsing, Fairy Tail, Naruto, Escaflowne* and the all-conquering *One Piece* – quite a lot of it is simply things exploding and smashing.

Now, if the 2004 *Appleseed* had a terrific script, and properly thought-out characterizations (and character development, and inter-actions, and conflicts, etc), it would likely be hailed as a masterpiece. It

22 Takeuchi also designed the first *Appleseed animé,* and worked on many of the *Ghost In the Shell* adaptations.

has everything going for it: a team of *animé* veterans, a decent schedule and budget, marvellous source material from Shirow-sensei, and an impressive vision of the future (with some stellar design work).

Unfortunately, script-wise, the ending of the 2004 *Appleseed* is a skyscraper being kicked to bits by a spider platform's leg: the Elders, bless their wrinkly form of wisdom, are going to end all of humanity with a virus! Eh? What gives these old coots the right to nix three million years of human history just like that?!

This is a really vicious send-up of that perennial favourite motif in *animé* and *manga* – the conflict between the older and the younger generation. So the city fathers are going to commit suicide? And render humanity infertile?! (Are the filmmakers really saying that the 'sins of the fathers' means mass suicide? Are they really saying that the older generation in Japan is so feeble and without hope, it's going to sacrifice all of humanity, including all young humans?). No wonder Deunan turns in disgust and storms out (leaping off the building in a crowd-pleasing, Motoko Kusanagi dive, climbing into a mobile suit as she falls. This is one of several *hommages* to *Ghost In the Shell* here – another has Deunan wrenching open a hatch on the spider platform,which echoes the image of Motoko on top of the tank).

And who, in this incredible city of the future, would place a deadly virus in full view on the top of a tower?! And who would build colossal Mobile Fortresses that *can't* be switched off?! (unless you blast them apart, bring them down, and get your lovely heroine to hit the 'OFF' button?!).

Yes, there are numerous flaws in the script of *Appleseed*, with motives jumbled, goals garbled, characterizations scrambled, and relationships damaged (or downright creepy). The virus... the Elders... the 'sins of mankind'... the humans vs. bioroids... the spider platforms... It just doesn't make sense.

❖

Wait a second, am I complaining too much? No: it *is* possible for a single movie to have slambang action, incredible production design, superb imagery, dazzling visual effects, and technical brilliance – *AND* a cracking story, big themes and compelling characters.

I give you: *Akira, Ghost In the Shell, Laputa: Castle In the Sky* and *Nausicaä of the Valley of the Wind*. (And all the other Hayao Miyazaki pictures). (Of course, it's not easy to produce pictures of that quality!).

Appleseed (2004)
(This page and over)

03

APPLESEED: EX MACHINA (2007)

The 2007 sequel to the 2004 *Appleseed* movie, subtitled *Ex Machina =
Ekusu Makina* (also directed by Shinji Aramaki), featured many of the
same elements as the 2004 movie, and many of the same production crew
(tho' this time it boasted the input of producer John Woo).[1] Production
companies: T.Y.O. Productions, Toei Company, Ltd, Toei Video Co., Ltd,
Tomy Company, Ltd, Digital Frontier, Micott & Basara and Sega. Script
by Kiyoto Takeuchi and Todd W. Russell. Produced by Sumiji Miyake
and Yasuhiko Kinoshita (exec), and Hidenori Ueki, John Woo, Joseph
Chou, Naoko Watanabe, and Terence Chang (Woo's regular producer).
Character design by Masaki Yamada. *Mecha* design by Takeshi
Takakura. Sound direction by Yota Tsuruoka. Sound design by Koji
Kasamatsu. Production design by Shinji Aramaki. Action choreography
by Tatsuro Koike. Editing by Ryuji Miyajima. Casting by Eiji Harada.
Music by Tetsuya Takahashi and many others. Released Oct 20, 2007. 105
mins.

In the cast, Ai Kobayashi was Deu, Kouichi Yamadera was Briareos,
Gara Takashima was Athena, Kuwata Kong was Aeacus, Miyuki
Sawashiro was Hitomi, Naoko Kouda was Dr. Xander, Rei Igarashi was
Nike, Rica Fukami was Yoshino, Shinpachi Tsuji was Lance, Takaya
Hashi was Dr. Kestner and Yuuji Kishi was Tereus.

Again, *Appleseed 2* was a computer-aided animation job using
motion capture input. But, again, too much of *Appleseed: Ex Machina*
comes across as a sophisticated and glossy but ultimately rather empty
version of a video game. The images of Deunan Knute running around
and blasting at anything in sight with her machine gun go on and on, and
the longer they run on, the further the movie descends into video gaming
(it's like watching a friend play a computer game, loud and full of

[1] John Woo was born in Guangzhou on May 1, 1946. His family moved to Hong Kong when
he was five. There are numerous *hommages* to the cinema of John Woo – of course, Woo and his
team (and his contemporaries like Ringo Lam, Tsui Hark and Wong Jing) were instrumental in
creating (or making famous) many of the gags and motifs that're used everywhere in action
cinema these days (the Mexican stand-offs, guns in both hands, shooting while diving in slo-
mo, motorcycles, etc). And of course the 'poetic' Woo elements, such as churches, Catholic
imagery, and doves (thus, the first big action scene in the 2007 *Appleseed* takes places in an
over-designed Gothic Cathedral).

movement, but you never feel like you're involved, and you never get a turn).

Altho' *Appleseed: Ex Machina* features Deunan Knute in many scenes, it still somehow seemed to shift the emphasis away from her, and away from Briareos Hecatonchires, and spends too much time with secondary characters (like Athena, Nike, or the villain Xander). For me, Deunan and Briareos are the core of *Appleseed*, and the movie adaptations lose much of their impact when they move away from them for too long.

Appleseed: Ex Machina was also hampered by a god-awful North American voice dub, in which the voice actors (Matranga, Christian, Guardiola *et al*) give new meaning to the term 'wooden'. That in turn affects the script and the storytelling. Also, the dialogue is abysmal, and the way it's expressed is just dreadful. (I haven't seen the Japanese version, and I loathe dubs. I've tried the German dub – it's not bad).

The *Appleseed* franchise and Masamune Shirow's work in general is supremely *Japanese*, no matter how many North American and European elements Shirow employs. The N. American voices add a layer of cultural ambiguity, so that *Appleseed: Ex Machina* exists in a limbo between Japan and the U.S.A., satisfying the cultural demands of neither culture. Because, coupled with those tired voices, the characters come across as dumb action movie stereotypes.

The result is that *Appleseed: Ex Machina* winds up utterly empty of value or meaning beyond its astonishing visuals and inventive *mecha* and designs. If the movie was shredded into little bits, maybe, or became just a bunch of stills, or was cannibalized and taken apart and re-molded into a new movie, or a new entity (like a cyborg in itself), it might be more effective. (But it's in the visuals and the *mecha* that the movie displays its meanings and values).

When you compare the 2004 + 2007 *Appleseed* movies to the *Ghost In the Shell* movies or the *Ghost In the Shell* TV series, you have to admit that all of those millions of Yen and all of those 1,000s of man hours have been utterly wasted. *Appleseed: Ex Machina* should be melted down in a giant furnace and a new movie or techno-cultural entity should be forged from the remains. A movie as bad as *Appleseed: Ex Machina* requires total demolition. Well, I guess you can't hit the jackpot every time.

The 2004 and 2007 *Appleseed* adaptations don't capture the spirit of the very wonderful *Appleseed manga* for me, altho' they do include many ingredients of Shirow-sensei's *manga*, and also make the Deunan-Briareos relationship central. There's a lot more humour in the *Appleseed manga*, and a lot about relationships, which the movies don't contain.

Playing the *Appleseed manga* so straight and so serious is a big mistake, I reckon, in the 2000s computer-aided *Appleseeds*: we miss the joshing interactions among the Extra Special Weapons and Tactics team, and, most of all, the goofy humour of Deunan Knute (and Briareos, too, has his wry remarks and his jokes. But, you know what?, Briareos does not laugh once in this movie, or crack a joke! Masamune Shirow states that Briareos never laughs – yet he is depicted laughing several times in the *Appleseed manga*. Anyway, some laughter could've been added to the movie versions).

The 2000s *Appleseed* movies overwhelm the characters and the story with over-fussy, over-detailed designs, layouts and visuals. The characters and their relationships are literally swamped by the visuals, which belong to a book of rock album designs from the 1970s, or an exhibition of new digital art at a swanky art gallery in Chicago or Berlin. In amongst all of that gleaming, intricate hardware and those vast, obsessively-detailed cityscapes, Deunan, Briareos, Athena *et al* are buried.

The decision to leave out the 2-D look of the human/ bioroid characters (using Toon Shading in the 2004 *Appleseed*), resulted in the familiar but dissatisfying 3-D computer-aided approach, which makes humans look like dolls. Yes, dolls and puppets might fit the thematic aspirations of Masamune Shirow's *manga*, but I don't think this was the intention! The compromise between 2-D and 3-D animation for the faces and human figures is a step backwards from the 2004 flick, which used 2-D animation for the humans (in the main).

Looks-wise, Deunan has been tweaked again, so now her hair has orange tints (the hair of all of the charas in *Ex Machina* is horrible. It looks like the plastic helmets or hair-pieces you stick on toy figurines). Deunan sports two costumes specially designed by fashionista Miuccia Prada, no less. One is an evening outfit for Hitomi's birthday party (the sort of dress that Deunan wouldn't be seen dead in, complete with high heels, which she trips over, in one of the several scenes where she acts like a bratty teenager).[2] Deunan in 2007 is notably more aggressive socially, whingeing at her superiors, such as Nike. (Lance, sidelined in the 2004 flick, plays a much bigger role in the sequel).

In the action scenes in *Appleseed 2*, Deunan Knute now performs numerous impossible dives, spins, jumps and other gymnastics,[3] as if she's starring in a ballet, a circus or an Olympic athletics version of a Hong Kong martial arts movie version of a Japanese animated movie of a Japanese action *manga*. We know that Deunan is a superhero, but in the 2007 movie her movements are just too silly. (However, Shirow-sensei does portray Deunan leaping all over the place in the later sections of *Appleseed*, such as in chapter 25: *Shalom*. But in the notes to *Ghost In the Shell*, he reminds us that only total cyborgs can perform very high jumps – everyone else would be shredded).

Appleseed: Ex Machina is notable in *not* putting a face to the super-villain – Alcides/ Halcon. Instead, like the Puppeteer in *Ghost In the Shell*, everybody seems to be taken over by something or other: Briareos is overcome by deadly nano-machines, Aeacus goes nuts, Xander is entombed in a tentacular queen bee machine, and the populace of Olympus become raging zombies.

For Shirow fans, it's pleasing to see the involvement of Poseidon Industrial in the '07 movie – Poseidon being one of the colossal mega-corporations in the Shirowworld (with several shadowy/ sinister

2 There is a scene where Deunan dresses up in the comic.
3 And in *Appleseed XIII*, too.

affiliations). Poseidon isn't just a vast array of companies and businesses, it's also a realm or country of its own (there are fascinating views of Poseidon during the meeting between an envoy of Poseidon and Prime Minister Athena).

There's a lengthy and repeated *hommage* to *Blade Runner*, with the flying advertizing blimp (in the *Appleseed manga*, Masamune Shirow draws clusters of TV screens at street level to dispense news broadcasts).

❖

Like the 2004 *Appleseed* flick, the 2007 sequel opens with an all-out, video game-style shoot-out. The setting is the most memorable aspect of the 5/6 minute sequence: a Cathedral in the mediæval European, Gothic style.[4] Deunan storms the building as a one-woman army, freeing the hostages and wasting villains (cyborg terrorists) by the ton. It's a replay of the 2004 opening sequence in most respects (tho', this time, Briareos bursts thru a stained window, guns blazing in both hands, in the manner popularized by Hong Kong action cinema, including the films directed by John Woo, of course. The sequence features numerous motifs taken from Hong Kong movies. Both Deu and Bri're often airborne, doing their Cirque du Soleil version of a cyborg 'n' girl act).

So a new, young turk (Tereus) is introduced in the computer-aided *Appleseed* sequel, as a rival to Briareos Hecatonchires in both work and love. That the powers-that-be in Olympus have chosen to give their new, military-designed bioroids the pretty boy face[5] of Briareos[6] is intriguing as well as simply ridiculous (Nike explains that Briareos this time has been the basis biologically for the new military bioroids, as Deunan's father Karl was in the 2004 movie). But it does give the 2007 movie the intriguing prospect of Deunan contemplating a guy who looks like her cyborgized lover. And Lance and co. force Deunan to take Tereus on as her partner (while Briareos recovers in hospital following the Cathedral shoot-out, reprising again the subplot, taken from the *manga*, of Briareos being injured). Alas, the narrative concept of Tereus as a double or clone or copy of Briareos goes... absolutely nowhere. (There are some terrific movies with copies/clones of lovers, including the most critically acclaimed movie of them all, *Vertigo*. But this isn't *Vertigo*).

With Deunan being paired up uneasily with Tereus, Briareos has his own sparring partner, in the form of Extra Special Weapons and Tactics member Aeacus, one of those wise-cracking, super-macho guys that're mandatory in North American-style, men-on-a-mission movies (Aeacus sports a part-cyborgized face that would type him as a villain in a *James Bond* movie, and Arges, who appears later, is also a scarred movie villain type, but he aids our heroes on the raid on the Halcon facility).

❖

In the second act of *Appleseed: Ex Machina*, the big set-piece is another

---

4 Don't ask what a Gothic Cathedral of the European Middle Ages is doing in the shiny, new realm of Olympus.
5 Tereus resembles a young John Travolta – which in turn evokes *Face/Off*, a 1997 movie dir. by John Woo.
6 Tereus is a *bishonen* version of Briareos, complete with irritating strings of hair that hang down at his temples.

terrorist attack on Olympus (which just happens to take place when Athena is presiding over a meeting of the nations of Earth, hoping to link everybody up with their satellite systems[7]). In the 2007 *Appleseed*, technology is the forefront of the terrorists' attempts to disrupt Olympus: they use the Connexus gizmos – little gadgets that clip to the ears and provide entertainment and communications (like a heads-up version of cel phones,[8] I-Pads and computers). Of course, everybody has a Connexus device (Olympus, an idealized version of super-capitalist Japan, is a gadget-obsessed society), so the terrorists have a hot-line to the populace. And, in a bitter satire on humanity's devotion to TV, phones and the media, they are turned into mindless zombies, staggering along the streets. (The people who *don't* become slaves to the Connexus/ the media, are the cops and the administrators. The people in power).

The second act of *Appleseed 2* also includes many of the clichéd scenes of the thriller/ cop/ action genre, such as training scenes (in the gym and on the shooting range – gun training is very Shirowian); a (yawnable) police briefing scene; and a funeral (of Aeacus). Yes, it's raining in the cemetery. Of course! A burial scene where it's a glowing, sun-bright day simply does not exist in *animé!*

In the second act of *Appleseed 2*, Briareos and Tereus spar in the training gym at Extra Special Weapons and Tactics (a rather boring, macho rivalry scene, with kickboxing moves out of a video game like *Tekken*). Deunan and Briareos ask Tereus to come out for a drink with them (the rather feeble pretext is to get the characters onto the streets, so Briareos can be attacked by a runaway, driverless vehicle).

So here in the second act of *Seedy Apple 2*, Briareos goes nuts: well, sort of: the terrorists take him over (using nano-machines), and have him act as their terminal into the super-computer Gaia. His cyborgization's affected, giving him the bulging veins of angry people in *manga* on his outer shell. And he goes on the run, as a fugitive (and Extra Special Weapons and Tactics have to hunt him down – minus Deunan, of course).

It's another way of giving the characters something to do that's personally-based, and not simply battling the terrorists within the context of the Extra Special Weapons and Tactics outfit, or the over-arching humans vs. bioroids/ technology theme. Yes, the second act is the tough one in an action movie, and that's true here, as the producers and writers cast about for significant acts for their characters to do).

Lance orders Deunan to stay put while the rest of the Extra Special Weapons and Tactics hunt down Briareos. In the comic, that would last about two milliseconds, but in the movie, Deunan complies.

In the Briareos On The Run plot (in the second half of act two), Bri escapes jail to seek out Dr Kestner (his design echoes Dr Matthew in the *manga*). Well, Kestner delivers lots of exposition, and then kills himself! It

---

7 Dizty liberal Prime Minister Athena even has all of the satellites join together to produce a giant olive tree made of lasers floating in the sky above Olympus. (Yes, this is a *peaceful* use of lasers and satellites in Japanese *animé!*).
8 Cel phones shouid have been fitted with heads-up displays years ago. Instead, people today walk around staring down and fiddling with their phones/ tablets, stumbling into people, falling off their bikes, and crashing their cars.

works chiefly because this is a *Japanese* product: in Japanese pop culture, the issue of suicide is extremely alarming yet quite common. Kestner's death is ridiculous – it's a screenwriter's joke about exposition characters: once they've done their bit, you can forget about them. But it does save the heroes the problem of what to do with him.

Meanwhile, Yoshitsune Miyamoto has been promoted from Akechi Motors garage mechanic to a member of Extra Special Weapons and Tactics (and he keeps his long, floppy, boy band hair!). So now Yoshi's their tech guy, who advises them on the terrorists' methods. (He's also promoted to the all-round helper figure – he has an antidote to the nano-machines driving Briareos crazy, for instance, taking over Dr Matthew's role).

In some points in act two of *Ex Machina*, the script and the pacing feels a little off – scenes look like they've been shifted around a tad, and some of the sequences (of scenes joined together), don't flow smoothly. There are redundant scenes, and scenes that repeat earlier scenes, too, which also weaken the second act.

❖

The third act of *Appleseed: Ex Machina* has Deunan and Briareos joined by Tereus for the mandatory Save The World scenario. The terrorists have Olympus' population acting as zombies, and attacking the authorities and police. It's another version of the civil war btn humans and bioroids, with the terrorists using humans as zombies assail Tartarus (the bioroid facility). Poseidon Industrial is involved, as is Halcon (invented for this movie). Only Briareos, Deunan and Tereus can Save The Day, flying into Halcon's HQ to bust some ass (tho' aided by a small team from Poseidon, headed up by Arges – not the same Arges as in the *manga*, tho').

The finale begins with a really boring talky scene, to set it all up: the heroic trio land on a Poseidon vessel at sea at night and receive pages of exposition from Poseidon's rep, about Halcon, Xander, bioroids, etc. It's one of those dull scenes where what the heroes have to do is set out for the audience.

The finale of *Appleseed 2* has the mandatory scenes of Heroes vs. Villains Fights, the Big Set (here it's Halcon's facility), the Heroes Battling Multiple Threats, the Meeting With the Super-villain, the Heroes Being Threatened/ Tortured, the Sacrifices and the Last Minute Rescues.

In the finale, so we can spot our heroine in amongst the flying mobile suits, debris, gunfire, smoke, spotlights, explosions, etc, she's given a pink power suit. Yes, *pink*. (Don't ask who would paint a machine costing billions of dollars pink. Certainly it picks up the high fashion element in *Appleseed 2*, with costumes designed by Prada).

Plot-wise, the finale of *Ex Machina* is not only routine and familiar, it's uninspired (and humourless). But the visuals, despite the video arcade game feel of the shoot-em-up scenes, are terrific.

Far more interesting than the scenes of Briareos, Deunan, Tereus, Arges *et al* flying around the enormous, rectilinear interior of the Halcon facility (tackling drones and cyborgs), is the encounter with the super-villain, Xander. This is portrayed very much in the manner of Masamune Shirow's art, with sleek, weirdo, cyberpunk designs (more in keeping with the *Ghost In the Shell: Man-Machine Interface manga* than *Appleseed*). Oh – and tentacles (here, coated in steel).

Now, we know what tentacles do in Japanese popular culture – they pin down girls and rape them. And certainly Masamune Shirow, bless him, has employed tentacles (including steel tenties just like these), in numerous rape scenarios. The finale of many of Shirow's erotic stories is a gang rape by tentacles (or spiders, bugs, aliens, ghosts, or hulking, black guys). In *Appleseed*, the slithery tentacles attack Deunan and force her to the ground, but – phew! – they don't go further.

Our heroes work together, and it's Deunan who gets to perform the decisive action, by nobbling the super-villain: Briareos is encased in a tentacle and metal structure, and Tereus is wounded, so it's all down to Deunan. The lads perform acts that aid the heroine: Briareos breaks free, and hurls the antidote to his girl; Tereus protects Deunan from more tentacles; and Deunan slams the green liquid into the creature.

The super-villain in *Ex Machina* is partly Xander, who's been taken over by Alcides *et al.* (Xander fulfils the mother role of the first *Appleseed* movie, as a scientist whose ideas have been exploited by the villains. As with Deunan's mother in the 2004 film, we see Xander mainly in flashbacks). Xander isn't all bad, however, and Deunan puts her out of her misery as a puppet in typical Japanese style – by shooting her in the head.

Which leaves our heroes free to flee and ride off into the sunset. Meanwhile, as a movie of the action-adventure or *James Bond* ilk, the villains' lair has to blow up and fall to pieces (now, folks, don't ask why, when the Xander puppet is killed, just *one* element in a vast enterprise, the *entire* structure has to collapse. It just does).

Here, the filmmakers offer a tribute to the finale of the classic Hayao Miyazaki movie *Laputa: Castle In the Sky* (Halcon floats above the sea, it has a blocky design, there's a computer at the centre, parts topple into the ocean, etc. There are nods to the Ghibli film in the *Appleseed manga*). But *Laputa: Castle In the Sky* possesses a charm and a delight that few movies can conjure, and despite its visual splendour (parts of *Ex Machina* are beautiful), it isn't a patch on the 1986 masterpiece.

❖

To be fair, the 2004/ 2007 *Appleseed* movies do contain many elements of Masamune Shirow's *Appleseed* comics – the Deunan-Briareos relationship, Briareos being injured and recovering in hospital, the terrorist/ rebels attacking the super-computers, Athena and her rivalry with the council of old coot Elders, etc. But they don't capture the true spirit of the *Appleseed manga* at all.

And that is such a pity. Because technically the *Appleseed* movies of 2004 and 2007 are very fine, and they look fabulous. If they were commercials for robotic technology manufacturers or car companies or computer software developers, they'd be lauded as masterpieces. But they just don't have the dramatic components necessary to make them work as movies and as stories. Their humourlessness is fatal, too, because that adds so much to the humanity of all of Masamune Shirow's *manga*. If you lose the humour, as the *Ghost In the Shell* movies and TV series also did, you lose so much of what makes *Appleseed* and *Ghost In the Shell* appealing and entertaining.

Masamune Shirow's *manga* aren't just about cool-lookin' robots and *mecha*, aren't just about chases and explosions, and aren't just about futuristic societies overly dependent on technology. They're very much about teams of people, how they interact, how they get their jobs done. They're about the slog of doing day-to-day work as well as the thrills. And they're about *characters*.

The *Appleseed* adaptations of 1988/ 2004/ 2007/ 2011/ 2014 don't put in the necessary effort of creating the characters and their relationships. Sometimes that doesn't matter, if there's plenty of other stuff going on (in a martial arts actioner, for instance, you don't have to care for the charas too much, because you've got amazing action to enjoy). But in the *Appleseed* movies it *does* matter, and the movies suffer for it. The charas never quite come alive, and they're dwarfed by the machines, the technofetishism, the splendid backgrounds, and the flashy visuals.

Appleseed: Ex Machina (2007)
(This page and over)

04

APPLESEED XIII, 2011

A TV series of 26 episodes based on *Appleseed*, entitled *Appleseed: Genesis*, was due to be released in 2006 (and then 2009). Disputes (and law suits) among the companies behind it (including *animé* houses Radix Mobanimation and Micott & Basara), led to the cancellation (the legal issues were resolved in 2012). This might-have-been *Appleseed* series would have had the incredible Romi Pak[1] voicing Deunan (she is Edward Elric in *Fullmetal Alchemist*), with a script by Toru Nozaki, Ryo Karasuma and Romanov Higa, direction by Romanov Higa[2] and character design by Haruhiko Mikimoto. The title alone – *Appleseed: Genesis* – suggests another origins or re-boot concept – which both the 2011 *Appleseed* series and the 2014 *Appleseed* movie took (the 2004 *Appleseed* movie was also titled *Appleseed: The Beginning*).

---

1 Romi Pak (b. 1972), a veteran of a *huge* number of *animés,* is well-known for voicing many young, often teen characters.
2 However, judged on the basis of the dreadful *TANK S.W.A.T. 01* (2006), which Higa helmed, I'm glad it didn't go ahead.

INTRO.

Appleseed XIII (*Appurushido Satin,* 2011-12) was a 13-episode animated TV series (of the usual 23-minute episodes) based on Masamune Shirow's *Appleseed manga.* The *Appleseed* TV shows were re-packaged as two movies: *Appleseed XIII: Tartaros* and *Appleseed XIII: Ouranos* (both 2011). There was also a spin-off *manga* (again, *not* by Shirow). *Appleseed XIII* was produced by Fields Corporation, Production I.G, Shochiku Co., Ltd, Starchild Records and Yomiko Advertising, Inc. Executive producer was Gen Fukunaga; the producers were Auchara Kijkanjanas, Aursook Thanruangsri, Hiroki Kawashima, Katsuji Morishita, Shinichi Ikeda and Tsuyoshi Hanzawa (6 producers!). Takayuki Hamana was director; Junichi Fujisaku was chief writer (Yoshiki Sakurai, Taishirou Tanimura, Eiji Umehara and Kosei Okamoto were the other writers),[3] music by Conisch; editing by Junichi Uematsu; character design by Takayuki Goto (the 'G' in Production I.G., and a key contributor to the *Ghost In the Shell* franchise); art director was Masanobu Nomura; animation director was Satoshi Takeno; mechanical design by Atsushi Takeuchi (designer for the *Appleseed* movies and *Ghost In the Shell*); and the sound director was Yota Tsuruoka. (Many in the crew also worked on the *Ghost In the Shell* adaptations).

Among the voice cast were Kouichi Yamadera as Briareos (an *animé* superstar, one of the key players in the *Ghost In the Shell* franchise, where he's Togusa; Yamadera was also Briareos in the 2007 *Appleseed* movie); Maaya Sakamoto as Deunan Knute (Sakamoto was chosen as Motoko Kusanagi in the *Ghost In the Shell* prequel *Arise* series, and had played Motoko in her younger guises in the *S.A.C.* TV series); Ami Koshimizu as Gina; Hiro Shimono as Yoshitsune; Mayumi Yanagisawa as Nike; Mikako Takahashi as Hitomi; Naomi Shindoh as Deia; Naoya Uchida as Lance; and Ryotaro Okiayu as Archedes.

Appleseed XIII features our heroes, Deunan Knute and Briareos Hecatonchires, already established in Olympus and working for Extra Special Weapons and Tactics. (there are flashbacks to their former lives). Once again, the filmmakers haven't really captured the central relationship of *Appleseed,* or the characterizations of the two main charas – tho' there is more time in the TV series to consider characterization (and back-story). The potential for character-based scriptwriting is frittered away in *Appleseed XIII* (despite the very high calibre of the producers and writers on this show, and that marvellous voice cast).

Too often Deunan Knute comes across as bratty and whiny, or just grumpy, which misrepresents the *Appleseed manga* considerably; this is simply *not* Deunan in Masamune Shirow's comic;[4] similarly, Briareos takes on possessive, jealous and angsty personality traits in the 2011-12

---

3 Yes, I know, it's hard to believe that writers such as Sakurai and Fujisaku, who worked on the *Ghost In the Shell* TV series, also scripted *Appleseed XIII.*
4 You want to slap Deunan Knute as she's portrayed in *Appleseed XIII,* or drag her kicking and screaming into a *really good,* properly imagined version of *Appleseed.*

anime which aren't in the *manga* (and seem ill-fitted to his characterization in the *Appleseed manga*). And in later episodes of *Appleseed XIII*, Briareos fades into the background, with Deunan being the focus of attention; sure, that wouldn't be a problem if Deunan was given interesting things to *do*, but the possibilities for her character, as for Briareos' character, are squandered.

There's a lot you could do with Deunan and Briareos, surely? Yes, there *is*! But not here. (Even *anime* voice stars Yamadera and Sakamoto struggle to elevate this series).

Also, the filmmakers of *Appleseed XIII* simply *can't* (or won't) accept that Deunan Knute and Briareos Hecatonchires are a loving couple. The idea of two people who simply love each other is just hateful to dramatists! So, as with so many other movies/ TV shows/ plays/ stories, friction is shoe-horned into the relationship (and becomes the dramatic engine for some of the episodes of *Appleseed XIII*).

Not only are Deunan and Briareos fudged in every single *Appleseed* screen adaptation, many of the secondary charas are either dropped or altered beyond recognition (in which case, why bother to even call this 'Appleseed'?). No version of *Appleseed* uses Hitomi, for instance, as she is in the *manga* by Masamune Shirow, or her companion at the Akechi garage, Yoshitsune Miyamoto. In the *Appleseed manga,* for instance, Yoshi is included in a lot of the story, including the central action sequence where all hell is breaking loose in Olympus, and the spider platforms are going A.W.O.L. But none of the *animés* seem to want to use Yoshi like this.[5]

Yoshitsune Miyamoto (Hiro Shimono) makes a teensy bit more of an impact in this version of *Appleseed*, but he's still not the over-eager *mecha* nut/ helper of the *manga*. The Elders, Presidents, politicos, officers *et al* (a big part of the 2004 and 2007 computer-aided version of *Appleseed*) are ditched.

Deia (Naomi Shindoh) is one of the principal villains of *Appleseed XIII* – jumping into an enormous, bright red mobile suit to create havoc; Athena does nothing more'n stand in her vast office (decorated in the mandatory neo-fascist style), and stare out of the window[6] (while Nike/ Nikki (Mayumi Yanagisawa), Athena's P.A., has even less to do). The scenes in the E.S.W.A.T. briefing room, overseen by Lance (Naoya Uchida), where our heroes're given their missions, are handled with feeble mundaneity (of all the ways you can tackle the boss-explains-the-story scene, near the top of each show, these are so uninspired and plain *boring*! But this is <u>Masamune Shirow</u> we're talking about – the guy who wrote *Ghost In the Shell*, and *Orion*, and *Dominion: Tank Police* – and *Appleseed*!).

The animation, the character designs and the visuals in *Appleseed XIII* veer from a little patchy to downright pathetic[7] (as with other Shirow-based *animés*, such as *Real Drive* and *Pandora*). In many spots, the animation is too-obviously cut corners, looking as cheap as a screen saver

5 The first *Appleseed* sequel, of 2007, employed Yoshi more than the others.
6 Which's also how we first meet Athena in the 1988 *Appleseed anime*.
7 Consider the rendering of charas such as Athena and Lance.

or a crummy video game. Once again, the faces and figures have a plasticky, doll-like feel (but look at how much love and attention has been heaped on the mobile suits!). Sadly, altho' this is a show coming out of Production I.G., Shochiku and others, regarded in the *animé* business as pioneers in animation, it has to be one of the ugliest shows of recent years. (How could *Appleseed XIII* pass the quality tests of any decent animation house?).

This adaptation is very much animation with a lot of digital techniques applied to it in approach (and look), as with another Shirow adaptation, 2008's *Real Drive*. In some ways, that suits the concepts and the visual style of Masamune Shirow's fiction, but in other ways it falls short of really engrossing the viewer. Too much of *Appleseed XIII* plays like a predictable and unimaginative cop show, with Deunan and Briareos as the main cops brought in to confront a Threat Of The Week in each episode. While the police show format *is* the basis of *Appleseed* (and *Ghost In the Shell* – <u>and</u> *Dominion: Tank Police*), *Appleseed* is also *more* than Just Another Cop Show. There are fascinating thematic, ideological and even metaphysical aspects to *Appleseed*, which *none* of the movie/ TV adaptations quite gets to grips with.

Where the filmmakers of each *Appleseed* adaptation *do* succeed, however, is at the level of world-building, technology, architecture and backgrounds (tho' perhaps not the 1988 *Appleseed* so much). Like Masamune Shirow, the filmmakers are *mecha* nuts who like nothing better'n designing flying machines, skyscrapers, consoles, floaty heads-up displays (tons of these), machine guns and motorcycles (the first episode of *Appleseed XIII* has all of that technofetishism, and more).

One of the reviews of *Appleseed XIII* (in Anime News Network) notes that there is not much 'fan service' in the 2011-12 series. Are you kidding?! There is *tons* of 'fan service' in *Appleseed XIII*! This is, after all, an adaptation of Masamune Shirow's *manga*! Where *everything* is 'fan service'! For *mecha*-based technofetishism, all of the *Appleseed* outings (well, *all* of Shirow's work!), can't be beat.

Meanwhile, for erotic 'fan service', there are images of Deunan in bed in lingerie, Deunan wiggling her ass at the viewer to show off a new outfit to Briareos,[8] and Deunan wearing a ridiculous cutaway Tee shirt and dungarees combo (that rides just under her breasts, and has braces), so she looks like a farm girl from the good, ol' Mid-West. A tomboy who's gorgeous *and* a warrior! A farm girl with a gun! Ah, how *otaku* love their heroines to be ultra-tomboyish yet also babes – and handy with a Seburo, of course.

One of the most curious aspects of the *Appleseed XIII* is the music by Conisch (with music production by Starchild Records). Instead of the usual pinky-plonky piano (which Conisch is best known for), Conisch (b. 1981) opted for harp-like sounds (as if to distance the music from the typical *animé* score). So that, instead of the usual drippy piano music that plays behind so many TV drama shows, we have a harp (and variations

8 The scene was taken directly from the *Appleseed manga* – well, the layout of the room and the stairs, plus Deunan on the left and Briareos on the right, was.

on harps). It's interesting, but not always successful (interesting at first; later, you loathe that stupid harp sound). And too many of the music cues in *Appleseed XIII* are too repetitive, too samey, and undistinguished. Like the cut-corners animation, there's seem to be a lack of care in the music production in *Appleseed XIII*.

Plus, the filmmakers of *Appleseed XIII* make the Great Mistake of Hollywood movies and North American television – they have the music playing *ceaselessly* through scenes, and through groups of scenes. Oh, this is *so* irritating! Especially when you know that much of Japanese *anime* is sparing with its use of music, and very often has lengthy sections of silence (or near-silence). Is this because the *Appleseed XIII* series was aimed at the U.S./ international market as well as the home market?

THE EPISODES OF *APPLESEED XIII*

The first episode of *Appleseed XIII* (*The Nemean Lion*, broadcast June 23, 2011), opens by focussing on Deunan Knute, and for much of the series we take her viewpoint in most matters (to the point where we are in her mindscreen, and also see her dreams). The use of flashbacks takes us back to the couple's life in 'Badside', and back further, to Briareos before he was mangled and cyborgized. There are also brief glimpses of Deunan's father Karl (Taiten Kusunoki). (Deunan is given a different origins story in this version of *Appleseed*, but she's still a product of mixed race, with African roots on one side).

There are also visions/ dreams (again from Deunan Knute's point-of-view), which include images of Ancient Greek-style[9] statuary (of Hercules), of Roman/ Greek frescoes (some with tiles and mosaics), and of stained glass (some with pseudo-African imagery). These layers sort of derive from Masamune Shirow's fiction (but not really); they act as 'flat art' in the Japanese style, as interludes in the 'pillow moments' manner, and as commentaries on the thematic elements of *Appleseed* (such as ancient world civilizations, the ideals of Ancient Greek civilization, and the concept of Olympus trying to build a utopia based on artificial and human-enhanced lifeforms such as bioroids and super-computers).

But when the filmmakers cut back yet again to the statuary hovering in a circle above Olympus, or to yet another stained glass or fresco artwork, it gets tiresome (it's irritating even in the first episode). So that, instead of acting as a commentary on the drama, or as a 'pillow moment', or even as the cheapo trick of using still frames instead of full (or partial) animation, it's simply wearying. The filmmakers over-use the device – so that every time little Deunan gets upset, we cut to something from the display cases of the British Museum or the Vatican! Yes, yes, we *know* that

9 The episodes have Greco titles like *The Apples of Hesperides*, *The Capture of Cerberus* and *The Girdle of Hippolyta*. Which probably mean zilch to the audience!

Masamune Shirow – bless him – liked to cram Ancient Greek mythology into *Appleseed* (what a show-off!), but talk about milking an idea! (Besides, the statuary only have resonance if you *fully* understand Ancient Greek mythologies – having a character explain them doesn't quite do the trick).

The filmmakers are veterans, yes, and, true, Junichi Uematsu was the editor of the *Stand Alone Complex* series, where he did a brilliant job – but episode one of *Appleseed XIII, The Nemean Lion,* seems awkwardly put together, in terms of editing, concepts and writing. We are cutting all over the place: to Deu and Bri in 'Badside' in the past, to Deunan's memories of happier times with Briareos, to contemporary Olympus, to further back in time to when Briareos was whole, to those sodding Greek statues and mosaics, and more.

The first show in a new season of animation is all-important. Amazing first episodes of recent shows include *Nurarihyon's Grandson, Space Dandy, Death Note, Fullmetal Alchemist, Heaven's Lost Property* and *Highschool of the Dead* (yes, even over-the-top comedies like *Highschool of the Dead* were expertly edited!). Shows like *Death Note* and *Fullmetal Alchemist* open with absolutely scorching narrative hooks.

Alas, *Appleseed XIII*'s opener, *The Nemean Lion,* seems bungled: the story elements don't blend in a satisfactory manner; the characters aren't given proper introductions; and, fatally, the *animé* relies on the audience knowing quite a bit about this franchise (for example, there's little exposition to describe the would-be utopia of Olympus).

Also, humour is thin on the ground – there are only one or two attempts at humour in ep. 1. (However, seeing Deunan very drunk was a novelty – in the *manga*, Deunan is very fond of alcohol, such as wine. In *Appleseed XIII*, Deunan calls on her female buddy Hitomi (Mikako Takahashi) for a night in with the girls bitching about men, or one man in particular – Briareos).

✻

The second episode of 2011-12's *Appleseed XIII* (*The Augean Stables*) depicts a terrorist scenario with obvious links to 9/11 – a hijacked plane is making its way to Olympus, probably to crash into the city, and into Tartaros (this story idea comes from the *Appleseed* comic *Called Game* included in the *Appleseed: Illustration and Data* book, and also the hostage scenario of the *Appleseed manga*, which in turn was dramatized in the 1988 *Appleseed* cartoon). It seems that there are terrorists in Olympus (called the Human Liberation Front) who're biological humans that loathe the idea and the reality of bioroids (introduced in the first episode). So they have taken control of a plane-load of bioroid embryos which they're going to crash into the Tartarus bioroid facility in Olympus. This particular issue – humans versus bioroids – is one of the over-arching themes of *Appleseed XIII*.

On the personal subplot front, Deu's longed-for vacation is nixed just as she and her man are heading for the beach on their hog (Lance orders them back to E.S.W.A.T. to deal with the plane hijacking). And Deunan's visit to a restaurant with a view is literally rained on in the *dénouement*.

❊

By the third episode of *Appleseed XIII* (titled *The Ceryneian Hind*), several elements are seriously grating in this animated TV series: the off-puttingly unattractive animation, the uninspired, cliché-ridden screen-writing, and that dreadful music from Conisch (the harp music cues rapidly lose their charm and become irritating). Plus, episode 3 is shoddily directed (by Akito Sato) – consider the pacing and the editing, the storyboarding, and the writing (it was scripted by Yoshiki Sakurai. He wrote some of the great episodes of the *Ghost In the Shell* TV series, but this show is so lame).

Two issues are raised in ep. three: one is suicide, a recurring and very disturbing theme in Japanese popular culture. In *Appleseed XIII*, it's the bioroids who're suiciding (seemingly with assistance). The issue also crops up in *Ghost In the Shell: Stand Alone Complex,* when cyborgs commit suicide (a suicide was depicted in the prologue of the 1988 *Appleseed animé*).

The other theme in ep. 3 is that staple of drama everywhere, jealousy and the romantic triangle. Or, here, Briareos experiencing a bout of adolescent sexual envy, imagining that Deunan is possibly seeing someone else. Ah, poor Briareos! Doesn't he realize that Deunan is utterly devoted to him?! No, apparently, he does not! – and he takes to doing very un-Briareos-like things (such as sneaking about and spying on her. This stalker behaviour is *not* Briareos!).

Such puerile shenanigans aren't worthy of Masamune Shirow's apple-flavoured *manga*, or the characters he created (or, really, worth our time in watching this TV show!). The one Shirowian element of ep. 3, tho', is the father complex aspect, plus the motif of a gun (guns are a *big* deal in Shirow's art). Deunan has an old pistol that she's fond of – it was her father's gun. (Talk about adding a phallic subtext to a father complex subplot!). So Deunan takes daddy's weenie – sorry, I mean, daddy's *gun* – to a firearms store (very Shirowian) to have it fixed.[10] And, lo and behold, the guy who's servicing her weapon, Lark Ceryne (yes, this *is* very Freudian!), just happens to look like her father Karl (or his son! He has some of Daddy Karl's genes). Ouch!

Ceryne is of course one of the nefarious dudes in Olympus who're involved with the assisted suicides of bioroids. So the two plots/ issues come together, and Briareos in his stalker mode gets to do his bit by stopping bullets meant for Deunan. (Thus, it turns out that Deunan was working on her days off, getting close to Lark Ceryne, and Briareos redeems himself as a stalker by doing his bit).

❊

Episode 4 of *Appleseed XIII* is one of the low-points in adaptations of Masamune Shirow. The animation is just horrible, and the story is utter dreck. The show exacerbates the antagonism between Deunan and Briareos even more, and has the girl leaving her life-long lover, and

---

10 This part's like a scene from *Gunsmith Cats*!

staying over with Hitomi, the friendly, neurotic, excitable bioroid (conceived in *Appleseed XIII* as a girlfriend character like someone out of *Sex In the City* or *Cosmopolitan* magazine). Typing Briareos as the jealous, possessive boyfriend is simply naff (or the way it's played here is naff). It's soap opera-ish and trivial, and it also turns Deunan a little bratty and snippy. Which isn't Deunan at all in the *Appleseed manga*!

Even worse, tho', is the primary narrative in *Appleseed XIII* ep. 4 concerning a small girl who befriends a dumb, goofy but well-meaning robot cop (a rejigged Kotus[11] from the *Appleseed manga*). It's a child and a robot again – a human (well, a bioroid – near-as-damn-it) and a friendly ogre, a perennial favourite of Japanese popular culture (and it's Franken-stein's monster and the girl, when they go a-wandering in *Frankenstein* – tho' without the murder). Even worse, Deunan and Briareos are sidelined as secondary charas.

This has – needless to say – nothing to do with Masamune Shirow and his *Appleseed manga* whatsoever,[12] and even the addition of a kidnapping plot (by two useless finks who dress up as doctors), doesn't convince. Oh dear, this is an episode where two charas stand on a hill at sunset and blow dandelion seeds out over the city. You might do that in a hearts and flowers *shojo manga*, you might do it in *Oh! My Goddess* or, if you're bored, in *Love Hina*, but you do *not* do that in a hi-tech, cop show *manga*! Hmmm. Let's... move on (quickly!).

❃

Episode 5 of *Appleseed XIII* is a more traditional fantasy/ horror outing – actually, there's quite a bit of horror, with grisly evocations culled from zombie and vampire movies. So we have Deunan Knute running about in a nightmarish world of corridors and shadows, becoming a feral creature herself (the motif of the Minotaur in the labyrinth from Greek mythology is employed in this episode called *The Cretan Bull*). The show snakes in between waking dream and sleeping nightmare, so we're not sure which reality is which (until the too-pat and too lengthy explanations at the end).

The premise of this show is simply to put Deunan into a horror movie scenario, where she's the vamp and the zombie – and who cares how to explain it all? The scientific reasons for humans becoming slathering zombies offered here are – as always in zombie movies – completely ridiculous.

Also, episode 5: *The Cretan Bull* maintains the terrible appearance of the animation of the previous shows, as well as those mind-numbing shots of statues and mosaics (please, you are begging now, never, *ever* show me another image of an Ancient Greek mosaic again. I doubt those insert shots of statues and mosaics were part of the storyboard: what producer would pass a storyboard as OK that cut to a mosaic in the middle of an action scene?).

---

11 Who designed a police robot that can't speak?! Instead, Kotus holds up a screen to communicate.

12 Oh, OK, there *is* a part of *Appleseed* where Deunan encounters a Kotus robot cop, and there's an explosion, and the Kotus defends Deunan from it (at the start of the second volume).

By now, the series is also revealing its lack of a decent schedule or budget – many shots are shamelessly recycled. Pity the editor of *Appleseed XIII* (Junichi Uematsu), who have to cobble together a show which must run 23 minutes, but the material he's been given bleeds to death after ten minutes. Even a professional editor like Uematsu can't stretch out the footage without gaping holes appearing.

❉

The romantic antagonism between Deunan and Briareos continues in the next episode of *Appleseed XIII*. So boring! So predictable! So not-going-anywhere! It's a sub-plot that adds nothing to the *Appleseed* franchise, it's as fake as the memories of the replicants in *Blade Runner* (no, *faker*!).

In this episode, *Cute Tomboy*[13] *With a Gun*,[14] Deunan K. gets to go on a mission on her own, infiltrating the community of the Argonauts. Are they terrorists? Idealists? Activists? Pro-humans? Chefs? Doesn't really matter – but it is cheering to see some further scenes of Deunan's father Karl (so that we are switching btn flashbacks and Deunan in the present).

Yep, Deunan Knute is on a father quest in this corner of the *Appleseed* universe. A father quest is, well, as commonplace as romantic bickering in *animé* (father quests are especially popular – well, mandatory – in fantasy and sci-fi, where every girl has an Elektra complex – and the boys, too). But at least the father quest is a much juicier plot (and visually more engaging) than the soap opera-ish arguments btn Deunan and her lover Briareos).

The *Appleseed XIII* series finally introduces segments of the main plot, with the anti-bioroid folk, the big Landmate, and a potential assault on Olympus. *Banzai*! But we still have to hear that dreadful harp music, sit thru too much recycled footage, and rest our beautiful, precious peepers on some really sub-standard character design and animation.

❉

So in the next episode of the 2011-12 *animé* (*The Stymphalean Birds*), the Argonauts unleash an attack on Olympus and Tartaros (the facility where bioroids are developed). It's an act of terrorism by the Human Liberation Front, who want to redress the bioroid-human balance. Now comes the slambang action we'd expect from an adaptation of *Appleseed*, as Extra Special Weapons and Tactics tries to stop the H.L.F.'s giant, red Landmate assaulting Olympus. Machine guns and laser beams zip and zap all over the place in the sky above the city, and many E.S.W.A.T. agents are fried in the process.

How to place Deunan and Briareos in the midst of all this? The filmmakers come up with a very silly concept: Deunan's heartbeat is used as part of the code for the Human Liberation Front's technology.[15] However dumb this is (and it is *exceedingly dumb*!), it does put Deunan where the filmmakers want her: in the villains' machine, the princess to be

---

13 Yes, Deu's still wearing her horrible pants and cutaway Tee shirt combo!
14 Oh yeah, *that* gun again – Daddy's big, long pistol.
15 A similar concept was used in the *Appleseed: Alpha* movie, where the cyborg Iris is the ignition key for the spider platform.

rescued by Briareos.

By this time in the *Appleseed XIII* series, the repetitive cutting to images of Greek statues and frescoes is getting *very* irritating (it takes Japanese animation's use of still frames in the midst of action scenes to a tiresome extreme!), and Conisch's plonky-plunky, pseudo-harp music grates.

You get sick of the relentless cutting back to still pictures of pretty frescoes and statuary (15 shots in some episodes[16]) – they have long since lost their dramatic power (was editor Junichi Uematsu also fed up with cutting back to those bloody statues?! *Don't make me stick in another shot of a blasted* statue *in the middle of a slambang action scene!*).

In the action sequence, there simply isn't enough money for all of the shots required, so we get numerous cutaways to the statues and mosaics, *plus* numerous flashbacks. Now, OK, yes, in the midst of many an action sequence flashbacks will be inserted. Sometimes several – usually to thicken the thematic or dramatic soup. In *Appleseed XIII*, the *same* flashbacks are reprised, telling us the same guff, and all of this occurs in the middle of a big, loud action sequence! It kills the show: you want to grab your Seburo 9 millimetre machine gun and blast this shoddy series to pieces.

Meanwhile, altho' Deunan, cute and blonde as ever, is in the centre of the *Appleseed* series, each episode becomes repetitive and dull. And the harping on of the issues and themes – like the human vs. bioroid issue – is handled with sledgehammer tactics. Every so often Deia pops up in her bright red, over-size Landmate (mobile suit), to create a suitably over-the-top villain, but it doesn't make a lot of difference.

◆

Submarines!

It's impossible for any group of filmmakers to ruin an adventure set aboard a submarine – *come on*, submarines have everything you could wish for in terms of drama and excitement! A submarine story virtually writes itself! And so there isn't a bad film or TV show about submarines, is there?

...Oh yes, there is: episode 8: *The Mares of Diomedes* of this awful TV series. Alas, this is not *Blue Submarine 6* (or even a mid-level *animé* featuring subs, like *Black Lagoon* or *Full Metal Panic*). But it ought to be: we've got our heroine trapped in a submarine that's been sabotaged by an unseen enemy, and is picking off the crew one by one.

Eh? You'd think it was creatively impossible for a Japanese film or television crew to deliver a rubbish story about submarines (or robots or demons or swords or high schools). They feature in several Shirow stories – he gives Motoko a secret submarine base in *Ghost In the Shell: Man-Machine Interface*, for instance. Well, yes, there are many ingredients from the standard narrative approach to submarines in ep. 8: *Mares*, but it all amounts to absolutely nothing.

◆

---

16 Yes, I'm so bored by *Appleseed XIII* sometimes I count the shots!

Is it me or does the quality of the animation in *Appleseed XIII* degrade as the series continues? The schedule and the budget seems to be flying out of the window, with the series looking more like the product of a bunch of talentless amateurs trying out 3-D computer-aided animation on their home computers.

Considering the quality of the personnel involved, this really is dreadful. In this episode, 10: *The Girdle of Hippolyta*, a terrorist-or-ambassador from Poseidon visits Olympus. She's called Deia Cide (the name's a clue, folks!).

The show opens with another pointless rash of imagery of statues and artwork (and more loathsome harp 'music'), and closes with a preposterous assassination scenario: the target of Deia Cide, a diplomat, one of the remaining candidates for something or other, falls to his doom. How? Because he rushes out to rescue his daughter from a walkway 100s of feet in the air.

Oh dear. Is this the best Fujisaku and four other writers can do? Who built this stupid walkway, with no handrails? Who let a child wander onto it? What kind of parents allow their girl to roam about (and during an intense time of negotiations)?

In ep. 11: *We Can't Be Bothered*, something might be happening – I mean, there are sounds and images on the screen which might have some value or substance to someone somewhere. But anyone expecting anything resembling entertainment will be disappointed, because in this show…

…Deunan looks at a compass in her palm… Deunan murmurs 'Deia'… Deunan looks at Briareos anxiously… And then we repeat (for 23 minutes!). Add some shots of Deia looking anxious. And of course the mandatory Greek, mythological art.

The inclusion of some noisy, shooty, blammy action in the final minutes of this pitiful excuse for an animated show does not redeem it in the slightest.

◆

The climactic episode, 12: *The Capture of Cereberus*, is dissatisfying and feeble. It looks like the production's schedule was cut drastically, because most of this show is recycled footage. It's recycled for the inevitable flashbacks in the midst of a climactic battle; it's recycled when Deunan thinks about Deia; and it's recycled because that's what this series has been doing all of the way along.

In ep. 12: *We Still Really Can't Be Bothered*, Deia is defeated… an ugly, doll-like baby cries in Hitomi's arms… and Deu and Bri pontificate in wistful murmurs about what's happened.

❀

The *Appleseed XIII* series crumples to a dismal, weedy halt in the last (13th) episode, *Paradeisos* (broadcast on Jan 25, 2012) with that ultimate in cop-out scriptwriting, the virtual reality test. So the was-that-a-dream? sequence, where Gaia goes into meltdown and our heroes have to blast their way thru 100s of robot guards, is nothing but a training exercise simulation for the E.S.W.A.T. team. And – what a jip! – poor Deunan and

Briareos *still* don't get their days off to find their paradise (or least to relax a little). 'This sucks!' whinges Deunan in the whiny, awful American dub (but it's no better in the Japanese version).

For some reason, in the *animé* adaptations of *Appleseed*, Gaia the super-computer that runs everything in the near-utopia of Olympus, which was, presumably, created by humans (or bioroids), becomes a murderous villain from time to time. Who gave this super-computer 100s of battle robots and defence systems? (Errr, humans? Squirrels? Snails?). Why is there so much weaponry in this supposed utopia? Who allowed this super-computer to become autonomous to the point where it threatens all life in Olympus?

Thus, we have absurd scenes of E.S.W.A.T. agents shooting at Gaia-led robot guards. It's like having a washing machine in your kitchen that can whip out a Magnum pistol when it feels antsy and blow you to smithereens. It's like having a cel phone which, if it doesn't like what you just said, a knife flies out of the earpiece and digs into your brain.[17]

Yeah, sure, build a super-computer to run some of the systems in your city, but don't also arm it to the teeth,[18] and allow it have sole control of vicious weaponry and colossal spider platforms!

The return to the storylines of Masamune Shirow's *Appleseed manga* in the final show of *Appleseed XIII* brings us back to Shirow Land after many meanderings in uninspired fan fiction. As if the producers can assert, see, folks, *Appleseed XIII* <u>is</u> based on Shirow-sensei's *Appleseed* – we've got lots of material straight out of the *manga* here. But it's far too late.

◆

Even among terrible (and over-rated) *animé* shows – *Nadia: Secret of the Blue Water, Elfen Lied, Gantz, Afro Samurai, Hack/ Sign, Serial Experiments Lain*, etc –*Appleseed XIII* is one of the worst.

Appleseed XIII stumbles in several key areas: the concept, the writing, the direction, the music, the animation, the editing, and some of the visuals. The over-arching conception of this series is weak, and when that flaky concept is delivered with poor direction, ugly animation, and other technical areas not up to scratch, it's pretty poor.

These are not easy fixes; better to scrap it all, forget it ever happened, and move on to something else. And here endeth my whinge about the *Appleseed XIII* (2011-12) series.

Right. Enough! Now it's time for *One Piece*! Yes, after watching something as mind-rotting and depressing as *Appleseed XIII*, you will need to cleanse your soul with the greatest animated show ever to come out of Japan: Monkey D. Luffy and the gang in *One Piece*.

---

17 Which's how Deunan nails the out-of-control Landmates.
18 Similarly silly let's-arm-our-city-to-the-teeth ideas occur in the 2001 *Metropolis* remake.

Appleseed XIII TV series (this page and over)

05

APPLESEED: ALPHA (2014)

Appleseed: Alpha (2014)[1] was a prequel to the previous two computer-aided animated *Appleseed* movies of 2004 and 2007. It was produced by Lucent Pictures Entertainment/ Kodansha/ Sola Digital Arts[2]/ Sony Pictures Home Entertainment. Executive producers: John Ledford, Hidetoshi Yamamoto and Takashi Oya. Producers: Eiichi Kamagata and Joseph Chou. It was directed by Shinji Aramaki and written by Marianne Krawczyk.[3] Music by Tetsuya Takahashi. Chara des. by Masaki Yamada. (Some in the crew – the director, char. designer, composer, etc, worked on all three computer-aided *Appleseeds*). Released 2014.7.15. 93 minutes.

Junichi Suwabe was Briareos Hecatonchires, Yuka Komatsu was Deunan, Hiroki Takahashi was Olson, Tesshô Genda was Two Horns, Hirokli Touchi was Talos, and Aoi Yuki was Iris.

Technically, *Appleseed: Alpha* was very sophisticated, rendering the post-WW3 world of the future in a photorealist manner (which also scuppers part of the appeal of Japanese animation in the first place – that it is so abstract and other-worldly and fantastical). So that *Appleseed: Alpha* comes across as even closer to live-action (and again with an obsessive emphasis on detail, filling the screen with way too much information. Which of course Masamune Shirow has been doing throughout his artistic career. But not in this same fashion; here, it comes across as detail for the sake of it).

Tho' *Appleseed: Alpha* is in the main a Japanese production, there are plenty of attributes which look towards Western (and specifically, North American) movie-making. One decision was to record the sound in the U.S.A., and to make the movie in English – but English of course means North American English, delivered by North American voice actors (U.S. actors were also used for some of the motion capture sessions).[4] But there was a Japanese version, of course.

The DVD of *Appleseed: Alpha* that I watched didn't have a Japanese

---

1 *Appleseed: Alpha* was mangafied (by Iou Kuroda), tho' the art was ugly.
2 Aramakin and Chou run Sola.
3 Written by a woman – unusual, but actually it doesn't seem to make the slightest difference.
4 In the audio commentary, the filmmakers note that North American actors move differently from Japanese actors, and deliver their dialogue differently.

voice track (except for the filmmakers' commentary). But it did have French, German, Italian, Spanish and other dubs. As I can't bear North Amerikan voices being plastered over Japanese movies (for *many* reasons), I used the French voice track[5] (which's actually really good. In fact, film directors such as Hayao Miyazaki have enjoyed the French dubs of their movies – the French version of *Porco Rosso* had Jean Reno as the hero Marco the pig-man. Miyazaki was impressed by the French cast, even more than the Japanese talent)[6]

DESIGNS.

Masamune Shirow advised on the production, offering suggestions. He had opinions on issues such as Deunan Knute's costume, for instance. It was his idea that Deunan and Briareos could approach the war machine facility by sniping the guards outside from afar, in the Humvee, then simply hurtling onto the underground ramp (a gag right out of *Dominion: Tank Police*).

Saddled with one costume for the entire duration of the movie, poor Deunan Knute sports one of those ridiculous outfits that *animé* character designers in Tokyo just love to create: a military tunic cut open over the chest, so that the croptop underneath can reveal Deunan's breasts and belly button. (Inevitably, Deunan's wardrobe was one of the aspects of *Appleseed: Alpha* that *mangaka* Masamune Shirow had some ideas about! Shirow likes things to be practical and combat-ready, of course, but he likes plenty of clingy outfits showing plenty of skin. None of the adaptations, needless to say, have followed Shirow-sensei's penchant in recent times for warrior women to go into battle naked between the ankles (boots) and the waist (panties or a thong). The *Appleseed* movies happily show blood splattering all over and guns blazing, but they're curiously restrained when it comes to the human body and clothing).

The computer-aided animated *Appleseed* movies do contain lots of Masamune Shirow's designs and *mecha* that he's very fond of: there're tanks (of course!), the mobile suits (Landmates),[7] the tilt-rotor aircraft (a key vehicle in *Ghost In the Shell*), and of course guns a-plenty, from giant rifles which can take out a tank, to Deunan Knute's machine gun and pistol. The finale portrays a giant spider machine, one of Shirow's favourite motifs (some of the images of the spider leviathan come directly from Shirow's *manga*). Few *mangaka* can rival Shirow when it comes to depicting weapons in all their deadly beauty, and the animated movies certainly pay tribute to that scary techno-fetishism (close to war-as-porn for some observers), by heaping the scenes with enough hi-tech detail to satisfy the most obsessive gun nut (all of Shirow's works could be used as commercials for the Asian arm of the National Rifle Association).

5 The French dub had Jean-Michel Vovk as Briareos and Mélanie Dermont as Deunan.
6 'Those characters really need French voices,' Miyazaki explained: 'There's a quality in the French voice that you really need for those roles. The French Gina was even better than the Japanese – there's something wonderful in her voice. That's a woman who could stand on her own two feet, by herself, and yet she's a very feminine woman.'
7 *Appleseed: Alpha* manages to squeeze in a mobile suit, such an iconic motif of the *Appleseed* series. And there's a doctor/ engineer to help out, too (again drawing on the *manga*, but reworked). This time Dr Matthew is a creepy guy who boozes and jokes around.

One of the background artists offers an interesting point in the 'making of' documentary on *Appleseed: Alpha* – that he hasn't been out of Japan, so how can he recreate New York City? (Director Shinji Aramaki said he was the only one in the staff who had been to New York). It's worth remembering that nearly all Japanese people have *not* travelled off their island. Japan might be a super-capitalist nation, with tons of Yen washing around the upper echelons of society, but even so many Japanese folk aren't that bothered about overseas travel. (But in *Appleseed: Alpha* they do a creditable job of imagining Gotham from thousands of miles away, and better than some other *animés*).

❖

Appleseed: Alpha was conceived very much as 're-boot' of the *Appleseed* franchise by the film producers (Hidetoshi Yamamoto, John Ledford, Takashi Oya, Eiichi Kamagata and Joseph Chou). That they opted for an 'origins' story is in keeping with many movie franchises in the West which aim to 're-boot' their ailing franchises (and not all of those 'origins' or re-boots work: *Star Trek, X-Men, The Hulk*, etc).

So the producers of *Appleseed: Alpha* took up the opening chapters of Masamune Shirow's *Appleseed manga*, to look at what Deunan Knute and Briareos were doing before they arrived in Olympus. Having said that, in the third act, and with the introduction of Talos and the Triton mob (Triton is a rival community to Olympus), we are back with the later chapters in the *Appleseed manga*, when giant forces and machines are unleashed and run amok.

However, the 'origins' story only goes back a short period before Deunan Knute and Briareos Hecatonchires head for Olympus (which they're depicted doing at the end of *Appleseed: Alpha*). And *Appleseed: Alpha* and the other computer-assisted *Appleseed* movies offer glimpses of further back, to the time when Briareos was a human (which're seen in the dream/ nightmare sequences in the 2004 *Appleseed* movie).

But the 2000s-2010s computer-aided *Appleseeds* *don't* use the back-story of Deunan and Briareos from Masamune Shirow's *manga*, where Briareos worked for Deunan Knute's father (Deunan is another Shirow's heroines with a father complex).

Yes, it's disappointing that, even after trying *three times*, the filmmaking team headed up by director Shinji Aramaki for these animated *Appleseed* outings *still* can't capture the relationship of Deunan Knute and Briareos Hecatonchires, or their individual personalities, or their Shirowian designs. If you take *Appleseed: Alpha* as a stand-alone, action-adventure movie set in a futuristic, post-apocalyptic world, with a grim, gritty, militaristic mission involving soldiers and tanks and gangsters, it works fine. But the *Appleseed* series created by Masamune Shirow is *more* than that, is *more* than a run-of-the-mill, join-the-dots cyber-thriller.

Appleseed: Alpha is *far* too 'serious', and doesn't capture the charm and delight of the *manga* of *Appleseed*. And if you're *not* going to do that, then why bother calling this '*Appleseed*' at all? Why not write your own amalgam of 1970s American road movies, WW2 'men on a mission' movies, and cyber-fantasies like *Total Recall, Starship Troopers* and the inevitable (indeed, mandatory) *Blade Runner*?

For instance, Deunan Knute and Briareos Hecatonchires are introduced in *Appleseed: Alpha* riding a subway train: notice, tho' that they do not sit opposite each other, do not look at each other, and seem somewhat miserable: *Appleseed: Alpha* introduces the heroes at a low point, and by the end of the 2014 movie they are heading for Olympus, but they still don't seem happier or more fulfilled. Briareos is sulky and grumpy to the point of being a pain in the ass; this is not the Briareos in the *manga* at all (yes, he does have technical glitches with his cyborgization, but the Bri in the *manga* is never as moany and humourless as this. Even when he's injured (which's often), he's stoic, sanguine, determined). And Deunan comes over as a long-suffering woman who'd been promised Much Better Things, but has to make do with Briareos and his incessant whingeing (Deu tries to make jokes and be friendly, but Bri scuppers all chances. Where's the Deunan of the *manga*, who would yell at Briareos now and again? Why are the charas played at the same dramatic tone throughout the piece?). Really, the pair of characters needs a sidekick to carry all of that part of the relationship (in *this* conception of the Deunan-Briareos partnership, that is. In the *manga*, tho', it's something else).

For me, if you don't get the Deunan-Briareos relationship *right*, you subvert the whole point and essence of the *Appleseed* concept and franchise, and then you've got soldiers vs. robots/ bioroids in a video game shoot-em-up scenario in a post-apocalytic world. Actually, that sounds good! But *Appleseed* is even more than that.

❖

The character designs in *Appleseed: Alpha*, once again, depart from Masamune Shirow's *manga*: why is it that the animators and designers in Neo-Tokyo cannot capture the look or the personality of Deunan Knute, the heart of the *Appleseed* franchise? (However, they do better with Shirow's densely detailed *mecha* – the guns, vehicles, machinery and aircraft that're such an important element in the Shirowian future cosmos. The two missions in the first act of *Appleseed: Alpha*, for instance, foreground guns – and ammo – to a striking degree. After all, Uncle Shirow included a four-page discussion of guns and weapons in the *Appleseed Databook*).

Character designer Masaki Yamada (who worked on the previous *Appleseeds*) drops the *animé* look for Deunan Knute, because, I guess, the photorealistic approach to the show required a more 'realistic' (or non-stylized) take on Deu's design. But this Deunan is a completely different look from the *manga* (and from the previous *Appleseed* movies). She looks like a grumpy, Scandinavian actress from a dreary soap opera (where's the busy hair? The beautiful eyes?). Why is Deunan permanently sour, flinching at everything? The way Deunan moves (influenced by the motion capture footage, presumably), seems too nervous and self-conscious – it misses the natural, animal-like quality of Deunan in the *Appleseed* comic (we don't believe that this movie-Deunan is a brilliant warrior, either.

She's also too thick-set, and lacks the muscles and tone of the comic-Deunan). In the published work, Deunan is a force of nature; in the movie, she's a neurotic soap actress.

How the movie-Deunan physically and psychologically relates to Briareos is also particularly irritating: consider how the characters interact in close proximity in the 2014 movie. Deunan acts warily and nervously, as if she's expecting Briareos to lose it and blow up at any moment. In the comic, the couple have a graceful ease with each other (again, some of this perhaps comes from the motion capture material).

Deunan is the heart and soul of *Appleseed*, and you have to get her characterization and design just right – none of the movies or TV series have achieved that.

Once again, the filmmakers of *Appleseed: Alpha* missed the essential warmth and humour in the Deunan Knute-Briareos Hecatonchires relationship, which contributes so much towards the charm of Masamune Shirow's *manga* of *Appleseed*. Instead, we get a tired and dejected Briareos and a long-suffering Deunan who's putting up with him (look at Deunan's face in many scenes: she is so fed up!). But this is *not Appleseed* at all! These charas belong in an American-Japanese hybrid movie where everything is sarcastic, depressed, and exhausted.

◆

Anyway, the scenario has *Appleseed: Alpha* taking place not long after the world war that's decimated much of the civilized world. So everywhere is run-down, bombed-out, and junked all over, in the usual post-apocalyptic manner. However, there is a major switch in *Appleseed: Alpha* – this is set not in Olympus but long ways from Japan – New York City (thus, for the Big Reveal of Gotham, our heroes emerge in Times Square, just as Aki did in the *Final Fantasy* movie of '01). This concept takes as its starting-point book three of Shirow-sensei's *manga*, which featured a delightfully scuzzy, post-apocalyptical Big Apple (where a team hunts the killer bioroid Artemis. In *Appleseed: Alpha*, there are three assassin cyborgs, for the customary shooty-shooty opening scene of the three computer-aided *Seedy Apple* movies).

And instead of the hi-tech world of Olympus with its panoply of gleaming skyscrapers, hemispherical Arcologies, sweeping freeways and shiny bioroids, we have a dirty, beat-up *mise-en-scène* (needles to say, that kind of environment is very much a part of the futuristic vision of Masamune Shirow, as well as the slick, moneyed future).

Best of all, we have Deunan Knute and Briareos taking centre stage – they begin the first act of *Appleseed: Alpha* on a couple of missions (we are introduced to the pair on an empty subway train trundling thru an equally empty Gotham – not like the *manga*, where the streets're still lived in by a host of damn-it-all survivors and hangers-on. Yes, I reckon in a post-apocalyptic scenario, people would still insist on living in New York! There must be some treasures in the wreckage there).

One undertaking has our miserable heroes delivering a vaccine to a petty, slimy mob boss, Two Horns, who runs rackets in New York City; the second job has our heroes being ordered by the tycoon to help clean up the badlands beyond Manhattan (and now Noo Joisey looks like the deserts of the American West – or maybe it always was like that! Or have we suddenly skipped 2,500 miles, and are in Nevada already?).

And not only are Deunan Knute and Briareos placed at the centre of *Appleseed: Alpha*, it also means that the over-rich environment of Olympus as visualized in the 2000s *Appleseeds*, with its bioroids, Elders, Presidents, politicos, officers, cops, lackeys, doctors and the like, are left aside. Which means more screen time for Deunan and Briareos (which's all to the good). This being a prequel, Knute and Hecatonchires haven't reached Olympus yet – it remains a mirage, a lure, which Deu is far more fascinated by than the much more cynical Briareos (that, at least, does accurately reflect the early chapters of the *Appleseed manga*, where Bri remains sceptical about Olympus and its utopian dream).

Two Horns is a genuine piece of Shirowian characterization, apparently meant to be Sokaku[8] from *Appleseed*, but also clearly based on the villain Buaku in the *Dominion: Tank Police manga*[9] (Masamune Shirow is fond of squat, bullish, desperate-to-be-cool villains who're callous but also with a dry wit, and the teeniest bit of a soft heart. And out-there character designs for cyborgs – which Two Horns certainly has! – are one of Shirow's specialities. Tho' why a cyborg would be fat, when you could select any sort of body type, is bizarre). Two Horns – expertly voiced by Tesshô Genda – steals the movie[10] (and is the most memorable character in all three *Appleseed* movies).

However, Sokaku in *Appleseed* was a rather foolish weapons expert robot, and certainly not a crime lord, and absolutely no way was he someone that Deunan Knute or Briareos Hecatonchires would work for![11] In the *Appleseed manga*, for instance, Deu blows up Sokaku's car for a prank. In another scene, Sokaku hides under the debris on the floor, so he can watch his handiwork with booby traps in the hostage sequence (Briareos rumbles him). Thus, in *Alpha,* Two Horns is really a wholly new character.

The doctor, Matthew (Katsunosuke Hori), pops up, in the guise of a kooky helper figure. In Masamune Shirow's *manga*, Matthew is certainly odd, taking to pontificating on the human-bioriod issue. And, as usual, the doctor is fixing up Briareos (part-way thru act one), as he does several times in the *Appleseed manga*.

❊

In the second act of *Appleseed: Alpha*, Deunan Knute and Briareos team up uneasily with Olson and Iris, two survivors of an ambush in the badlands (the action scene where the Humvee is waylaid forms the climax of act one. This is, of course, another version of the Deu-and-Bri versus the tank scene of the start of Masamune Shirow's *Appleseed* comic, with action gags that pay *hommage* to that scene).

8 He has three horns, like Sokaku.
9 Who makes a cameo in *Appleseed.*
10 Not too difficult when everybody else seems manically depressed.
11 In fact, they wouldn't work for a sleazy crime lord at all.

So we're into a sort of *Road Warrior*, post-apocalyptic road movie (but in a Humvee, of course!). There is grim talk about 'the mission' of Olson and Iris, and Briareos and Deu ponder on whether it's a good idea doing this at all. (Iris is the sulky, loner teenager that is a staple in a large proportion of *animé*. She takes on some of the function of the bioroid Hitomi in the *Appleseed manga* (and Greenpeace in the *Dominion: Tank Police manga*), tho' her downbeat personality is very different).

A bunch of villains're introduced, cyborgs or something similar, faceless and impassive, and clad in sleek, space suits and helmets with a distinctly 1970s, retro feel (which's *very* Shirowian, of course. They might've walked out of a *sentai*/ team-based action/ fantasy show like *Power Rangers*. Their design also echoes the yellow spacesuits that the private detective team wear in Shirow's erotic book *W Tails Cat 2*, and the designs that Shirow has produced of robots for Nintendo and other video games). Their leader is Talos (the second-in-command is the slinky Nyx), and they come from Triton, another hi-tech community (a version of Poseidon Industrial in the *manga*). They fly a tilt-rotor craft, a way of getting the iconic aircraft from Shirow Land into the mix.

The Big Set-Piece in the second act of *Appleseed: Alpha* involves another Deunan-and-Briareos-versus-a-tank scenario (another nod to the opening chapters of the *Appleseed manga*). In fact, it's pretty much a replay of the start of Masamune Shirow's apple-flavoured *manga*, to the point where Knute and Briareos split up, Briareos carries Deunan in his arms as he jumps btn buildings, and Briareos is hurtling around the rooftops while the tank tries to blow him out of the sky. This tank sequence also reprises the moment in the *manga* where Hitomi pops a grenade thru the hatch of the tank and it blows up (which Iris performs[12]).

Wisely, the filmmakers bring back the mobster Two Horns from the dead (after the Triton cyborgs tried to assassinate him). Because Two Horns is a good value, and the 2014 movie livens up when he's around. (Sokaku in the *manga* of course tended to survive multiple explosions). On a niggly note – Two Horns wouldn't personally trek out to the badlands to run down two minor employees, he's too busy running his crime syndicate in Gotham. And that Two Horns would track down Iris himself also doesn't convince. But there's more dramatic meat when it's Two Horns in the tank, and not a bunch of bland and disposable cyborgs.

FLAWS.

There are plenty of flaws in the script of *Appleseed: Alpha*. A behemoth military machine which requires a teenage bioroid to activate it is ridiculous. (Masamune Shirow does use Hitomi, however. It was sort of re-used in *Appleseed XIII*). That Iris is also sullen, withdrawn and a peacenik[13] who's self-righteously anti-war makes the concept even stupider. (Thus, Iris is the treasure or MacGuffin everyone's hunting for in *Appleseed: Alpha*, a bargaining chip and the key to a weapon for Talos/

---

12 Improbably, Olson leaves Iris with a grenade when he rushes to help. Not a gun or a knife or a cruise missile?

13 Reminiscent of Hitomi in the *Escaflowne* movie and Shinji in *Evangelion*.

Triton. Having cute girls as the special key to something (usually something dangerous) is a minor trope in *animé*).

Have something to say – this is Jean-Luc Godard's advice to filmmakers. And how few filmmakers and producers follow that advice! And, you have to admit, that in *Appleseed: Alpha* the team haven't really got that much to say (this team has already said it anyway in the previous two *Appleseed* movies. And they're repeating themselves – they even bring back the spider behemoth).

The flaws in the script are exposed in the slower scenes, where the characters talk (scenes where a good screenwriter can really show their stuff). Like the nighttime scene round the fire in the badlands,[14] when Iris and Deunan chat. Not much is said (tho' Deunan is fascinated to hear that, yes, Olympus really does exist. Structurally, all sorts of plots and emotional material could be inserted here). Meanwhile, the animation of Iris is impressive (the rendering of skin is a tricky challenge for computer-aided animation, for instance, and this is marvellously done). But the technical mastery isn't in the service of anything particularly profound, or interesting, in this scene. (Iris spouts the well-worn rhetoric that 'war is baaad').

Motivations – the motives of Deunan Knute and Briareos are skipped over: they are surviving in 'Badside', yes, and they're reduced to working for manic mobsters like Two Horns (in Masamune Shirow's *manga*, they are working for themselves, and much of their effort goes into simply surviving). But just why they suddenly become heroic and take off to pursue Iris when Talos and his cronies have kidnapped her is a mystery (especially as the bonds between them have been shaky, and Iris is autistically withdrawn. Has Deunan gone all motherly on us, and decided that Iris needs protecting?). At the end of the 2014 picture, Deunan tells Iris that she has given them hope. Well, sort of. But, actually, no: the motives of the heroes just aren't really explained at all (and motive is crucial in Japanese animation). And the Deunan in the *manga* isn't like that at all – she bounces back from every challenge.

The issue of hope comes from the *manga*, tho' in a different context: it's used by the Elders as the name of their plan. In the 2004-2014 movies, the 'Hope' scheme is changed to 'Appleseed' – partly to explain just what 'Appleseed' refers to. But in Shirow's typically obscure manner, 'Appleseed' is so-called because Briareos used the seeds of apples to plug up the Gaia computer before it melts down.

THE FINALE.

Just what Talos and his crew of maudlin, shiny baddy cyborgs are after is unclear, too: oh, Talos makes a Big Villain's Speech about war and humans loving war (the boring, Nietzschean 'war for war's sake', 'mankind is violent' argument), and that's why he wants to control the spidery leviathan. Meanwhile, when the machine is unleashed, what does it do?! It heads to New York City in order to destroy it! But it's already

14 There's a joke about Deunan's cooking – one of the few flurries of humour in an otherwise too-serious affair.

been pummelled! Because that's the default mechanism when the spider-robot thinks it's been captured by the enemy! (Like a mad, Japanese, military suicide ritual – if my country's been defeated, I'm gonna take all the other mothers down with me!). This, too, is plain dumb screenwriting. (Yes, it echoes Masamune Shirow's *manga* in having the spider platform act as a Titan assaulting the abode of the Gods, Olympus, and, yes, the producers have gone back to the middle section of the *manga* (as they did in the 2004 *Appleseed*),[15] but... it's *bluergh*!).

Meanwhile, what is Two Horns doing turning up in the finale of *Appleseed: Alpha*? This guy is a gangster who's introduced in his office, surrounded by armed flunkies, with his boots up on the desk, who looks like he never gets his hands dirty. Is it revenge on Talos? Does he want to flush Talos out of the city, so he can run it as he likes? Is there something that Two Horns hopes to snitch from the underground facility? Who knows!? (Two Horns talks about being humiliated by Talos and his crew, but really Two Horns should not appear in the finale – not when you've got Briareos and Deunan in full action mode, and Deu's in a Landmate suit! However, it looks like the production team enjoyed Two Horns, and thought it might be a good idea to bring him back).

Thus, Deunan Knute (in the powered suit) forms a one-woman assault team on the spider platform running amok, but Two Horns helps her with a chase along a smashed freeway (they leap onto the spider platform from the jeep. Two Horns offers aid again, with a circus trapeze stunt). Really, this should be Briareos alongside of Deu – instead, Briareos is in the tilt rotor craft, ready to snipe the spider fortress. (Besides, the finale of the first *Appleseed* movie had Bri and Deu on the spider platform trying to Save The World. Earlier, Bri has a duel with Nyx,[16] a kicking and punching form of combat).

❉

Appleseed: Alpha has many of the elements in place for a Great Movie. But of course, it's nearly always the script and the concept that's the biggest challenge (along with casting), and *Appleseed: Alpha* stumbles on that issue. It could do with a lot more work on the characterizations, and on the interactions btn Deunan and Briareos; it could deliver the clichés more imaginatively; it could add some reversals and twists (the script is simply too unadorned, structurally, moving from A-to-B with nary a filip); and it could include a more compelling subtext or theme than 'hope'.

Because you are waiting for *Appleseed: Alpha* to take off, and it never does. The concepts, the characters, the themes and the story don't get their hooks into you. There is also the feeling, as often with a sequel (and a second sequel), that We Have Been Here Before. Well, that's fine if you're talking about enjoying being there (as with a sequel to a successful

---

15 On the audio commentary, the filmmakers joke that the idea was to keep *Appleseed: Alpha* small-scale, but somehow they ended up with a large-sized finale.
Aspects of the production of *Appleseed: Alpha* seem designed to reduce the budget by re-using costly elements already created in the computer. Such as: there are two scenes in Two Horns' office, two visits to Dr Matthew, two war-torn cities (the second town visited, in act two, looks like the New York set redressed), and so on.
16 That's why two cyborg villains were invented.

franchise, like *Harry Potter, Star Wars* or *Naruto*).

Or is the feeling of airlessness, lifelessness, and energylessness to be found in the animation of the characters? Is because computer-aided animation that tries for photorealistic approaches to humans feels not only weird and plastic but also doll-like and bereft of life? (Even with motion capture data powering some of the animation – they might sort of move like humans, but they look like dolls).

The irony is that the closer that producers and filmmakers try to get to 'real life' or to a photorealistic simulacrum of life, the more it comes over as artificial and clunky. (And yet, in Japanese pop culture, it seems that this is just fine – partly because there's a special, unusual attitude towards dolls, puppets and robots in Nihon, and partly because Japanese films and animations are not obsessive about 'realistic' forms of representation).

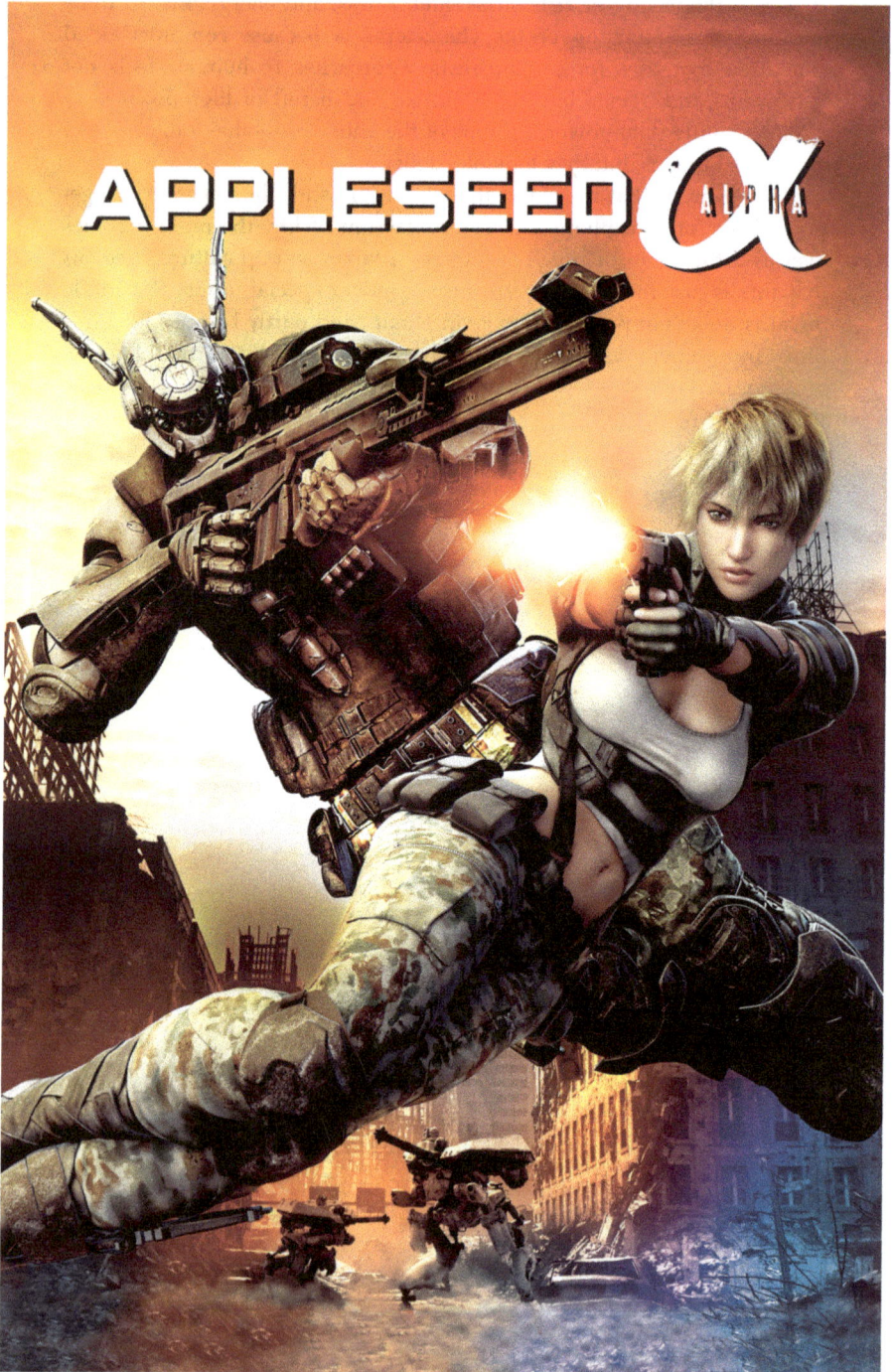

Appleseed: Alpha (2014)
(This page and over)

RESOURCES

WEBSITES

Masamune Shirow's own website is Shirowledge: shirowledge.com
Useful websites for the *Ghost In the Shell* franchise include:
• ghostintheshell.tv
• manga.com
• kenjikawai.com
• productionig.com.
• motorballer.org/shirow
• shirowsama.blogspot.com.es (Spanish)

One of the best sources on the internet for *animé* information is Anime News Network: animenewsnetwork.com. It is excellent, and the first stop for any online research on *animé*. Anime News Network has the fullest credits on the web for animation, and each entry is linked, so you can follow your favourite actors, directors, producers and artists, across numerous shows.

Also:
Japanese Cinema Database.
Japanese Movie Data Base.
Anime Web Turnpike: anipike.com.
Gilles Poitras's site: koyagi.com.
Fred L. Schodt's site: jai2.com.
Otaku News: otakunews.com.
Midnight Eye (for Japanese cinema): midnight eyec.com.
There are fan sites, of course. See the list of websites in the bibliography.

BOOKS ON *ANIMÉ*

Many of Masamune Shirow's *manga* are available in the West, including the three *Ghost In the Shell* volumes.

Books by Frederik Schodt, Helen McCarthy, Trish Ledoux, Patrick Drazen, Fred Patten, Jonathan Clements, Simon Richmond, Antonia Levi, Susan Napier, Jason Thompson and Gilles Poitras are standard works. But apart from those key authors, there is surprisingly little available on *animé* in English.

And most film critics tend to focus on characters, stories, and the biographies of the filmmakers. So many books on *animé* simply tell us the stories. Very few critics grapple with the industrial, social and cultural aspects of *animé* (and even less with theory and philosophy). Which's why critics such as Fred Schodt and Helen McCarthy are so important, because they address issues such as the modes of production, the audience and the market, and social-cultural contexts.

The single most useful book on *animé* is *The Animé Encyclopedia* (2001/ 2006/ 2015) by Jonathan Clements and Helen McCarthy. If you buy one book on Japanese animation, get this one. *The Animé Encyclopedia* provides entries on pretty much every important *animé* show, Original Video Animation and movie to come out of the Japanese animation industry, as well as numerous minor shows and oddities. This is the equivalent of a Leonard Maltin/ *Time Out/ Virgin/ Oxford/ Variety* guide to cinema. Clements and McCarthy are *animé* experts as well as fans (I would also recommend any of Clements' other books, including his history of *animé*, and his entertaining account of working in the *animé* business in translation and dubbing,

Schoolgirl Milky Crisis).

All of Helen McCarthy's books have become standard works: *Anime! A Beginner's Guide To Japanese Animation, The Animé Movie Guide, The Erotic Animé Movie Guide, 500 Manga Heroes & Villains* and *500 Essential Anime Movies* (some of these were co-authored with Jonathan Clements). They contain facts, credits and background to *animé* and *manga* which will greatly enhance your studies (and enjoyment) of Japanese comics and cartoons.

Other standard works on *animé* include: *The Art of Japanese Animation* (from Animage, 1988-89), and the *Dictionary of Animation Works* (2010).

Fred Schodt is one of the most valuable commentators on Japanese *animé* and *manga* in the West. His pioneering study of *manga, Manga! Manga! The World of Japanese Magazines,* is a marvellous book. Before it, there was virtually nothing. Because of the huge crossover between *manga* and *animé,* many of the chapters on *manga* in Schodt's studies also apply to *animé.* Schodt also offers one of the fullest and most detailed accounts of the history of *manga* and visual art in Japan. (*Manga! Manga!* also includes samples from some famous *manga,* including *Barefoot Gen* and *The Rose of Versailles,* and the illustrations – from the history of Japanese art as well as from *manga* – are stunning).

Fred Schodt's follow-up, *Dreamland Japan: Writings On Modern Manga,* is equally riveting. It includes a huge number of illuminating studies of individual artists and their works (with illustrations), as well as another history of *manga. Dreamland Japan* is also probably the finest, most intelligent and best-informed analysis of the *manga* market in both Japan and overseas. As well as Osamu Tezuka, Frederik Schodt also discusses Hayao Miyazaki, the relation of *manga* to *animé,* artistic styles, Japanese publishers, and the big *manga* magazines. It enhances Schodt's books that he has also interviewed many of the chief artists of *manga,* including the 'god of manga' himself, Osamu Tezuka.

Trish Ledoux and Doug Ranney edited an early guide to *animé, The Complete Anime Guide,* that is now a standard work. It is packed with fascinating snippets, as well as hard information, credits, etc. The companion volume, *Anime Interviews,* culled from *Animerica* magazine, is wonderful, featuring many of the key practitioners in animation (such as Masamune Shirow, Shoji Kawamori, Mamoru Oshii, Leiji Matsumoto, Rumiko Takahashi and Hayao Miyazaki).

Gilles Poitras has produced a number of works on *animé,* including *The Animé Companion* and *Animé Essentials.* Poitras offers vital links between Japanese animation and Japanese culture and society. There are objects, gestures, words and customs in *animé* that often surprise or bemuse Western viewers: Poitras' books help to explain them. You will find yourself recognizing all sorts of elements in *animé* that Poitras includes in his books (which contain many illustrations).

Antonia Levi's *Samurai From Outer Space* is stuffed with information on Japanese society as well as Japanese animation. Clearly written and with an appealing sense of humour, Levi's book is a lesser-known but invaluable work. *Samurai From Outer Space* discusses all of the celebrated *animé* shows that've made the leap across the Pacific to the Western world. Published in 1996, you wish that Levi (like many other authors whose books came out in the 1990s), was able to update it. Many great shows have been released since 1996!

Simon Richmond's *The Rough Guide To Anime* is a superb, general introduction to the wild world of *animé.* Like other *Rough Guides,* it selects fifty must-see TV shows and movies, plus providing discussions of related topics like *manga,* adaptations of *animé,* and a history of animation.

Jason Yadao's *The Rough Guide To Manga* is a companion guide to *The Rough Guide To Animé.* It has the same format and is a terrific general introduction to the world of Japanese comics. Yadao's enthusiasm is infectious: you will want to hunt out many of his recommendations. Both *Rough Guides* were published in the 2000s, so they're able to include recent classics like *Fullmetal Alchemist, Cowboy Bebop, Love Hina* and the masterpieces of Satoshi Kon.

Manga: The Complete Guide (Jason Thompson and others) is another illuminating book, packed with short reviews and longer pieces on topics like games, sci-fi, martial arts, sport, religion, crime, *mecha, shojo,* and *yaoi.*

Zettai! Anime Classics is another of those books that looks at 100 classic movies: Brian Camp and Julie Davis spend more time, however, on each of the familiar masterpieces of Japanese animation, exploring the films, Original Video Animations and TV shows in much more detail than the usual single paragraph review.

Manga Impact! from Phaidon is an entertaining survey of Japanese animation, with a format focussing on characters and personnel. *Manga Impact!* has short text entries, but features numerous wonderful illustrations in colour.

Susan Napier's *Anime: From Akira To Princess Mononoke* is much more theoretical, and somewhat dry. (If you are familiar with theoretical approaches to Western animation (see the studies noted below), you will findthe same approaches here to Japanese animation from a philosophical point-of-view).

The guides to the art of comics by Scott McCloud (including *Understanding Comics*), are highly recommended general introductions to how comics work (delivered in the form of a comic, with plenty of humour).

BOOKS ON ANIMATION

On animation in general, I would recommend the following studies: P. Wells' *Understanding Animation*; E. Smoodin's *Animating Culture: Hollywood Cartoons From the Sound Era*; Leonard Maltin's *Of Mice and Magic: A History of American Animated Cartoons*; James Clarke's *Animated Films*; *From Mouse To Mermaid: The Politics of Film, Gender and Culture* (edited by E. Bell *et al*); *Animation Art* (edited by J. Beck); and *Reading the Rabbit: Explorations in Warner Bros. Animation* (edited by K. Sandler).

For information on Walt Disney, the standard works include: Leonard Maltin's *The Disney Films*; Richard Schickel's *The Disney Version: The Life, Times, Art, and Commerce of Walt Disney*; R. Grover's *The Disney Touch*; Project on Disney's *Inside the Mouse: Work and Play at Disney World*; *Disney Discourse: Producing the Magic Kingdom* (edited by E. Smoodin); and *Walt Disney: A Guide to References and Resources* (edited by E. Leebron*et al*).

BOOKS ON CINEMA

For a study of cinema, there is one book that towers above *every other book* on film (even tho' the competition is fierce!): David A. Cook's *A History of Narrative Film*. If you want one book that covers everything, this is it.

David Bordwell and Kristin Thompson have written many meticulously researched and beautifully crafted books on cinema: *Film Art: An Introduction, Narration In the Fiction Film, Film History: An Introduction, The Classical Hollywood Cinema: Film Style and Mode of Production to 1960* and *Storytelling In the New Hollywood*. Anything by Bordwell and/ or Thompson is excellent.

I would also recommend Bruce Kawin's *How Movies Work*, Gerald Mast's *Film Theory and Criticism: Introductory Readings*, and Mast & Kawin's *A Short History of the Movies*.

David Cook, David Bordwell, Kristin Thompson, Gerald Mast and Bruce Kawin will give you all you could need for an in-depth study of cinema. Read their books: it's the equivalent of a degree or PhD in cinema!

FILMOGRAPHIES

APPLESEED (1988)

Appurushido. 1 episode. 75 mins.

CREW

Produced by A.I.C., Bandai Visual, M.O.V.I.C., Tohokushinsha Film Corporation, Gainax
Executive produced by Hirohiko Sueyoshi, Shinji Nakagawa and Yutaka Takahashi
Produced by Atsushi Sugita, Masaki Sawanobori, Taro Maki and Toru Miura
Kazuyoshi Katayama – director and writer
Norimasa Yamanaka – music
Kiyomi Tanaka – *mecha* designer
Yumiko Horasawa – character designer. and animation director
Hiroaki Ogura – art director
Yasumasa Date – sound director

JAPANESE VOICE CAST

Masako Katsuki – Deunan Knute
Yoshisada Sakaguchi – Briareos Hecatonchires
Mayumi Shou – Hitomi
Norio Wakamoto – A J. Sebastian
Toshiko Sawada – Athena
Toshio Furukawa – Calon
Kenichi Ono – Police Officer
Kouji Totani – Terrorist Leader
Kumiko Takizawa – Nike
Tamio Ohki – Nereus
Mika Doi – Fleia

APPLESEED (2004)

Appurushido. 102 mins.

CREW

Produced by Micott & Basara, Geneon Entertainment, Mainichi Broadcasting System, T.B.S., T.Y.O., Toho, Yamato and Digital Frontier
Produced by Hidenori Ueki, Fumihiko Sori, Naoko Watanabe and S.O.R.I.
Executive produced by Sumiji Miyake
Written by Haruka Handa and Tsutomu Kamishiro
Directed by Shinji Aramaki
Music – Tetsuya Takahashi
Sound design – Koji Kasamatsu
Sound director – Yota Tsuruoka
Production design – Shinji Aramaki
Character design – Masaki Yamada
Mecha design – Takeshi Takakura and Atsushi Takeuchi
C.G.I. director – Yasuhiro Ohtsuka
Background design – Nobuhito Sue

JAPANESE VOICE CAST

Ai Kobayashi – Deunan Knute
Jurota Kosugi – Briareos
Mami Koyama – Athena
Miho Yamada – Nike
Yuki Matsuoka – Hitomi
Yuzuru Fujimoto – Uranus
Emi Shinohara – Dr. Gilliam
Tadahisa Saizen – Kudou

APPLESEED: EX MACHINA (2007)

Appurushido: Ekusu Makina. 105 mins.

CREW

Production by T.Y.O. Productions, Toei Company, Ltd, Toei Video Co., Ltd, Tomy Company, Ltd, Digital Frontier, Micott & Basara and Sega
Executive produced by Sumiji Miyake and Yasuhiko Kinoshita
Produced by Hidenori Ueki, John Woo, Joseph Chou, Naoko Watanabe, and Terence Chang
Script by Kiyoto Takeuchi and Todd W. Russell
Directed by Shinji Aramaki
Character design – Masaki Yamada
Mecha design – Takeshi Takakura
Production design – Shinji Aramaki
C.G.I. directors – Yasuhiro Ohtsuka and Yasushi Kawamura
Music – Tetsuya Takahashi *et al*
Music producer – Shin Yasui
Action choreography – Tatsuro Koike
Casting – Eiji Harada
Editing – Ryuji Miyajima

JAPANESE VOICE CAST

Ai Kobayashi – Deunan
Koichi Yamadera – Briareos
Gara Takashima – Athena
Kuwata Kong – Aeacus
Miyuki Sawashiro – Hitomi
Naoko Kouda – Dr. Xander
Rei Igarashi – Nike
Rica Fukami – Yoshi
Shinpachi Tsuji – Commander Lance
Takaya Hashi – Dr. Kestner
Takaya Kuroda – Arges
Yasuyuki Kase – Yoshitsune
Yuuji Kishi – Tereus

APPLESEED XIII (2011)

Appurushido Satin. 13 episodes.

CREW

Produced by Fields Corporation, Production I.G., Shochiku Co., Ltd, Starchild Records and Yomiko Advertising, Inc.

Executive producer – Gen Fukunaga

Producers – Auchara Kijkanjanas, Aursook Thanruangsri, Hiroki Kawashima, Katsuji Morishita, Shinichi Ikeda and Tsuyoshi Hanzawa.

Head writer – Junichi Fujisaku, plus Yoshiki Sakurai, Taishirou Tanimura, Eiji Umehara and Kosei Okamot

Directed by Takayuki Hamana

Music – Conisch

Editing – Junichi Uematsu

Character design – Takayuki Goto

Art director – Masanobu Nomura

Animation director – Satoshi Takeno

Mechanical design – Atsushi Takeuchi

Sound director – Yota Tsuruoka

JAPANESE VOICE CAST

Maaya Sakamoto – Deunan Knute
Koichi Yamadera – Briareos
Ami Koshimizu – Gina
Hiro Shimono – Yoshitsune
Mayumi Yanagisawa – Nike
Mikako Takahashi – Hitomi
Naomi Shindoh – Dia
Naoya Uchida – Lance
Ryotaro Okiayu – Archedes

APPLESEED: ALPHA (2014)

Appurushido: Alpha. 93 mins.

CREW

Produced by Lucent Pictures Entertainment, Kodansha, Sola Digital Arts and Sony Pictures Home Entertainment
Executive produced by John Ledford, Hidetoshi Yamamoto and Takashi Oya
Produced by Eiichi Kamagata and Joseph Chou
Written by Marianne Krawczyk
Directed by Shinji Aramaki
Music – Tetsuya Takahashi
Character design – Masaki Yamada
Production design – Daisuke Matsuda
Concept design – Shinji Usui
C.G.I. director – Masaru Matsumoto
Military action advisor – Masato Hosokawa
Sound design – Chris Bourque and Bryan Leach

JAPANESE VOICE CAST

Yuka Komatsu – Deunan
Junichi Suwabe – Briareos Hecatonchires
Hiroki Takahashi – Olson
Tesshô Genda – Two Horns
Hirokli Touchi – Talos
Aoi Yuki – Iris
Kaori Nazuka – Nyx
Katsunosuke Hori – Matthews

MASAMUNE SHIROW

KEY WORKS

ART

Black Magic, 1983.
Appleseed, 1985-89.
Dominion, 1986.
Appleseed Databook, 1990.
Ghost in the Shell, 1991.
Orion, 1991.
Neuro Hard, 1992-94.
Intron Depot 1, 1992. *2*, 1998. *3*, 2003. *4*, 2004. *5*, 2012. *6*, 2013. *7*, 2013. *8*, 2018. *9*, 2019.
Appleseed Databook, 1994.
Dominion: Conflict 1 (No More Noise), 1995.
Cybergirls Portfolio, 2000.
Ghost in the Shell 2: Man-Machine Interface, 2001.
Galgrease, 2002.
Galhound 1, 2003. *2*, 2004.
Ghost in the Shell 1.5: Human-Error Processor, 2003.
Appleseed: Illustration and Data, 2007.
Pieces 1, 2009. *2*, 2010. *3*, 2010. *4*, 2010. *5*, 2011. *6*, 2011. *7*, 2011. *8*, 2012. *9*, 2012.
W-Tails Cat 1, 2012. *2*, 2013. *3*, 2016.
Pieces Gem 1, 2014. *2*, 2015. *3*, 2016.
Greaseberries 1, 2014. *2*, 2014. *3*, 2018. *4*, 2019.

ADAPTATIONS

Black Magic, 1987.
Appleseed, 1988.
Dominion: Tank Police, 1988.
New Dominion: Tank Police, 1994.
Ghost In the Shell, 1995.
Ghost In the Shell: Stand Alone Complex, 2002-05.
Ghost In the Shell: Stand Alone Complex, movies, 2005 & 2007
Ghost In the Shell 2: Innocence, 2004.
Appleseed, 2004, 2007, 2014.
Ghost In the Shell: Stand Alone Complex: The Laughing Man, 2005.
Ghost In the Shell: Stand Alone Complex: 2nd G.I.G.: Individual Eleven, 2006.
Ghost In the Shell: Stand Alone Complex: Solid State Society, 2006.
Ghost Hound, 2007.
Real Drive, 2008.
Ghost In the Shell: Arise, 2013-15.
Ghost In the Shell: The New Movie, 2015.
Pandora in the Crimson Shell: Ghost Urn, 2015-16.

Ghost In the Shell, 2017.
Ghost In the Shell: S.A.C. 2045, 2020.

BIBLIOGRAPHY

MASAMUNE SHIROW

MANGA WORKS

Areopagus Arther, published in *ATLAS*, 1980
Yellow Hawk, published in *ATLAS*, 1981
Colosseum Pick, published in *Funya*, 1982/ *Comic Fusion Atlas*, 1990
Pursuit, published in *Kintalion*, 1982
Black Magic, Seishinsha, 1983
Optional Orientation, published in *ATLAS*, 1984
Battle On Mechanism, published in *ATLAS*, 1984
Metamorphosis In Amazoness, published in *ATLAS*, 1984
Alice In Jargon, published in *ATLAS*, 1984
Appleseed, Seishinsha, 1985-89/ Dark Horse, 1995
Bike Nut, published in *Dorothy*, 1985
Dominion, Hakusensha, 1986
Gun Dancing, published in *Young Magazine Kaizokuban*, Kodansha, 1986
Pile Up, published in *Young Magazine Kaizokuban*, Kodansha, 1987
Appleseed Databook, 1990
Ghost in the Shell, Kodansha, 1991/ Dark Horse, 2007
Orion, Seishinsha, 1991
Neuro Hard - The planet of a bee, published in *Comic Dragon*, 1992-94
Interview. *Manga Mania*, Feb, 1994
Interview. Dark Horse, 1995
Dominion: Conflict 1 (No More Noise), Hakusensha, 1995
Appleseed Databook, Dark Horse, 1994/ 1995
Ghost in the Shell 2: Man-Machine Interface, Kodansha, 2001
Ghost in the Shell 1.5: Human-Error Processor, Kodansha, 2003
Appleseed: Illustration and Data (a.k.a. *Hypernotes*), Dark Horse, 2007
Pandora In the Crimson Shell: Ghost Urn, Newtype Ace magazine, 2012 (art by Koshi Rikudo)

ART BOOKS

Intron Depot 1 Seishinsha, 1992
Intron Depot 2: Blades, Seishinsha, 1998
Cybergirls Portfolio, Norma/ Dark Horse, 2000
Intron Depot 3: Ballistics, Seishinsha, 2003
Intron Depot 4: Bullets, Seishinsha, 2004
Kokin Toguihime Zowshi Shu, Seishinsha, 2009
W-Tails Cat 1, G.O.T., 2012
Intron Depot 5: Battalion, Seishinsha, 2012
Intron Depot 6: Barb Wire 1, Seishinsha, 2013
Intron Depot 7: Barb Wire 2, Seishinsha, 2013
W-Tails Cat 2, G.O.T., 2013

W-Tails Cat 3, G.O.T., 2016
Intron Depot 8: Bomb Bay, Seishinsha, 2018
Intron Depot 9: Barrage Fire, Seishinsha, 2019

GREASEBERRIES/ GALGREASE/ PIECES

Galgrease, Uppers Magazine, 2002
Galhound 1, Kodansha, 2003
Galhound 2, Kodansha, 2004
Pieces 1 - Premium Gallery, Kodansha, 2009
Pieces 2 - Phantom Cats, Kodansha, 2010
Pieces 3 - Wild Wet Quest, Kodansha, 2010
Pieces 4 - Hellhound 1, Kodansha, 2010
Pieces 5 - Hellhound 2, Kodansha, 2011
Pieces 6 - Hell Cat, Kodansha, 2011
Pieces 7 - Hellhound 1 & 2, Kodansha, 2011
Pieces 8 - Wild Wet West, Kodansha, 2012
Pieces 9 - Kokon Otogizoshi Shu Hiden, Kodansha, 2012
Pieces Gem 1: Ghost In the Shell Data, Seishinsha, 2014
Greaseberries 1, G.O.T., 2014
Greaseberries 2, G.O.T., 2014
Pieces Gem 2: Neuro Hard, Seishinsha, 2015
Pieces Gem 3, Kodansha, 2016
Greaseberries 3, G.O.T., 2018
Greaseberries 4, G.O.T., 2019

TIE-IN *MANGA*, NOVELS AND RELATED WORKS

Dominion: Tank Police by Nemuruanzu, Kadokawa Shoten, 1994
Ghost In the Shell by Akinori Endo, Kodansha, 1995, 1998
Ghost In the Shell: Stand Alone Complex by Junichi Fujisaku, 3 novels, Tokuma Shoten, 2004-05
Black Magic by Hideki Kakinuma, Softbank Creative, 2005-08
Real Drive by Yoshinobu Akita, Kodansha, 2008
Ghost In the Shell: Stand Alone Complex by Yu Kinutani, Kodansha, 2009
Ghost In the Shell: Stand Alone Complex: Tachikoma na Hibi by Yoshiki Sakurai and Mayasuki Yamamoto, Kodansha, 2009
Appleseed XIII by Yoshiki Sakurai, T.O. Entertainment, 2012
Ghost In the Shell: Arise: Sleepless Eye by Junichi Fujisaku and Takumi Ooyama, Kodansha, 2013
Appleseed: Alpha by Iou Kuroda, 2014
Ghost In the Shell: Comic Tribute, Kodansha, 2017
Ghost In the Shell: Perfect Book, Kodansha, 2017
Ghost In the Shell: The Human Alogorithm by Yuki Yoshitomo and Junichi Fujisaku, Kodansha, 2019

BIBLIOGRAPHY

OTHERS

Animage. *The Art of Japanese Animation*, Tokuma Shoten, 1988-89
—. *Best of Animage*, Tokuma Shoten, 1998
L. Armitt, ed. *Where No Man Has Gone Before: Women and Science Fiction,* Routledge, 1991
A. Balsamo. *Technologies of the Gendered Body: Reading Cyborg Women*, Duke University Press, Durham, N.C., 1996
—. "Reading Cyborgs Writing Feminism", in J. Wolmark, 1999
M. Barr, ed. *Future Females, the Next Generation: New Voices and Velocities In Feminist Science Fiction Criticism* , Rowman & Littlefield, Lanham, M.D., 2000
R. Barringer: "Skinjobs, Humans and Radical Coding", *Jump Cut*, 41, 1997
J. Baxter. *Science Fiction In the Cinema* , Tantivy Press, 1970
J. Beck, ed. *Animation Art*, Flame Tree Publishing, London, 2004
D. Bell & B. Kennedy, eds. *The Cybercultures Reader*, Routledge, 2000
E. Bell *et al*, eds. *From Mouse To Mermaid: The Politics of Film, Gender and Culture*, Indiana University Press, Bloomington, I.N., 1995
G. Bender & T. Druckrey, eds. *Cultures On the Brink*, Bay Press, Seattle, 1994
M. Benedikt, ed. *Cyberspace: First Steps*, M.I.T. Press, Cambridge, M.A., 1991
I. Bergman. *The Magic Lantern: An Autobiography* , London, 1988
J. Bergstrom: "Androids and Androgyny", *Camera Obscura*, 15, 1986
J. Berndt, ed. *Global Manga Studies*, Seika University International Manga Research Center, Kyoto, 2010
C. Bloom, ed. *Gothic Horror* , Macmillan, 1998
D. Bordwell & K. Thompson. *Film Art: An Introduction*, McGraw-Hill Publishing Company, New York, N.Y., 1979
—. *Narration In the Fiction Film*, Routledge, London, 1988
—. *The Way Hollywood Tells It*, University of California Press, Berkeley, C.A., 2006
F. Botting. *Gothic*, Routledge, 1996
—. *Sex, Machines and Navels: Fiction, Fantasy and History In the Future Present,* Manchester University Press, Manchester, 1999
J. Bower, ed. *The Cinema of Japan and Korea*, Wallflower Press, London, 2004
S. Brewster *et al*, eds. *Inhuman Reflections: Thinking the Limits of the Human*, Manchester University Press, Manchester, 2000
R. Brody. *Everything Is Cinema: The Working Life of Jean-Luc Godard*, Faber, London, 2008
J. Brook & I. Boal, eds. *Resisting the Virtual Life: The Culture and Politics of Information*, City Lights, San Francisco, 1995
P. Brophy, ed. *Kaboom! Explosive Animation From America and Japan*, Museum of Contemporary Art, Sydney, 1994
J. Brosnan. *Future Tense: The Cinema of Science Fiction* , St Martin's Press, New York, N.Y., 1978
—. *Primal Screen: A History of Science Fiction Film* , Orbit, London, 1991
S. Bukatman. *Terminal Identity: The Virtual Subject In Postmodern Science Fiction*, Duke University Press, Durham, N.C., 1993
—. *Blade Runner*, British Film Institute, London, 1997
—. "The Ultimate Trip: Special Effects and Kaleidoscopic Perception", *Iris*, 25, 1998
J. Butler. *Gender Trouble: Feminism and the Subversion of Identity* , Routledge, 1990

—. & J.W. Scott, eds. *Feminists Theorise the Political*, Routledge, 1992

—. *Bodies That Matter*, Routledge, 1993

—. *Subjects of Desire: Hegelian Reflections In 20th Century France*, Columbia University Press, N.Y., 1999

D. Cartmell *et al*, eds. *Alien Identities: Exploring Differences In Film and Fiction*, Pluto, 1999

J. Caughie & A. Kuhn, eds. *The Sexual Subject: A* Screen *Reader In Sexuality*, Routledge, 1992

D. Cavallaro. *The Cinema of Mamoru Oshii: Fantasy, Technology and Politics*, McFarland & Company, 2006

—. *The Animé Art of Hayao Miyazaki*, McFarland, Jefferson, N.C., 2006

C. Chatrian & G. Paganelli, *Manga Impact!*, Phaidon, London, 2010

L. Cherny & E.R. Weise, eds. *Wired Women: Gender and New Realities In Cyberspace*, Seal Press, Seattle, 1996

J. Clarke. *Animated Films*, Virgin, London, 2007

J. Clements & H. McCarthy. *The Animé Encyclopedia*, Stone Bridge Press, Berkeley, C.A., 2001/ 2006/ 2015

—. *The Development of the U.K. Anime and Manga Market*, Muramasa Industries, London, 2003

—. *Schoolgirl Milky Crisis*, Titan Books, London, 2009

—. *Anime: A History*, British Film Institute, London, 2013

C. Clover. *Men, Women and Chain Saws: Gender In the Modern Horror Film*, Princeton University Press, N.J., 1992

J. Collins *et al*, eds. *Film Theory Goes To the Movies*, Routledge, N.Y., 1993

I. Condry. *The Soul of Anime*, Duke University Press, Durham, N.C., 2013

D.A. Cook. *A History of Narrative Film*, W.W. Norton, New York, N.Y., 1981, 1990, 1996

L. Cooke & P. Wollen, eds. *Visual Display*, Bay Press, Seattle, 1995

J.C. Cooper: *Fairy Tales: Allegories of the Inner Life*, Aquarian Press, 1983

J. Crary, ed. *Incorporations*, Zone Books, 1992

B. Creed. *The Monstrous-Feminine*, Routledge, 1993

C. Degli-Esposti, ed. *Postmodernism In the Cinema*, Berghahn Books, N.Y., 1998

T. de Lauretis & S. Heath, eds. *The Cinematic Apparatus*, St Martin's Press, N.Y., 1980

—. *Alice Doesn't: Feminism, Semiotics, Cinema*, Indiana University Press, Bloomington, 1984

—. *Technologies of Gender*, Macmillan, 1987

M. Dery, ed. *Flame Wars: The Discourse of Cyberculture*, Duke University Press, Durham, N.C., 1994

—. *Escape Velocity: Cyberculture At the End of the Century*, Hodder, 1996

C. Desjardins. *Outlaw Masters of Japanese Film*, I.B. Tauris, London, 2005

J. Dixon & E. Cassidy, eds. *Virtual Futures: Cyberotics, Technology and Post-human Pragmatism*, Routledge, 1998

J. Donald, ed. *Fantasy and the Cinema*, British Film Institute, London, 1989

P. Drazen. *Animé Explosion*, Stone Bridge Press, Berkeley, C.A., 2003

Mircea Eliade. *Shamanism: Archaic Techniques of Ecstasy*, Princeton University Press, Princeton, N.J., 1972

—. *Myths, Dreams and Mysteries*, Harper & Row, New York, N.Y., 1975

—. *From Primitives to Zen: A Sourcebook*, Collins, London, 1977

—. *Ordeal by Labyrinth*, University of Chicago Press, Chicago, I.L., 1984

—. *Symbolism, the Sacred and the Arts*, Crossroad, New York, N.Y., 1985

P. Evans. "Future Tense", *Manga Mania*, Feb 1994

M. Featherstone & R. Burrows, eds. *Cyberspace/ Cyberbodies/ Cyberpunk*, Sage, 1995

D. Fingeroth. *The Rough Guide To Graphic Novels*, Rough Guides, 2008

T. Foster. "Meat Puppets or Robopaths?", *Genders*, 18, 1983

C. Fuchs: "Death Is Irrelevant: Cyborgs, Re-production, and the Future of Male Hysteria", *Gender*, 18, 1993

H. Garcia. *A Geek In Japan*, Tuttle, North Clarendon, V.T., 2011

P.C. Gibson & R. Gibson, eds. *Dirty Looks: Women, Pornography, Power*, British Film Institute, 1993

W. Gibson. *Neuromancer*, Grafton, 1986

Ghost In the Shell: Stand Alone Complex Official Log, ed. R. Napton, Bandai Entertainment, 2005

F. Glass: "The 'New Bad Future': *Robocop* and 1980s Sci-Fi Films", *Science as Culture*,

5, 1989

L. Goldberg *et al*, eds. *Science Fiction Filmmaking In the 1980s*, McFarland, Jefferson, 1995

J.-L. Godard. *Godard on Godard*, eds., J. Narobi & T. Milne, Da Capo, New York, N.Y., 1986

J. González. "Envisioning Cyborg Bodies", in C. Gray, 1995

J. Goodwin, ed. *Perspectives On Akira Kurosawa*, G.K. Hall, Boston, M.A., 1994

B.K. Grant, ed. *Planks of Reason: Essays On the Horror Film*, Scarecrow Press, N.J., 1984

—. ed. *Crisis Cinema: The Apocalyptic Idea In Postmodern Narrative Film*, Maisonneuve Press, 1993

—. ed. *The Dread of Difference: Gender and the Horror Film*, University of Texas Press, Austin, 1996

P. Gravett. *Manga*, L. King, London, 2004

—. ed. *1001 Comics You Must Read Before You Die*, Cassell, London 2011

C. Gray, ed. *The Cyborg Handbook*, Routledge, 1995

E. Grosz. *Sexual Subversions*, Allen & Unwin, 1989

—. *Volatile Bodies*, Indiana University Press, Bloomington, 1994

—. *Space, Time and Perversion*, Routledge, 1995

J. Halberstam. *Skin Shows: Gothic Horror and the Technology of Monsters*, Duke University Press, Durham, N.C., 1995

D. Haraway. "A Manifesto For Cyborgs", *Socialist Review*, 15, 2, 1985

—. *Primate Visions: Gender, Race and Nature In the World of Modern Science*, Routledge, 1989

—. *Simians, Cyborgs, and Women*, Routledge, 1991

—. "The Promises of Monsters", in J. Wolmark, 1999

P. Hardy, ed. *The Aurum Encyclopedia of Science Fiction*, Aurum, London, 1991

N.K. Hayles: "The Life of Cyborgs", in M. Benjamin, ed. *A Question of Identity*, Rutgers University Press, N.J., 1993

E.R. Helford, ed. *Fantasy Girls: Gender In the New Universe of Science Fiction and Fantasy TV*, Rowman & Littlefield, Lanham, M.D., 2000

H. Hitoshi. *Mecha World*, in *Appleseed Databook*, 1990

V. Hollinger: "Cybernetic Deconstructions", *Mosaic*, 1990

D. Holmes, ed. *Virtual Politics*, Sage, 1997

Tze-yue Hu. *Frames of Anime*, Hong Kong University Press, HK, 2010

J. Hunter. *Eros In Hell: Sex, Blood and Madness In Japanese Cinema*, Creation Books, London, 1998

E. James. *Science Fiction In the 20th Century*, Oxford University Press, Oxford, 1994

F. Jameson. *Signatures of the Visible*, Routledge, N.Y., 1990

—. *Postmodernism, or the Cultural Logic of Late Capitalism*, Verso, 1991

S. Jeffords. *Hard Bodies: Hollywood Masculinity In the Reagan Era*, Rutgers University Press New Brunswick, 1994

R. Johnson. "Kawaii and kirei: Navigating the identities of women in *Laputa: Castle in the Sky* by Hayao Miyazaki and *Ghost in the Shell* by Mamoru Oshii", *Rhizomes: Cultural Studies in Emerging Knowledge*, 14, 2007

S. Jones, ed. *Virtual Culture*, Sage, 1997

E. Ann Kaplan, ed. *Psychoanalysis and Cinema*, Routledge, 1990

B.F. Kawin. *Mindscreen: Bergman, Godard and First-Person Film*, Princeton University Press, N.J., 1978

—. *How Movies Work*, Macmillan, N.Y., 1987

R. Keith. *Japanamerica*, Palgrave Macmillan, London, 2007

A. Kibbey *et al*. *Sexual Artifice: Persons, Images, Politics*, New York University Press, 1994

B. King. *Women of the Future: The Female Main Character In Science Fiction*, Scarecrow Press, 1984

G. King. *Science Fiction Cinema*, Wallflower, 2000

Sharon Kinsella. *Adult Manga*, University of Hawaii Press, Honolulu, 2002

P. Kirkham & J. Thumim, eds. *Me Jane: Masculinity, Movies and Women*, Lawrence & Wishart, 1995

P. Kramer. *The Big Picture: Hollywood Cinema From Star Wars To Titanic*, British Film Institute, 2001

J. Kristeva. *Desire In Language: A Semiotic Approach To Literature and Art*, ed. L.S. Roudiez, tr. T. Gora*et al*, Blackwell, Oxford, 1982

—. *Powers of Horror: An Essay On Abjection*, tr. L.S. Roudiez, Columbia University Press, N.Y., 1982

—. *Revolution In Poetic Language*, tr. M. Walker, Columbia University Press, N.Y., 1984

—. *The Kristeva Reader*, ed. T. Moi, Blackwell, Oxford, 1986

—. *Tales of Love*, tr. L.S. Roudiez, Columbia University Press, N.Y., 1987

—. *Black Sun: Depression and Melancholy*, tr. L.S. Roudiez, Columbia University Press, N.Y., 1989

A. & M. Kroker, eds. *Hacking the Future*. New World Perspectives, Montreal, 1996

—. *Digital Delirium*, New World Perspectives, Montreal, 1997

A. Kuhn, ed. *Alien Zone: Cultural Theory and Contemporary Science Fiction*, Verso, London, 1990

—. ed. *Alien Zone 2*, Verso, London, 1999

F. Ladd & H. Deneroff. *Astro Boy and Anime Come To the Americas*, McFarland, Jefferson, N.C., 2009

T. Lamare. *The Anime Machine*, University of Minnesota Press, Minneapolis, M.N., 2009

B. Landon. *The Aesthetics of Ambivalence: Rethinking Science Fiction Film*, Greenwood Press, 1992

—. *Science Fiction After 1900*, Twayne, N.Y., 1997

T. Ledoux & D. Ranney. *The Complete Animé Guide*, Tiger Mountain Press, Washington, D.C., 1997

—. ed. *Anime Interviews*, Cadence Books, San Francisco, C.A., 1997

S. Lefanu. *In the Chinks of the World Machine: Feminism and Science Fiction*, Women's Press, 1988

T. Lehmann. *Manga: Masters of the Art*, HarperCollins, London, 2005

J. Lent, ed. *Animation in Asia and the Pacific*, John Libbey, 2001

A. Levi. *Samurai From Outer Space: Understanding Japanese Animation*, Open Court, Chicago, I.L., 1996

L. Levidow & K. Robins, eds. *Cyborg Worlds: The Military Information Society*, Columbia University Press, N.Y., 1989

P. Macias. *The Japanese Cult Film Companion*, Cadence Books, San Francisco, C.A., 2001

—. & T. Machiyama. *Cruising the Anime City*, Stone Bridge Press, C.A., 2004

L. Maltin. *Of Mice and Magic: A History of American Animated Cartoons*, New American Library, New York, N.Y., 1987

—. *The Disney Films*, 3rd ed., Hyperion, New York, N.Y., 1995

A. Masano & J. Wiedermann, eds. *Manga Design*, Taschen, 2004

G. Mast *et al*, eds. *Film Theory and Criticism: Introductory Readings*, Oxford University Press, New York, N.Y., 1992a

—. & B. Kawin. *A Short History of the Movies*, Macmillan, New York, N.Y., 1992b

L. McCaffery, ed. *Storming the Reality Studio: A Casebook of Cyberpunk and Postmodern Fiction*, Duke University Press, Durham, N.C., 1991

H. McCarthy. *Anime! A Beginner's Guide To Japanese Animation*, Titan, 1993

—. *The Animé Movie Guide*, Titan Books, London, 1996

—. & J. Clements. *The Erotic Animé Movie Guide*, Titan Books, London, 1998

—. *Hayao Miyazaki: Master of Japanese Animation*, Stone Bridge Press, Berkeley, C.A., 2002

—. *500 Manga Heroes & Villains*, Barron's, Hauppauge, New York, 2006

—. *500 Essential Anime Movies*, Collins Design, New York, N.Y., 2008

S. McCloud. *Understanding Comics*, Harper, London, 1994

—. *Reinventing Comics*, Harper, London, 2000

—. *Making Comics*, Harper, London, 2006

H. Miyazaki. *Points of Departure, 1979-1996*, Tokuma Shoten, Tokyo, 1997

—. *Starting Point, 1979-1996*, tr. B. Cary & F. Schodt, Viz Media, San Francisco, C.A., 2009

—. *Turning Point, 1997-2008*, tr. B. Cary & F. Schodt, Viz Media/ Shogakukan, San Francisco, C.A., 2014

T. Moi. *Sexual/ Textual Politics: Feminist Literary Theory*, Methuen, 1985

A. Morton. *The Complete Directory To Science Fiction, Fantasy and Horror Television Series*, Other Worlds, 1997

J. Murray. *Hamlet On the Holodeck: The Future of Narrative In Cyberspace*, M.I.T. Press, Cambridge, M.A., 1997

S. Napier. *Anime: From Akira To Princess Mononoke*, Palgrave, New York, 2001

—. "Excuse Me, Who Are You?", in S. Brown, 2006

—. "Interviewing Hayao Miyazaki", *Huffington Post*, Jan, 2014

S. Neale & M. Smith, eds. *Contemporary Hollywood Cinema*, Routledge, London, 1998

C. Odell & M. Le Blanc. *Studio Ghibli: The Films of Hayao Miyazaki and Isao Takahata*, Kamera Books, Herts., 2009

—. *Anime*, Kamera Books, Herts., 2013

I. & P. Opie: *The Classic Fairy Tales*, Paladin, 1980

T. Oshiguchi. "The Whimsy and Wonder of Hayao Miyazaki', *Animerica*, 1, 5 & 6, July, 1993

Oshii Mamoru, Kawade shobo shinsha, Tokyo, 2004

M. Oshii. Interview, in T. Ledoux, 1997

A. Osmond. "*Nausicaä* and the Fantasy of Hayao Miyazaki", *SF Journal Foundation*, 73, Spring, 1998

—. "Hayao Miyazaki", *Cinescape*, 72, 1999

—. "Will the Real Joe Hisaishi Please Stand Up?", *Animation World Magazine*, 5.01, April, 2000

— *Spirited Away*, British Film Institute, London, 2003a

—. "Gods and Monsters", *Sight & Sound*, Sept, 2003b

—. *Satoshi Kon*, Stone Bridge Press, San Francisco, 2009

K. Ott *et al. Artificial Parts, Practical Lives: Modern Histories of Prosthetics*, New York University Press, 2001

L. Pearce, ed. *Romance Revisited*, Lawrence & Wishart, London, 1995

D. Peary & G. Peary, eds. *The American Animated Cartoon*, Dutton, New York, N.Y., 1980

C. Penley, ed. *Feminism and Film Theory*, Routledge, 1988

—. *et al*, eds. *Close Encounters: Film, Feminism and Science Fiction*, University of Minnesota Press, Minneapolis, M.N., 1991

—. & A. Ross, eds. *Technoculture*, University of Minnesota Press, Minneapolis, 1991

C. Platt. *Dreammakers: Science Fiction and Fantasy Writers At Work*, Xanadu, 1987

G. Poitras. *The Animé Companion*, Stone Bridge Press, Berkeley, C.A., 1999

—. *Animé Essentials*, Stone Bridge Press, Berkeley, C.A., 2001

D. Porter, ed. *Internet Culture*, Routledge, 1997

N. Power. *God of Comics: Osamu Tezuka and the Creation of Post-World War II*, University of Mississippi Press, 2009

K. Quigley. *Comics Underground Japan*, Blast Books, New York, N.Y., 1996

E. Rabkin & G. Slusser, eds. *Shadows of the Magic Lamp: Fantasy and Science Fiction In Film*, Southern Illinois University Press, 1985

—. *Aliens: The Anthropology of Science Fiction*, Southern Illinois University Press, 1987

D. Richie. *The Films of Akira Kurosawa*, University of California Press, Berkeley, C.A., 1965

K. Robins & L. Levidow. "Soldier, Cyborg, Citizen", in J. Brook, 1995

J.M. Robinson. *The Cinema of Hayao Miyazaki*, Crescent Moon, 2015

—. *Cowboy Bebop: The Animé TV Series and Movie*, Crescent Moon, 2015

—. *Spirited Away*, Crescent Moon, 2016

—. *Princess Mononoke*, Crescent Moon, 2016

— *The Akira Book: Katsuhiro Otomo*, Crescent Moon, 2018

—. *The Art of Katsuhiro Otomo*, Crescent Moon, 2018

—. *The Art of Masamune Shirow*, 3 vols., Crescent Moon, 2020/ 2022

M. Rose. *Alien Encounters*, Cambridge University Press, Cambridge, 1981

P. Rosenthal. "Jacked In: Fordism, Cyberpunk, Marxism", *Socialist Review*, Spring, 1991

A. Ross. *Strange Weather: Culture, Science and Technology In an Age of Limits*, Verso, 1991

C. Rowthorn. *Japan*, Lonely Planet, 2007

N. Ruddick, ed. *State of the Fantastic*, Greenwood Press, 1992

B. Ruh. *Stray Dog of Anime: The Films of Mamoru Oshii*, Palgrave Macmillan, 2004

J. Rusher & T. Frentz. *Projecting the Shadow: The Cyborg Hero In American Film*, University of Chicago Press, 1995

D. Rushkoff. *Cyberia: Life In the Trenches of Cyberspace*, HarperCollins, 1994

K. Sandler. *Reading the Rabbit: Explorations In Warner Bros. Animation*, Rutgers University Press, Brunswick, N.J., 1998

C. Sandoval. "New Sciences: Cyborg Feminism and the Methodology of the

Oppressed", in C. Gray, 1995

Z. Sardar & J. Ravetz, eds. *Cyberfutures*, Pluto, 1996

—. "Alt.Civilizations.FAQ: Cyberspace As the Darker Side of the West", in Z. Sardar, 1996

P. Schelde. *Androids, Humanoids and Other Science Fiction Monsters*, New York University Press, 1993

R. Schickel. *The Disney Version: The Life, Times, Art, and Commerce of Walt Disney*, Pavilion, London, 1986

R. Shields, ed. *Cultures of the Internet*, Sage, 1996

M. Schilling. *The Encyclopedia of Japanese Pop Culture*, Weatherhill, Boston, M.A., 1997

—. *Contemporary Japanese Film*, Weatherhill, New York, N.Y., 1999

F. Schodt. *Manga! Manga! The World of Japanese Magazines*, Kodansha International, London, 1997

—. *Dreamland Japan: Writings On Modern Manga*, Stone Bridge Press, Berkeley, C.A., 2002

—. *The Astro Boy Essays*, Stone Bridge Press, C.A., 2007

G. Schwab: "Cyborgs", *Discourse*, 9, 1987

C. Shiratori, ed. *Secret Comics Japan*, Cadence Books, San Francisco, C.A., 2000

K. Silverman. *The Subject of Semiotics*, Oxford University Press, N.Y., 1983

—. *The Acoustic Mirror: The Female Voice In Psychoanalysis and Cinema*, Indiana University Press, Bloomington, 1988

C. Sinclair. *Net Chicks: A Small Girl Guide To the Wired World*, Henry Holt, N.Y., 1996

T. Smith. "Miso Horny: Sex In Japanese Comics", *Comics Journal*, Apl, 1991

E. Smoodin. *Animating Culture: Hollywood Cartoons From the Sound Era*, Roundhouse, 1993

—. ed. *Disney Discourse: Producing the Magic Kingdom* , Routledge, London, 1994

V. Sobchack. *The Limits of Infinity: The American Science Fiction Film*, A.S. Barnes, N.Y., 1980

—. *Screening Space: The American Science Fiction Film* , Ungar, N.Y., 1987/ 1993

—. "Cities On the Edge of Time: The Urban Science Fiction Film", *East-West Film Journal*, 3, 1, Dec, 1988

—. *The Address of the Eye: A Phenomenology of Film Experience*, Princeton University Press, N.J., 1992

—. ed. *The Persistence of History: Cinema, Television, and the Modern Event*, Routledge, 1995

—. "New Age Mutant Ninja Hackers", in D. Bell, 2000

Z. Sofia. "Virtual Corporeality", *Australian Feminist Studies* , 15, Adelaide, 1992

C. Springer. "The Pleasure of the Interface", *Screen*, 32, 3, 1991

—. *Electronic Eros*, Athlone, 1996

G. Stewart. *Between Film and Screen: Modernism's Photo Synthesis*, University of Chicago Press, Chicago, I.L., 1999

J. Stieff & A. Barkman, eds. *Manga and Philosophy*, Open Court, Chicago, I.L., 2010

Y. Tasker. *Spectacular Bodies: Gender, Genre and the Action Cinema* , Routledge, 1993

J. Telotte: "*The Terminator, Terminator 2* and the Exposed Body", *Journal of Popular Film & Television*, 20, 2, 1992

—. *Replications: A Robotic History of the Science Fiction Film*, University of Illinois Press, Urbana, 1996

—. *A Distant Technology: Science Fiction Film and the Machine Age* , Wesleyan University Press, Hanover, 1999

J. Thompson. *Manga: The Complete Guide*, Del Rey, New York, N.Y., 2007

K. Thompson & D. Bordwell. *Film History: An Introduction*, McGraw-Hill, New York, N.Y., 1994

—. *Storytelling In the New Hollywood*, Harvard University Press, Cambridge, M.A., 1999

A. Tudor. *Monsters and Mad Scientists*, Blackwell, Oxford, 1989

P. Virilio & S. Lotringer. *Pure War*, Semiotext(e), N.Y., 1983

—. *Lost Dimensions*, tr. D. Moshenberg, Semiotext(e), N.Y., 1991a

—. *The Aesthetics of Disappearance*, tr. P. Beitchman, Semiotext(e), N.Y., 1991b

—. *War and Cinema*, Verso, 1992a

—. "Aliens", in J. Crary, 1992b

—. *The Vision Machine*, tr. J. Rose, Indiana University Press, Bloomington, 1994a

—. "Cyberwar, God and Television", *CTHEORY*, http:// www/aec/at/ctheory/a-cyberwar_god. html, 1994b

—. *The Art of the Motor*, tr. J. Rose, University Press, Minnesota, 1995a

—. "Speed and Information", *CTHEORY*, http:// www/aec/at/ctheorya30-cyberspace_alarm.html, 1995b

P. Warrick: *The Cybernetic Imagination In Science Fiction* , M.I.T. Press, 1980

J. Wasko. *Hollywood In the Information Age*, Polity Press, 1994

P. Webb. *The Erotic Arts*, Secker & Warburg, London, 1983

P. Wells. *Understanding Animation*, Routledge, London, 1998

C. Winstanley, ed. *SFX Collection: Animé Special* , Future Publishing, London

J. Wolmark. *Aliens and Others: Science Fiction, Feminism and Postmodernism*, Harvester Wheatsheaf, 1993

—. "The Postmodern Romances of Feminist Science Fiction", in L. Pearce, 1995

—. ed. *Cybersexualities: A Reader On Feminist Theory, Cyborgs and Cyberspace*, Edinburgh University Press, Edinburgh, 1999

T. Woods. *Beginning Postmodernism*, Manchester University Press, Manchester, 1999

K. Woodward. "From Virtual Cyborgs To Biological Time Bombs", in G. Bender, 1994

S. Zizek. *Looking Awry*, Verso, 1991

—. *Enjoy Your Symptom: Jacques Lacan In Hollywood and Out*, Routledge, N.Y., 1992

—. *Tarrying With the Negative: Kant, Hegel, and the Critique of Ideology*, Duke University Press, Durham, N.C., 1993

—. *The Metastases of Enjoyment*, Verso, 1994

—. *The Indivisible Remainder*, Verso, 1996

—. *The Fright of Real Tears: The Uses and Misuses of Lacan In Film Theory* , British Film Institute, 1999

J. Zipes. *Fairy Tales and the Art of Subversion: The Classical Genre for Children and the Process of Civilization*, Heinemann, London, 1983

—. *The Brothers Grimm: From Enchanted Forests To the Modern World*, Routledge, New York, N.Y., 1989

—. ed. *The Oxford Companion To Fairy Tales*, Oxford University Press, 2000

—. *Breaking the Spell: Radical Theories of Folk and Fairy Tales*, University of Kentucky Press, Lexington, 2002

—. *Sticks and Stones: The Troublesome Success of Children's Literature from Slovenly Peter To Harry Potter*, Routledge, London, 2002

—. *The Enchanted Screen: The Unknown History of Fairy-tale Films*, Routledge, New York, N.Y., 2011

—. *The Irresistible Fairy Tale*, Princeton University Press, Princeton, N.J., 2012

WEBSITES

MASAMUNE SHIROW

Shirowledge (Shirow's own website): shirowledge.com
gallery.shirow.net
mshirow.free.fr

GHOST IN THE SHELL

ghostintheshell.tv
production-ig.com
kenjikawai.com
darkhorse.com
appleseed13.jp
worldwide-yk.com (Yoko Kanno)

ANIMÉ

manga.com
animenewsnetwork.com
anipike.com
koyagi.com
jai2.com
otakunews.com
midnighteyec.com
www.moribito.com
www3.nhk.or.jp/anime/moribito

JEREMY ROBINSON has published poetry, fiction, and studies of J.R.R. Tolkien, Samuel Beckett, Thomas Hardy, André Gide and D.H. Lawrence. Robinson has edited poetry books by Novalis, Ursula Le Guin, Friedrich Hölderlin, Francesco Petrarch, Dante Alighieri, Arseny Tarkovsky, and Rainer Maria Rilke.

Books on film and animation include: *The Akira Book* • *The Art of Katsuhiro Otomo* • *The Art of Masamune Shirow* • *The Ghost In the Shell Book* • *Fullmetal Alchemist* • *Cowboy Bebop: The Anime and Movie* • *The Cinema of Hayao Miyazaki* • *Hayao Miyazaki: Pocket Guide* • *Princess Mononoke: Pocket Movie Guide* • *Spirited Away: Pocket Movie Guide* • *Blade Runner and the Cinema of Philip K. Dick* • *Blade Runner: Pocket Movie Guide* • *The Cinema of Donald Cammell* • *Performance: Donald Cammell: Nic Roeg: Pocket Movie Guide* • *Pasolini: Il Cinema di Poesia/ The Cinema of Poetry* • *Salo: Pocket Movie Guide* • *The Trilogy of Life Movies: Pocket Movie Guide* • *The Gospel According To Matthew: Pocket Movie Guide* • *The Ecstatic Cinema of Tony Ching Siu-tung* • *Tsui Hark: The Dragon Master of Chinese Cinema* • *The Swordsman: Pocket Movie Guide* • *A Chinese Ghost Story: Pocket Movie Guide* • *Ken Russell: England's Great Visionary Film Director and Music Lover* • *Tommy: Ken Russell: The Who: Pocket Movie Guide* • *Women In Love: Ken Russell: D.H. Lawrence: Pocket Movie Guide* • *The Devils: Ken Russell: Pocket Movie Guide* • *Walerian Borowczyk: Cinema of Erotic Dreams* • *The Beast: Pocket Movie Guide* • *The Lord of the Rings Movies* • *The Fellowship of the Ring: Pocket Movie Guide* • *The Two Towers: Pocket Movie Guide* • *The Return of the King: Pocket Movie Guide* • *Jean-Luc Godard: The Passion of Cinema* • *The Sacred Cinema of Andrei Tarkovsky* • *Andrei Tarkovsky: Pocket Guide.*

'It's amazing for me to see my work treated with such passion and respect. There is nothing resembling it in the U.S. in relation to my work.'
(Andrea Dworkin)

'This model monograph – it is an exemplary job, and I'm very proud that he has accorded me a couple of mentions… The subject matter of his book is beautifully organised and dead on beam.'
(Lawrence Durrell, on *The Light Eternal: A Study of J.M.W. Turner*)

'Jeremy Robinson's poetry is certainly jammed with ideas, and I find it very interesting for that reason. It's certainly a strong imprint of his personality.'
(Colin Wilson)

'*Sex-Magic-Poetry-Cornwall* is a very rich essay... It is a very good piece… vastly stimulating and insightful.'
(Peter Redgrove)

CRESCENT MOON PUBLISHING

web: www.crmoon.com e-mail: cresmopub@yahoo.co.uk

ARTS, PAINTING, SCULPTURE

The Art of Andy Goldsworthy
Andy Goldsworthy: Touching Nature
Andy Goldsworthy in Close-Up
Andy Goldsworthy: Pocket Guide
Andy Goldsworthy In America
Land Art: A Complete Guide
The Art of Richard Long
Richard Long: Pocket Guide
Land Art In the UK
Land Art in Close-Up
Land Art In the U.S.A.
Land Art: Pocket Guide
Installation Art in Close-Up
Minimal Art and Artists In the 1960s and After
Colourfield Painting
Land Art DVD, TV documentary
Andy Goldsworthy DVD, TV documentary
The Erotic Object: Sexuality in Sculpture From Prehistory to the Present Day
Sex in Art: Pornography and Pleasure in Painting and Sculpture
Postwar Art
Sacred Gardens: The Garden in Myth, Religion and Art
Glorification: Religious Abstraction in Renaissance and 20th Century Art
Early Netherlandish Painting
Leonardo da Vinci
Piero della Francesca
Giovanni Bellini
Fra Angelico: Art and Religion in the Renaissance
Mark Rothko: The Art of Transcendence
Frank Stella: American Abstract Artist
Jasper Johns
Brice Marden
Alison Wilding: The Embrace of Sculpture
Vincent van Gogh: Visionary Landscapes
Eric Gill: Nuptials of God
Constantin Brancusi: Sculpting the Essence of Things
Max Beckmann
Caravaggio
Gustave Moreau
Egon Schiele: Sex and Death In Purple Stockings
Delizioso Fotografico Fervore: Works In Process 1
Sacro Cuore: Works In Process 2
The Light Eternal: J.M.W. Turner
The Madonna Glorified: Karen Arthurs

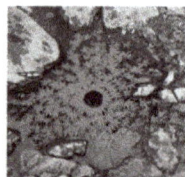

MEDIA, CINEMA, FEMINISM and CULTURAL STUDIES

J.R.R. Tolkien: The Books, The Films, The Whole Cultural Phenomenon
J.R.R. Tolkien: Pocket Guide
The Lord of the Rings Movies: Pocket Guide
The Cinema of Hayao Miyazaki
Hayao Miyazaki: Princess Mononoke: Pocket Movie Guide
Hayao Miyazaki: Spirited Away: Pocket Movie Guide
Tim Burton : Hallowe'en For Hollywood
Ken Russell
Ken Russell: Tommy: Pocket Movie Guide
The Ghost Dance: The Origins of Religion
The Peyote Cult
Cixous, Irigaray, Kristeva: The Jouissance of French Feminism
Julia Kristeva: Art, Love, Melancholy, Philosophy, Semiotics and Psychoanalysis
Luce Irigaray: Lips, Kissing, and the Politics of Sexual Difference
Hélene Cixous I Love You: The Jouissance of Writing
Andrea Dworkin
'Cosmo Woman': The World of Women's Magazines
Women in Pop Music
HomeGround: The Kate Bush Anthology
Discovering the Goddess (Geoffrey Ashe)
The Poetry of Cinema
The Sacred Cinema of Andrei Tarkovsky
Andrei Tarkovsky: Pocket Guide
Andrei Tarkovsky: Mirror: Pocket Movie Guide
Andrei Tarkovsky: The Sacrifice: Pocket Movie Guide
Walerian Borowczyk: Cinema of Erotic Dreams
Jean-Luc Godard: The Passion of Cinema
Jean-Luc Godard: Hail Mary: Pocket Movie Guide
Jean-Luc Godard: Contempt: Pocket Movie Guide
Jean-Luc Godard: Pierrot le Fou: Pocket Movie Guide
John Hughes and Eighties Cinema
Ferris Bueller's Day Off: Pocket Movie Guide
Jean-Luc Godard: Pocket Guide
The Cinema of Richard Linklater
Liv Tyler: Star In Ascendance
Blade Runner and the Films of Philip K. Dick
Paul Bowles and Bernardo Bertolucci
Media Hell: Radio, TV and the Press
An Open Letter to the BBC
Detonation Britain: Nuclear War in the UK
Feminism and Shakespeare
Wild Zones: Pornography, Art and Feminism
Sex in Art: Pornography and Pleasure in Painting and Sculpture
Sexing Hardy: Thomas Hardy and Feminism

The Light Eternal is a model monograph, an exemplary job. The subject matter of the book is beautifully
organised and dead on beam. (Lawrence Durrell)
It is amazing for me to see my work treated with such passion and respect. (Andrea Dworkin)

CRESCENT MOON PUBLISHING
P.O. Box 1312, Maidstone, Kent, ME14 5XU, Great Britain. www.crmoon.com

cresmopub@yahoo.co.uk   www.crescentmoon.org.uk

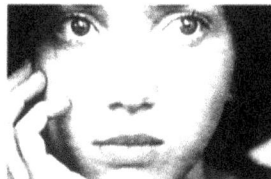